A Confucian

Constitutional

Order

THE PRINCETON–CHINA SERIES

DANIEL A. BELL, SERIES EDITOR

The Princeton–China Series aims to open a window on Chinese scholarship by translating works by the most original and influential Chinese scholars in the humanities, social sciences, and law. The goal is to improve understanding of China on its own terms and create new opportunities for cultural cross-pollination.

Yan Xuetong–*Ancient Chinese Thought, Modern Chinese Power*

A CONFUCIAN CONSTITUTIONAL ORDER

HOW CHINA'S ANCIENT PAST CAN SHAPE ITS POLITICAL FUTURE

Jiang Qing

Edited by Daniel A. Bell and Ruiping Fan
Translated by Edmund Ryden

PRINCETON UNIVERSITY PRESS
PRINCETON & OXFORD

Copyright © 2013 by Princeton University Press

Published by Princeton University Press, 41 William Street,
Princeton, New Jersey 08540

In the United Kingdom: Princeton University Press,
6 Oxford Street,
Woodstock, Oxfordshire OX20 1TW

press.princeton.edu

Jacket photograph: *Oversight*, Forbidden City gates,
Tiananmen Square, July 2, 2005.
© Eric Jonathan Walker

Jacket art: Ancient Chinese painting of Confucius, China.
© Panorama / The Image Works

All Rights Reserved

Library of Congress Cataloging-in-Publication Data

Jiang, Qing, 1953–
A Confucian constitutional order : how China's ancient past can
shape its political future / Jiang Qing;
edited by Daniel A. Bell and Ruiping Fan ;
translated by Edmund Ryden.
p.cm. — (The Princeton-China series)
English translation of materials from a workshop on
Confucian constitutionalism in May 2010 at the
City University of Hong Kong
Includes bibliographical references and index.
ISBN: 978-0-691-15460-2 (hardcover : alk. paper)
1. China—Politics and government—Philosophy.
2. Confucianism and state—China. 3. Jiang, Qing 1953—
Political and social views. I. Bell, Daniel (Daniel A.), 1964–
II. Fan, Ruiping. III. Ryden, Edmund. IV. Title.
JQ1510.J528 2012
320.951—dc23
2012005795

British Library Cataloging-in-Publication Data is available
This book has been composed in Verdigris MVB Pro Text
Printed on acid-free paper. ∞
Printed in the United States of America
10 9 8 7 6 5 4 3 2 1

Contents

Acknowledgments

The chapters by Jiang Qing as well as the four critical commentaries included in this book were discussed at a workshop titled "Confucian Constitutionalism and the Future of China" held in Hong Kong, May 3–5, 2010. The workshop was sponsored and funded by the Department of Public and Social Administration of the City University of Hong Kong. We are grateful also for the funding of the Center for Studies in Culture, Ethics and the Environment in Alaska and the Confucius Family Net in mainland China. We thank Professor Hon Chan, the head of the Department of Public and Social Administration at City University of Hong Kong, Professor Brian Partridge, the director of the Center for Studies in Culture, Ethics and the Environment, and Mr. Kong Weidong, the webmaster of the Confucius Family Net, for their support of the workshop.

We greatly appreciate Mr. Jiang Qing's hard work in contributing to this book. Confucianism is both an intellectual effort and a way of life, and nobody we know brings these two aspects better than Mr. Jiang Qing. We (the two editors), along with our families, had the pleasure of visiting the Confucian Academy (Yangming Jingshe) that Mr. Jiang Qing set up in the mountains of southwestern China, and we are grateful for Mr. Jiang's hospitality, friendship, and inspiration.

We would also like to thank the four commentators who wrote in-depth critical evaluations of Jiang Qing's essays. Princeton University Press sent earlier versions of the manuscript to three anonymous referees, and we are very grateful for their reports, which helped us to improve the book. We would also like to thank Stephen Angle, Ci Jiwei, David Elstein, and P. J. Ivanhoe for helpful comments on an earlier draft of the introduction.

We were lucky that Dr. Edmund Ryden accepted the offer to translate the manuscript with his usual brilliance and efficiency. We are also grateful to Ms. Erika Yu, who spent many, many hours proofreading, checking notes, and standardizing terminology.

We are very grateful to Princeton University Press for funding the translation, and special thanks are owed to Peter Dougherty, Rob Tempio, and Ian Malcolm for their support and interest in this translation series.

A Confucian

Constitutional

Order

Introduction

Daniel A. Bell

In 1912, Kang Youwei (1858–1927)—the most prominent political reformer of his day—founded the Confucian Religious Society. During China's brief experiment with parliamentary debate in the newly established Republic of China, the society twice proposed institutionalizing Confucianism as the state religion but narrowly failed to garner the required two-thirds majority of the vote in the national assembly.[1] A century later, Jiang Qing (b. 1952)—the most prominent Confucian political thinker of our day—has revived Kang's cause. Similar to Kang, Jiang argues that nothing less than an official embrace of Confucianism can save China from its moral and political predicament. Whereas Kang was somewhat vague about how to implement his idea of a constitutional monarchy with Confucianism as the official state religion, Jiang has developed the institutional implications in great detail. Jiang's views are intensely controversial in mainland China,[2] but a conversation about political change among intellectuals and political reformers in China rarely fails to turn to Jiang's proposals. Jiang's political Confucianism has generated an extensive Chinese-language secondary literature of comments and criticisms.[3] It may not be an exaggeration to say that Jiang Qing has almost single-handedly succeeded in enriching debates about China's political future. Prior to Jiang, the discourse about politics with "Chinese characteristics" was usually shallow rhetoric meant to buttress the status quo. The main alternative was put forward by liberal democrats, who tend to think that China's political future comes down to an empirical issue of when and how to adopt Western-style liberal democracy in the form of elections and multiparty competition.[4] But Jiang's modern-day adaptation of Confucian constitutionalism is the most detailed systematic alternative to both the current regime and Western-style liberal democracy.

In view of Jiang's originality and influence, Fan Ruiping and I organized a workshop on Confucian constitutionalism in May 2010 at the City University of Hong Kong (due to the political sensitivity of this material, it would have been difficult to secure official permission or funding for such a workshop in mainland China). Jiang developed his proposals for the purposes of the workshop, and four leading Chinese intellectuals wrote detailed critical comments. Jiang then wrote a detailed response, and the material was translated by Dr. Edmund Ryden and polished by Erika Yu.

This book is Jiang's most detailed and systematic work on Confucian constitutionalism. Jiang does not spend much time directly criticizing the political status quo in China because he does not consider it to be viable for the long term (not to mention the fact that it would be politically dangerous to do so). However, he worries about its main competitor—liberal democracy—and seeks to develop a morally desirable and politically realistic alternative. This introduction summarizes Jiang's Confucian constitutionalism, followed by a discussion of his debates with liberal Confucians and socialists. The last section suggests a "middle way" between Jiang and his critics.

A BRIEF INTELLECTUAL BIOGRAPHY

But before we turn to the substance of Jiang's ideas, it is worth asking how Jiang came to embrace Confucianism.[5] After all, Confucianism has come under sustained attack in mainland China by both Chinese liberals and Marxists since the early twentieth century, and Jiang was clearly swimming against the tide. In fact, Jiang started out his intellectual journey as a committed Marxist. Jiang's father was a high-ranking Communist official, and he had a comparatively comfortable childhood in Guiyang, the capital city of Guizhou province. Jiang went to high school during the Cultural Revolution and spent most of his time on manual labor and "revolutionary" meetings. He responded to Mao's call to "wholeheartedly serve the people" and joined the army, where he served as a truck repairman in Yunnan province. Jiang read Karl Marx's *Das Kapital* in his spare time and became convinced that Marx's masterpiece would lead him to the final truth about human society. His growing commitment to study Marxist theories prompted him to apply for a clerical post that would leave more time for study, and Jiang immersed himself thoroughly in the study of Marxist works for two and a half years.

Jiang's grandmother was another significant influence during the Cultural Revolution. She came from an intellectual family and was still active writing classical poetry in her seventies. Jiang was at first puzzled by the fact that she was reading Confucian classics that were officially criticized and banned at the time. But soon he came to hold that pursuit of such knowledge should not be restricted by the political authorities. In his last year in the army, Jiang began to read non-Marxist Chinese classical works that he obtained from the underground market and became disillusioned with the official version of Marxist ideology propagated by the army.

In 1978, Deng Xiaoping assumed power amid signs of political change. Jiang resigned from the army and took the National College Entrance Examination. His outstanding results earned him admission to the Southwest University of Politics and Law in Chongqing (then Sichuan province), the only Key Law School recognized by the state at the time. Jiang immersed himself more deeply in the works of the young Karl Marx on humanism and alienation and became fascinated by the ideas of individual liberty, equality, and human rights developed by Western classical liberal philosophers such as Locke and Rousseau. He believed that all these different perspectives could be integrated into a coherent liberal Marxist doctrine that could save China from turmoil. Jiang became an activist in the democratic movement and developed a reputation as a student leader at the forefront of criticizing China from the perspective of human rights.

In 1980, Jiang wrote an essay titled "Back to Marxism" that was published on the campus notice board. He drew inspiration from the young Marx's *Economic and Philosophical Manuscripts* and Western theories of Marxism to argue that Marxism was a theory of humanism rather than class struggle and that Marxism was consistent with individual rights, equality, and democracy. The essay inspired fellow students, but it was condemned and suppressed by the authorities. Jiang was offered a chance to confess his "mistake" in writing, but he refused and insisted that individual rights, humanism, and a critique of alienation are central to Marxism. Jiang submitted a thesis titled "A Critique of Stalinism," defending the same argument as his earlier essay, and the authorities promptly failed the thesis. To earn his degree, Jiang wrote on the topic that would define the rest of his life: "A First Look at Confucius's Humanism."

Most of Jiang's fellow law graduates were assigned to important positions in Beijing or other major cities,[6] but he was assigned to a post in a remote rural court in Guizhou province. Jiang became disillusioned with the political world and turned to questions of ultimate concern, and he experienced a spiritual crisis over the next few years. He spent most of his days meditating and reading Daoist and especially Buddhist religious works that could hold the key to the true meaning of life. But Jiang eventually decided that he could not side with Buddhism. Even if the Buddhist claim that the world cannot stand still even for an instant is correct, Jiang could not agree that *sunyata* (emptiness) is the ultimate truth. Rather, he recognized with Confucianism that the ever-changing world is a result of a creative universe with history and culture. Hence, Jiang concluded that Buddhism fails to give any guidance for solving problems of mankind inherited from history and culture. Jiang also tried to draw spiritual nourishment from Christianity. He translated a Christian work from English into Chinese, became moved by Jesus's spirit of charity, and tried to join a Christian church. In the end, however, he failed to become a Christian believer because, as he put it, "the spirit of Chinese culture drags my legs behind."

Jiang's full commitment to Confucianism was set off by his exposure in 1984 to the works of Tang Junyi, a prominent neo-Confucian scholar in Hong Kong. Before then, he was unaware that the Confucian tradition had been maintained by scholars in Taiwan and Hong Kong. He read more works by neo-Confucian scholars, even though some were officially banned in mainland China because they were explicitly anticommunist. The twentieth-century neo-Confucians inherited the basic thoughts of neo-Confucianism in the Song and Ming dynasties (eleventh to seventeenth centuries). Due to the influence (and challenge) of Buddhism, they tended to focus on the cultivation of the mind and attempted to reinvent the Confucian tradition by highlighting its metaphysical, transcendent, spiritual, and religious aspects.[7] The twentieth-century neo-Confucians distinguished themselves from their predecessors by drawing resources from modern Western philosophies to synthesize a new Confucian doctrine for modern China. In particular, they contended that Confucian values can develop and shape Western liberal-democratic values in their full force from the central commitments of Confucianism.[8]

Jiang was determined to advance such neo-Confucianism in mainland China. In 1985, he met Liang Shuming, the most courageous and influential neo-Confucian scholar in mainland China in the twentieth century,[9] and Liang encouraged Jiang to pursue his effort to revive Confucianism in mainland China. The traumatic political upheavals in 1989, however, caused Jiang to change focus.[10] For Jiang, political disorder in the actual empirical world became the key concern that called for the reconstruction of a legitimate and stable polity. The bloody repression of the student-led movement meant that the government had lost substantial legitimacy, but Jiang was also critical of the call for Western-style liberal democracy. Even those Chinese intellectuals who claimed to be tolerant and open-minded liberal democrats did not really behave as such, and Jiang was upset by Chinese liberal intellectuals who begged overbearing U.S. legislators to impose a liberal democracy in China, regardless of China's historical, cultural, and social circumstances. For Jiang, it was superficial to view the 1989 political turmoil simply as a failed call for democratic politics. Rather, it was one of several tragedies ultimately dating from the early twentieth century in which an alien Western ideology was imposed on the Chinese people. The Chinese people had been asked to forsake their traditional cultural life and reject Chinese political ideals so that they could become "modern" Marxists or liberals. No other civilization had been subject to such sustained attack for nearly a century; it was no wonder that Chinese people felt disoriented and in turmoil. The same could have happened in Western countries if, say, there had been a concerted effort to impose a Saudi-style Islamic regime on them. A political transition, in Jiang's view, must draw on already existing cultural resources in order to legitimize a long-lasting constitutional order.

At that point, Jiang explicitly parted company with the modern neo-Confucians in Hong Kong and Taiwan. For one thing, their focus on self-cultivation was too abstract to be relevant for the particular political needs of contemporary China. More importantly, they were wrong to think that traditional culture could be maintained within a liberal-democratic political framework. That framework itself needed to be questioned: surely an adaptation of political ideals developed within the Confucian tradition is more likely to secure a Confucian way of life. Hence, Jiang coined the term "political Confucianism" in contrast to the "self-cultivation Confucianism" (or "heart-mind Confucianism") emphasized by the neo-Confucians. Jiang argues that both traditions are necessary, but the most pressing task now is to revive "political Confucianism" that focuses more directly on the betterment of social and political order by legislating and legitimizing political institutions. Jiang argues that "political Confucianism" was founded by the *Gongyang* school, a commentary on the *Spring and Autumn Annals* (allegedly compiled by Confucius himself) that chronicled the history of the state of Lu from 722 BCE to 481 BCE. Jiang argues that "political Confucianism" was developed by Xunzi in the Warring States period, Dong Zhongshu in the Han dynasty, Huang Zongxi in the late Ming/early Qing dynasties, and Kang Youwei in the early twentieth century. After a break of nearly a century, Jiang has revived this tradition, and he has devoted the past few years to working out the justification and institutional implications of a Confucian constitutional order appropriate for contemporary China.[11]

In China's political context, it takes a great deal of courage to put forward such ideas. Jiang continued to experience political difficulties and eventually quit his teaching job at the Shenzhen College of Administration. In 2001, the forty-eight-year-old Jiang established a privately funded Confucian academy in a remote mountainous area in his home province of Guizhou.[12] The academy allows Jiang to pursue his work inspired by the natural scenery and relatively unimpeded by political constraints. Let us now turn to Jiang's work. The next section summarizes Jiang's account of "Wangdao," the highest Confucian political ideal that we can translate as the "Way of the Humane Authority."[13]

THE WAY OF THE HUMANE AUTHORITY

In chapter 1, Jiang makes it clear that his main target is Western-style democracy. Although democracy—more specifically, a form of government

that grants ultimate controlling power to democratically elected representatives—is built on the separation of powers, the separation, Jiang argues,
is a matter of implementation rather than legitimization. In a democracy,
legitimacy is based on the sovereignty of the people. But Jiang objects to the
idea that there is only one source of legitimacy. He claims that the modern
notion of sovereignty of the people is similar in form to the medieval notion
of the sovereignty of God, but with the content changed from God to the
people: "In fact, the sovereignty of the people is simply the secular equivalent of the sovereignty of God."

In political practice, the overemphasis on popular sovereignty translates
into the politics of desire: "[I]n a democracy, political choices are always
down to the desires and interests of the electorate." This leads to two problems. First, the will of the people may not be moral: it could endorse racism,
imperialism, or fascism. Second, when there is a clash between the short-
term interests of the populace and their long-term interests or the common
interests of all mankind, the former have political priority. Jiang specifically
worries about the ecological crisis. It is difficult if not impossible for democratically elected governments to implement policies that curb energy
usage in the interests of future generations and foreigners. If China were
to follow the American model in terms of per capita carbon emissions, for
example, the world would be damaged beyond repair. But "it is impossible
for Green Parties to fully—through legitimization and implementation—
realize ecological values in a Western democracy, without radical change
in both the theory and structure of western democracy." Hence, a political
system must place more emphasis on what Jiang calls "sacred values" that
are concerned with the well-being of the environment, the welfare of future
generations, and humanity as a whole.

Jiang's political alternative is the Confucian Way of the Humane
Authority. The question of political legitimacy, he argues, is central to Confucian constitutionalism. He defines legitimacy as "the deciding factor in
determining whether a ruler has the right to rule." But unlike Western-style
democracy, there is more than one source of legitimacy. According to the
Gongyang Commentary, political power must have three kinds of legitimacy—
that of heaven, earth, and the human—for it to be justified. The legitimacy
of heaven refers to a transcendent ruling will and a sacred sense of natural morality. The legitimacy of earth refers to a legitimacy that comes from
history and culture. And the legitimacy of the human refers to the will of
the people that determines whether or not the people will obey political
authorities. All three forms of legitimacy must be in equilibrium, but Jiang
notes that the equilibrium is not one of equality. According to the *Book of
Changes*, the multiplicity of things comes from the one principle of heaven,

hence the sacred legitimacy of the way of heaven is prior to both the cultural legitimacy of the way of earth and that of the popular will of the human way.

In ancient times, the Way of the Humane Authority was implemented by the monarchical rule of the sage kings of the three dynasties (Xia/Shang/Zhou). But changes in historical circumstances necessitate changes in the form of rule. Today, the will of the people must be given an institutional form that was lacking in the past, though it should be constrained and balanced by institutional arrangements meant to implement the other two forms of legitimacy. Hence, Jiang argues that the Way of the Humane Authority should be implemented by means of a tricameral legislature that corresponds to the three forms of legitimacy: a House of the People that represents popular legitimacy, a House of *Ru* that represents sacred legitimacy,[14] and a House of the Nation that represents cultural legitimacy.

Jiang goes into more institutional detail. The members of the House of the People "are chosen according to the norms and processes of Western democratic parliaments," including universal suffrage and election from functional constituencies.[15] The leader of the House of *Ru* is a great scholar proposed by the Confucian scholars. The candidates for membership are nominated by the scholars, and then they are examined on their knowledge of the Confucian classics and assessed following a trial period of administration at lower levels of government, similar to the examination and recommendation systems used in China in the past. The leader of the House of the Nation should be a direct descendant of Confucius, who would select from "among the descendants of great sages of the past, descendants of the rulers, descendants of famous people, of patriots, university professors of Chinese history, retired top officials, judges, and diplomats, worthy people from society as well as representatives of Daoism, Buddhism, Islam, Tibetan Buddhism, and Christianity."

Each house deliberates in its own way and may not interfere in the running of the others. Jiang addresses the key issue of how to deal with political gridlock that may arise as a result of conflicts between the three houses of parliament. He says that a bill must pass at least two of the houses to become law. The priority of sacred legitimacy is expressed in the veto power exercised by the House of *Ru*. However, Jiang notes that the power of the *Ru* is restrained by the other two houses: for example, "if they propose a bill restricting religious freedom, the People and the Nation will oppose it and it cannot become law." In that sense, it differs from the Council of Guardians in theocratic Iran, where the sacred is the only form of legitimacy and "and so the council of guardians has power over the assembly and is not subject to its restraint."[16]

In chapter 2, Jiang puts forward a proposal for another institution—the Academy—that is meant to further restrain the power of parliamentarians. In Western constitutionalism, power is limited by means of rights. In Confucian constitutionalism, power is limited primarily by means of morality (Jiang is not against the protection of rights per se, but he says that it cannot be the sole aim of a constitution; put differently, the protection of rights will not be effective unless the power holders are primarily regulated by morality). Again, however, new historical circumstances dictate new institutions and practices: "Now that China has ended monarchical rule and begun republican rule, Confucian constitutionalism must create a new structure adapted to the times." The key institution designed to limit power today is what Jiang calls the "Academy," an institution that continues China's tradition and spirit of rule by scholarship.

Jiang explicitly invokes the seventeenth-century Confucian scholar Huang Zongxi's proposal for an Academy composed of scholar-officials who could question the emperor and appraise and adjudicate the rights and wrongs of his policies (Huang's proposal was too radical for his own day: it circulated samizdat-style for over 250 years, surfacing only in the late Qing period, with the dynasty in disarray). An Academy adapted to the present, Jiang argues, would have six functions. First, it would supervise all levels and organs of government by means of a Historical Records Office that would record the words and deeds of the highest decision makers so that they would be answerable to their own time, to history, and to future generations, and a Modern System of Posthumous Titles that would help to restrain the actions of the living.[17] Second, it would set the examinations to ensure that people in all state institutions have the basic qualifications for governing as well as train parliamentarians for the House of *Ru*. Third, it would preside at state ceremonies of a religious nature, sacrifices to heaven, to sages of the past, and to the natural world, and at the investiture of a new head of state. Fourth, it would have the supreme power of recall of all top leaders of state institutions in the event of dereliction of duty. Fifth, it would have the power to undertake mediation and issue final verdicts in the event of serious conflicts among state bodies. And sixth, it would have the power to uphold religion. Jiang is careful to note that "the Academy supervises, but does not run the state. Subordinate bodies exercise their own authority according to the principle of balance of powers and independence." The Academy does not interfere in these operations and hence its maintenance of religion and morality is different from that of a Taliban-style theocracy.[18] Ordinarily, the members of the Academy spend their time on the study of the Confucian classics, and only rarely intervene in the affairs of the state. Such work has special importance because Jiang argues that Confucian constitutionalism cannot be realized without a substantial body of scholars who keep to Confucian beliefs and practices.

In chapter 3, Jiang turns to the third feature of Confucian constitutionalism: the symbolic monarch. Kang Youwei had put forth a similar proposal a century ago, but Jiang defends it in unprecedented detail. According to Jiang, the state is a mysterious body from a distant past,[19] and present-day people have an obligation to maintain it and hand it down to future generations. A leader chosen by the current generation such as an elected president cannot express the state's historical legitimacy because the state also belongs to past and future generations. Hence, a hereditary monarch descended from a noble and ancient lineage is most likely to embody the historical and trans-generational identity of a state: "Inheritance alone bears the hallmarks of status and tradition demanded by the continuity of the state." But Jiang is not calling for the restoration of the imperial system. In traditional China, the monarch represented "both state and government, which means that the structure of the state and that of the government are confused and not very clearly separated." In modern-day Confucian constitutionalism, by contrast, the tricameral legislature would exercise real political (legislative) power, the Academy would exercise supervisory power, and the monarch would exercise symbolic power.

Symbolic power, however, is not really "nothing." The monarch will head the House of the Nation and influence the life of the nation by mediating conflicts between power holders and by "signing and concluding international treaties, proclaiming the law, naming civil and military officials, proclaiming amnesties and pardons, distributing honors, and the like." The monarch can also exercise moral power by speaking out on such issues as environmental degradation that affect future generations. Most important, the symbolic monarch contributes to the legitimacy of political power by instantiating the historical legitimacy of the state. The state is more likely to be legitimate in the eyes of the people if it is headed by a symbolic monarch who commands awe and respect. Jiang emphasizes that loyalty to the state—which underpins its legitimacy, hence the unity and stability of the state—is not purely rational, and it is better for people to project their psychological sense of belonging onto a symbolic monarch than onto those who hold real (legislative) power.

But who exactly should be the symbolic monarch? In today's China, Jiang argues, "the symbolic monarch will have to meet five conditions to be acceptable: (1) the monarch must have a noble and ancient blood lineage; (2) this lineage must be political in nature; (3) it must be clearly shown that the lineage is direct and unbroken; (4) the lineage must be so unique as to exclude competition from any other lineages; and (5) the citizens must universally respect and accept the person with this noble political lineage." Jiang shows that descendants of past emperors cannot meet those conditions. He then goes through each condition and argues that only one person qualifies to be the symbolic monarch in today's China: "the direct heir of Confucius."[20]

LIBERAL CONFUCIANISM VERSUS CONFUCIAN CONSTITUTIONALISM

The first three critics—Joseph Chan, Bai Tongdong, and Li Chenyang—have written sympathetically about aspects of political Confucianism in the past, but they take Jiang Qing to task for neglecting if not undermining key aspects of the liberal tradition. These critics—let us call them liberal Confucians—argue that any form of constitutionalism appropriate for the modern world must incorporate more aspects of the liberal tradition than Jiang Qing allows for.

Joseph Chan, professor of political theory at the University of Hong Kong, endorses the idea that Confucianism can positively shape political institutions, legislation, and policy making. However, he criticizes Jiang for promoting Confucianism as a comprehensive doctrine designed to regulate the constitutional order. According to Chan, Jiang is an "extreme perfectionist" who argues that the state should promote a Confucian conception of the good life that ranks human goods in a particular way and specifies concrete ways of realizing those goods. But promoting Confucianism as a comprehensive doctrine in a modern pluralistic society will damage civility. Free and equal citizens live according to various ways of life and hold different religious beliefs, and promoting Confucian values over and instead of other beliefs can lead only to social conflict. Instead, Chan favors a "moderate form of perfectionism" that allows the state to promote specific values in a piecemeal way. He proposes a kind of civility that requires citizens to be open-minded, to give reasons that others can share in justifying their views, and to seek common ground that underlies conflicting opinions and a common good that transcends partisan interests.[21] Within this context, it may be possible to promote particular Confucian values in a piecemeal way so that they can be accepted or understood by citizens without adopting Confucianism as a comprehensive doctrine. Such values should be widely accepted by many people in modern society and not ranked into a hierarchy of goods or tied to metaphysical or religious doctrines. And they should be modernized so that they are compatible with modern-day values. In traditional China, for example, the value of filial piety was tied to a comprehensive doctrine of the good life that called for obeying parental wishes, but today it should be made compatible with personal autonomy and not tied to any transcendent truths that serve as our moral standard. To the extent values are promoted in a legislative process, there should be a high degree of freedom of speech so that the citizens will be able to freely evaluate the merits of particular Confucian values.

In his response, Jiang Qing affirms the value of speech and debate: "What is today called 'response' was termed 'debate' in the old times. I can do nothing else but debate!" Jiang then accepts Chan's characterization of his theory as "comprehensive." However, he argues that any stable and civil society needs a "comprehensive" theory in the sense of a publicly affirmed philosophy with a set of values for human and social betterment. Without a set of such comprehensive values, society will disintegrate into "moral anarchy" and social conflict. Moreover, he argues that those calling for "specific and piecemeal adoption of Confucian values" in fact hold more comprehensive doctrines that they want to foist upon China. Chan, for example, adheres to a highly contested Rawlsian form of liberalism that prioritizes values such as equal democratic citizenship and personal autonomy that are supposed to set limits to and determine what is good and what is bad about Confucian values. The U.S. constitutional system, for its part, prioritizes a Protestant value system that sets limits to and structures what is acceptable and what is not in society and politics. The United States could not choose Islamic, Hindu, or Confucian religions, values, or political ideas as its mainstream values or constitutional principles. Yet the West won't admit to its hypocrisy. Could it be, Jiang asks, "that it wishes for specific and piecemeal adoption of Confucian values in order to allow it to spread its own liberal democracy as the comprehensive umbrella over all?"[22]

Just as liberal democracy may be appropriate for the West given its own culture and history, so Jiang argues that China should be allowed to make Confucianism into its own public philosophy. Moreover, Confucianism has its own way of securing some of the goods secured by liberal democracy. For example, it accomplishes tolerance for plurality and harmony among people by distinguishing between leading and nonleading values: "the former are the official teaching and have public significance in politics; the latter are confined to . . . private thoughts." In Chinese history, Confucianism had a leading role, but Buddhism and Daoism could flourish as "private, nonleading values" with the result that China never had the religious wars that characterized Western society. Today, official Confucianism might mean that only statues of Confucius are erected in state universities but Buddhist, Daoist, or Christian statues could be erected in their own temples and churches. Gay marriage is another issue that illustrates Jiang's point. The "thick" Confucian view of family relations might rule out open and formal legalization,[23] but Jiang says that homosexual partnerships should be tolerated in society without any interference by the state. On the issue of filial piety, Jiang argues that it should not be stripped of its traditional and metaphysical underpinnings: piety within the family is a kind of springboard of other forms of piety, including "running the state with piety, respecting spirits with piety, sacrificing to sages with piety, and treating things with piety." And Chan is wrong to think that piety translates into blind obedience. Confucius himself said, "When the father is unjust, the son contends with him. How can one say that one can be pious by obeying the father's commands?" Obedience, in other words, is conditional on doing the right thing. Here too Confucianism as a "comprehensive doctrine" might not have dangerous implications that liberals worry about.

Bai Tongdong, professor of philosophy at Fudan University (Shanghai), has written in defense of Confucian politics, but he rejects Jiang Qing's interpretation of Confucian constitutionalism. On the one hand, Bai charges Jiang with not being faithful to "original" Confucianism, notwithstanding his reputation as a "fundamentalist" Confucian. Jiang argues for a kind of Confucian constitutionalism that is grounded in "transcendent values" of the Han dynasty *Gongyang* school, but Bai argues that the true spirit of Confucianism should be located in the earlier pre-Qin Confucians such as Mencius and Xunzi who attempted to find a middle way between the sacred and the secular. The Han Confucians, Bai suggests, used heaven and Confucians' monopoly on the interpretation of heaven to obtain power for Confucians and govern the state with the emperor. On the other hand, Bai charges Jiang with dogmatically applying the ways of an outdated view of Confucianism to a modern-day pluralistic context. Bai argues that a Confucianism backed by a transcendent foundation could not be widely accepted in a modern-day society characterized by what Rawls called the "fact of pluralism." Bai worries along with Jiang that Chinese culture faces a serious threat from Christianity and the Westcentric modern world, but he argues that this threat can and should be met without appealing to contested transcendent values. Just as Rawls sought to defend an interpretation of liberal democracy that could command universal political agreement by freeing itself from 'comprehensive' Christian values, so Confucians should seek to defend Confucian codes of conduct and institutions not grounded in a priori systems of thought.[24] Bai specifically defends Mencius's idea that identifies heaven's will with the people's will and yet leaves an important role for the wise and virtuous elite to determine what the people's will is and what should be done with it. Institutionally, Mencius's idea translates into a hybrid regime that combines elements of popular will and involvement of the elite. Hence, Bai rejects Jiang's idea that political institutions such as the House of *Ru* and the Academy should represent heaven as separate from (and more important than) "the people." For Bai, it's a matter of how to interpret the people's will in a way that does justice to the original spirit of Confucianism while being acceptable to a wide group of people in China today.

Jiang's response is clear: he denies that there is disagreement about fundamental ideas between the pre-Qin and the Han Confucians, especially regarding the nature of a transcendent, sacred heaven. Hence, Bai is wrong to think that the earlier Confucians held a more "disenchanted and humanized" conception heaven that is supposedly more appropriate for our day. Jiang specifically questions Bai's reading of Mencius. He draws on several passages to argue that "the ultimate holder of the highest political power is heaven and not a human person, that is, sovereignty lies with heaven. . . . [Hence], it is natural that the transcendent, sacred legitimacy of heaven is higher in terms of legitimacy than legitimacy based on the people." How then can we know heaven's will? By the way things are done to express its sovereignty. One way is to win the hearts of the people, so that when the people are satisfied, we can say that heaven is satisfied. But the will of heaven can also be made manifest in other ways, such as "revealing auspicious omens, sending down disasters, or in the heart of the king and the will of the sages." In short, the will of the people is a way of identifying the will of heaven, but "it does not mean that sovereignty is owned by the people, still less that the will of the people is the will of heaven." Such a debate might seem esoteric to the nonexpert (or the nonbeliever), but it does have key political implications. For one thing, Jiang's view on the ultimate importance of the legitimacy of heaven grounds his view that institutions representing the legitimacy of heaven—the House of *Ru* and the Academy—have more political power than institutions representing the legitimacy of the people and the earth. Jiang argues that Bai's own reading of Mencius—influenced by Western liberalism—cannot produce a theory of legitimacy that would justify Bai's aim of giving extra power to the wise and virtuous. And it affects the way we think of the natural world. For Bai, the environment has value insofar as it is necessary for human flourishing. For Jiang, the environment has sacred value irrespective of its impact on humans.

Li Chenyang, professor of philosophy at Nanyang Technological University in Singapore, defends yet another interpretation of heaven that is neither transcendent nor anthropocentric: he argues that heaven is necessarily interrelated in a "heaven-earth-humanity" triad. Jiang's view that there is one transcendent heaven occupying a higher position that generates a differentiated heaven (along with earth and humanity) is problematic on two grounds. First, the idea of a transcendent and personalized heaven was developed in pre-Confucian times and was replaced by the idea of an immanent heaven that is part of the heaven-earth-humanity triad in classical Confucian times. The mainstream (and correct) understanding of heaven, according to Li, is heaven amid earth and humanity. Hence, Jiang's interpretation represents regress, not progress.[25] Second, the notion of a transcendent heaven is redundant and illogical. It makes no sense to say that heaven can be both one thing that generates something else and one part of something else (the heaven-earth-humanity triad) that is generated by it. Li speculates that the real reason for Jiang's metaphysical position is the need to justify an Academy that represents heaven and stands above the tricameral parliament. Instead of metaphysics generating politics, Li argues that politics generates the metaphysics, in violation of what ought to be the Confucian view of heaven.

Jiang responds by reaffirming his view of heaven as both the one and the many. Far from being redundant, Confucian metaphysics cannot do without one principle that stands above the heaven-earth-humanity triad: "[T]he heaven which is the one principle of the triad heaven-earth-humanity is the ultimate coordinator and synthesizer of the myriad things in the universe and gives them a universal purpose and meaning." Jiang recognizes Li's argument that his reading of heaven has the same logical difficulties as the Christian doctrine of the Trinity, where God is both One as well as the Father, the Son, and the Holy Spirit. But Jiang responds that such matters are matters of faith, whether in Christianity or Confucianism: "This faith must rely on a mystical intuition that transcends reason and a dark-seeing and mystical understanding in the depths of the heart before it can be known or grasped."

Again, such debates may seem somewhat obscure to people standing outside the Confucian tradition, but they have important political implications. Li fundamentally opposes a Confucian constitution that is sacred and transcendent in character and favors a constitution, along with government establishment, that is "mundane in nature." He opposes the idea that sage kings or scholar-officials are able to represent the transcendent heaven or act on behalf of it. In political practice, Li's ideal translates into "Confucian content with democratic form," referring to a society with Confucian social and moral ideals that adopts an electoral mechanism to choose political leaders. Confucianism, Li says, could adopt "the democratic political mechanism for governmental affairs, in some way similar to how Christianity adopts a democratic form in the West without changing its fundamental beliefs and ideals."

Jiang, not surprisingly, casts doubt on Li's ideal. General elections will generate leaders "who will represent the interests and desires of the masses." Put simply, it would be impossible for defenders of Confucian values to be elected without giving up on those values: "If sages, worthies, and gentlemen wish to mount the stage they must keep to the objective framework of the stage, that is, the form of democracy, and first make themselves into ordinary persons or small-minded persons, or else they cannot ascend the stage and hold the power to rule." Succeeding in democratic elections means taking part in "secularism, pursuit of interests, agitation, demagoguery, self-projection, performance, fawning, hypocrisy, pretence, pandering to the populace, including even absurdities, farce, and a great waste of money." Jiang points to the "chaotic phenomenon of Taiwan's realization of democracy" to illustrate the case that democracy undermines Confucian values. Hence, Jiang proposes "the opposite thesis, of a Confucian form with a democratic content. . . . [W]e must use the form of Confucian constitutionalism and selectively pick and choose elements of democratic content or of constitutional content, and not the other way around."

It is worth asking, however, if Li and Jiang are really as far apart as they suggest. Li's idea of "Confucian content" includes the idea that "Confucian values and convictions must be constitutionally guaranteed (e.g., integrity of the family and priority of citizen's livelihood in the agenda of the government)." In that sense, Confucianism sets the limits to democratic decision making. But what if elected politicians favor repealing Confucian values in the constitution on the grounds that, say, freedom of speech is more important than citizens' livelihood? Would Li then favor Jiang-style constraints on democratic decision making by Confucian worthies?

SOCIALISM VERSUS CONFUCIAN CONSTITUTIONALISM

In Chinese political discourse, the socialist or "new Leftist" thinkers seek inspiration from the Marxist tradition as well as China's Maoist heritage. Wang Shaoguang, professor of political science at the Chinese University of Hong Kong, is one of the leading "new Left" thinkers in China. He is often (mis)taken as a strong supporter of the status quo in China, but Wang was sharply critical of the emphasis on privatization, the destruction of the Maoist-style emphasis on social welfare, and the growing gap between rich and poor in the 1980s and 1990s. The Hu Jintao era has seen somewhat of a (re)turn to the "Left"—elimination of taxes and improved health care in rural areas, more funding for basic education, and experiments with socialist forms of property rights in Chongqing and elsewhere—and that is the main reason Wang has become more supportive of the status quo. Still, he argues that more needs to be done to combat the inequalities generated by capitalist modernization in China (the gap between rich and poor has continued to worsen). Jiang Qing agrees with the critique of capitalism, though they disagree about whether socialism or Confucianism should set the political agenda for China's political future.

For Wang, political legitimacy is not something to be defined by moral philosophers in total abstraction from the political reality. Rather, it is a matter of "whether or not a political system faces a crisis of legitimacy depends on whether the people who live there doubt the rightness of its power, and whether they consider it the appropriate system for their country." In other words, Wang endorses a definition of legitimacy as the legitimacy of the popular will. But far from endorsing liberal-democratic political practice, this view of legitimacy provides a critical perspective on actually existing democracy. Wang turns the tables on Jiang, arguing that he naïvely endorses "the mainstream Western view that Western liberal democracy does enjoy the legitimacy of the popular will." In the United States and Europe, empirical studies show that institutions that represent the people have little popular legitimacy. Wang argues that the main problem lies with the expectation that elections per se can represent the people's will. In fact, capitalist interests tend to skew electoral outcomes: the wealthy elites participate more in politics, with the result that "the influence of elites on the government far surpasses that of the masses." Hence, the problem is not too much democracy (as Jiang argues), but too little.

Wang draws on extensive empirical evidence to show that the Chinese political system enjoys greater legitimacy—in the sense that people have confidence in their government—than most Western liberal democracies. He notes that such results were greeted with skepticism by Western scholars, but later inquiries were designed to prevent people from telling lies, and still the results show consistent support for the regime. In this sense, Wang questions Jiang's assumption that China has a legitimacy crisis. Wang seems to credit Mao Zedong's efforts to "destroy the capitalist class," and he quotes a study that shows more support for Maoism than for Confucianism or liberalism. But he worries that China has not done enough to combat the increasing power of the elite in politics. For example, the proportion of workers and farmers in the National People's Congress has fallen since the Cultural Revolution. For China, too, the solution is more democracy, not less. But democracy must be more than elections: "It should be a new form of democracy that tries to enable everyone to take part in politics through sortition, deliberation, and modern electronic forms of communication and that extends popular participation from the political realm to other areas, including that of the economy." If we were to use

Jiang's terminology, Wang concludes, "then 'socialism' would be the way of heaven (sacred legitimacy), 'democracy' the way of humanity (popular legitimacy), 'Chinese' the way of earth (cultural and historical legitimacy). Would this model of threefold legitimacy not be a 'more realistic utopia'?"

In his response, Jiang distinguishes between normative legitimacy and "subjective endorsement of the actual political situation by the masses." For Jiang, there are three forms of normative legitimacy that balance and check each other, unlike Western democratic politics that grants sole normative legitimacy to sovereignty of the people. Even in terms of popular legitimacy, however, Jiang does not share Wang's view that there is no legitimacy crisis in China. While the standard of living has made great progress as a result of the policy of reform and this has led to a rise of popular satisfaction, "popular legitimacy is broader than this. Besides the satisfaction of material life, it also includes the protection of some basic rights such as freedom of speech, of religion, of media and the press, freedom to form associations, and the like. It also includes the sense of security of the people, their happiness, their sense of fairness, and assessment of social and political morality. In this sense, the Chinese masses are clearly discontented."[26] And whereas Wang does not say whether he favors participatory democracy instead of competitive elections or as a supplement to them, Jiang is more straightforward about the need for elections to improve popular legitimacy: "The participation of all is granted a place in popular legitimacy and in the House of the People."

Still, Jiang notes that Confucianism and the new Left do hold some things in common: both are opposed to the capitalist alliance of political and financial elites who oppress the masses. But they hold different views about how to deal with the problem. For Maoists, the solution is to attack all forms of inequality in society. But this ideal is a destructive utopian fantasy, leading to such outcomes as the Terror of the French Revolution and the chaos and violence of the Cultural Revolution. For Confucians, the best way of challenging material inequality is to replace a financial elite with an elite of "worthy and capable scholar-officials [who] are able to truly represent the interests of the masses thanks to their moral virtue and political ability, and hence once in power they can forcefully oppose the monopoly of power of capitalism and the oppression that this brings to the masses." The realistic choice is not between an egalitarian society and an elitist one but rather between different kinds of elites. Confucians favor "an elitism of knowledge and ability, not of money or wealth." In that sense, Jiang's ideal of the Way of Humane Authority is a realistic utopia "that can be realized by reflection and effort."

A THIRD BEST WAY?

One of the great virtues of Jiang Qing is his willingness to engage in substantive debate with his critics. He tackles their arguments in elaborate detail and makes clear distinctions between his responses. One is tempted to say that Jiang's argumentative style is closest to the mode favored by Western (or Anglo-American) liberal thinkers, though he is no doubt inspired by earlier Confucian debaters such as Xunzi who wrote in a clear and systematic style. Still, there is an element of unease: Jiang seems adamant about sticking to his views; he fails to make even one concession to his critics.[27] He gives the impression that China (and maybe even the whole world) is doomed unless it endorses and implements the Way of the Humane Authority as a whole package.[28] So it is worth asking if Jiang *could* have made some compromises or modifications to his theory that would have at least partly satisfied his critics.

Jiang himself notes that the Way of the Humane Authority is already a compromised ideal. In an ideal world, an all-wise and virtuous sage king would decode Confucius's message in the *Spring and Autumn Annals* and seek to implement the blueprint for reform that could save the world (*tianxia*) from its current state of turmoil: "The highest political hope of Confucianism is for the return of a sage king who will restore the direct rule of the sage kings."[29] But Jiang recognizes that no such sage king has appeared since ancient times (he recognizes that Mencius, who claimed that sage kings come in five-hundred-year cycles and hence were overdue in his own day—the fourth century BCE—was too optimistic). Hence, Jiang does not theorize much about this possibility but rather puts forward what should be viewed as a second-best alternative—the Way of the Humane Authority—to be implemented in China first, with the hope that it could inspire the rest of the world. But Jiang explicitly reminds us that "Confucian constitutionalism is the interim Way of the Humane Authority that prepares for this direct rule by the sage kings. . . . [It] is not designed to last forever. It exists only in this interim period of republicanism."[30]

But if Jiang has compromised his ideal, why can he not make further compromises that accommodate some of the arguments of his critics? Why can he not consider the possibility of a third best way, something less good (from Jiang Qing's perspective) than the Way of the Humane Authority but that is still better than the status quo? In fact, Jiang Qing's own political interventions suggest that he is willing to consider the possibility of a third best way. He signed a petition that publicly criticizes plans to build a church in Qufu (the home of Confucianism) that would tower over the Confucian temple;[31] the rest of the power structure in China would not change, but presumably this effort to fight for the status quo is worthwhile. He has compiled a twelve-volume series of Confucian classics for children that is meant to shape education now, not just in the fully "Confucianized" future. He has praised the female academic Yu Dan's best-selling work on the *Analects* of Confucius on the grounds that she helps to popularize Confucianism among the masses even though he disagrees with her depoliticized interpretation of Confucianism.[32] And he has called for "Confucianizing" the Chinese Communist Party and more teaching of Confucian classics in Communist Party schools, and he has said that he would advise the current government if called upon to do so. On all these issues, he has been surprisingly pragmatic and willing to work within the contemporary social and political reality for improvements, even though the result would still not look anything like the Way of the Humane Authority. Of course, he would hope that these improvements would pave the way for the Way of the Humane Authority—just as the Way of the Humane Authority is a short-term (several thousand years?) political ideal that is meant to pave the way for a sage ruler—but the point is that he should also be open to modifications of his views that go some way to appeasing his critics. So what would a "third best alternative" look like? More precisely, how could Jiang Qing modify his views so as to accommodate some of the criticisms of his critics while still remaining true to his central normative (religious) commitments?

Let us first ask if Jiang can accommodate the views of his socialist critics. Jiang clearly aspires to a society governed by talented and virtuous elite. For the socialist, the downside is that the governed—the mass of mankind—seem to be perpetually condemned to a life of hard physical labor and toil. As Mencius (in)famously put it, "Those who labor with their brains govern others; those who labor with their brawn are governed others. Those governed by others, feed them. Those who govern others are fed by them. This is a principle accepted by the whole world" (*Mencius* 3A:4). Mao went to the other extreme and tried to abolish any division between those who work with their brains and those who work with their brawn. As Wang puts it, "[H]e was looking for a completely equal society in which the three great inequalities of workers and peasants, town and country, physical labor and mental labor would be destroyed." In the Cultural Revolution, it meant sending "intellectuals" to the countryside and "peasants" to universities. The result was ten years of violence and chaos that few Chinese would want to go through again.[33] Even advocates of Maoism now, Jiang notes icily, would not likely favor an outcome where "Professor Wang [works] on the assembly line in a factory in Dongguan and . . . an assembly worker from a factory in Dongguan [lectures] in the Chinese University of Hong Kong."[34]

But perhaps the "original Marx"—one still (at least partly) favored by Jiang[35]—holds some valuable insights. At the moral core of Marx's philosophy is the idea that we should strive for a society that frees the large mass of humankind from the need to slave in factories and fields. Marx opposed the capitalist mode of production because it treats workers as mere tools in the productive process and puts technology to use for the purpose of enriching a small minority of capitalists. But capitalism does have one virtue: it has the consequence of developing the productive forces (technology and the knowledge required to use it) more than any previous economic system, and hence lays the foundation for communist society. Once the productive forces are sufficiently developed, then capitalist property relations will be overthrown and humankind can begin to implement communism. The final goal is "higher communism": technology will be highly developed and machines will do most of the dirty work needed to meet people's physical needs, and people will finally be free to develop their creative talents. Unpleasant labor will be limited to the maintenance of machinery and other tasks required to keep the system going, but this "realm of necessity" would not take up most of the working day.

Jiang would no doubt reply that "higher communism" is a dangerous fantasy. Any attempt to bring it about by focusing exclusively on the development of the productive forces would end up destroying the environment (Marx, to be fair, was unaware of global warming). Plus there will always be a need for talented and virtuous elite to govern others,[36] and Marx's ideal of society where the state would have "withered away" is another utopian fantasy. Fair enough. But it does not follow that we should be satisfied with a capitalist economic system that is designed to maximize the profit of a minority of capitalists. To the extent possible, we should favor technological change and a property rights regime that frees workers from the need to engage in drudge labor. Of course, this aim would have to be balanced against other concerns, such as economic efficiency and environmental sustainability. This kind of decision making is likely to be empirically complex and would require, at the very least, knowledge of basic economics: precisely the sort of decision making that should be the concern of the talented and virtuous elite. However, the selection process of political elites—whether for the House of *Ru* or the Academy—would need to involve testing of basic economic knowledge,[37] not simply knowledge of the Confucian classics.

For Jiang's liberal critics—even those sympathetic to (parts of) the Confucian tradition—the key worry is that Jiang seems intent on institutionalizing a form of Confucianism that is founded on highly controversial transcendent values. Such a foundation for Confucian constitutionalism is not acceptable to those who view Confucianism as primarily social rather than religious ethics, not to mention those indifferent or hostile to the Confucian tradition. But it is worth noting that few of the criticisms were directed at Jiang's institutional proposals per se. In fact, these same critics have written works defending institutional frameworks that incorporate aspects of meritocratic (or elite) rule with democratic institutions.[38] So perhaps Jiang and his critics can agree to disagree about justifications for political institutions. The House of *Ru*, for example, could be justified with reference to a transcendent heaven for Jiang and his supporters, whereas it could be justified differently by nonreligious Confucians and others.[39] Politically speaking, what matters is to secure agreement on what the institution is supposed to do. For example, Jiang argues that democratic representation is limited because (even when it works well) it represents only the interests of voters. Hence, the House of *Ru* would have the task of representing the task of nonvoters who are affected by the policies of the government, including future generations and people living outside the boundaries of the state. In practice, one of the main tasks of the House of *Ru* would be to consider the environmental consequences of policies that are normally neglected or underemphasized in democratic decision making since the voters (and politicians chosen by them) are unlikely to favor policies that curb their own interests in cases of conflict with the interests of future generations and foreigners.[40] Jiang Qing's critics could agree to a house of parliament specifically entrusted with the task of deliberating about the interests of nonvoters, though they would agree for different reasons. For Jiang, the deputies in the House of *Ru* decide in favor of environmentally sustainable policies because they owe their allegiance to the moral truths enshrined by heaven. For his nonreligious critics, the deputies might reach similar decisions because they seek to consider the basic (evolutionarily determined?) human needs of those who are typically neglected by democratic decision making, as well as perhaps the needs of the animal and natural worlds. The latter might not agree that welfare of future generations, humanity as a whole, and the environment is a "sacred" duty, but it does not matter as long as they agree it is an important duty and there is a need for an institution that would have the task of being responsible for the needs of nonvoters affected by the policies of the government.

Of course, it is not so simple. For one thing, Jiang insists that the constitution should be explicitly based on sacred Confucian values, something his critics could not accept. But perhaps there is room for compromise. What matters is the substance of the values enshrined in the constitution, not the precise terminology. If the substance of Confucian values is protected without any explicit reference to the Confucian (sacred) tradition,

Jiang should be able to live with the result.[41] And when we do turn to the substance, it turns out that Jiang has much in common with his liberal critics. He favors the freedoms of speech and association, religious toleration, concern for the disadvantaged, and so on. He seems to allow for multiparty politics in the election mechanisms that select deputies for the House of the People. Pure liberals might object to a constitution that enshrines an element of elite rule (elites would be selected by nondemocratic mechanisms such as examinations and recommendations in the other houses),[42] but liberal Confucians such as Chan, Bai, and Li may be willing to go along.

Still, liberal Confucians almost certainly will not be willing to endorse the whole of Jiang's institutional proposals. Jiang's seemingly unshakeable confidence in the truth of sacred, transcendental Confucian values underpins his desire to empower Confucians in the House of *Ru*, the House of the Nation, and the Academy as well as his call to make Confucius's direct descendant into the symbolic monarch. But such confidence, to put it mildly, is not widely shared in China (or anywhere else); it may be a product of Jiang's own rather distinctive lifelong quest for an absolute moral truth that would make sense of the mysteries of the universe. Arguably, Jiang's own outlook goes against the grain of Chinese popular culture, which has been eclectic and pragmatic about religious outlooks for much of its history (the casual tourist to China cannot fail to notice temples that seem to incorporate, almost at random, aspects of Daoist, Buddhist, Confucian, and folk religions). So perhaps Jiang should allow for greater political power for non-Confucians in the name of being faithful to an important strand of Chinese culture and history.

To be fair, the House of the Nation is supposed to represent not just the Confucian tradition but also other traditions that have been influential in Chinese history, such as Buddhism, Daoism, and Christianity. Still, Jiang argues that the head of the House should be the direct descendant of Confucius (i.e., the symbolic monarch) who should have the power to approve and reject all proposals for the deputies in the house. Here, Jiang would need to compromise. Surely it is more respectful of traditions to let them choose their own representatives without fear of veto power: Buddhist organizations would choose Buddhist representatives to the House of the Nation, Daoist organizations would choose Daoist representatives, and so on. In fact, such practices could coexist with extra state sponsored support for Confucianism. What matters (for Jiang) is that Confucianism is the "first among equals," not that Confucians exercise direct control over other religions.

The Academy would also need to be somewhat "de-Confucianized" in order to be made acceptable to liberal Confucians. Jiang himself draws extensively on knowledge of different constitutional systems to defend (and compare) his proposals,[43] so it would not seem unreasonable to request that members of the Academy have some knowledge of comparative constitutionalism. Such knowledge can be helpful for thinking about how to mediate conflicts among the three houses of parliament.[44] Another task of the Academy is to check the power of the three houses of parliament, but Jiang's critics are not likely to agree that we can rely on the superior virtue of its members as a way of checking their own power. Such mechanisms as term limits and stiff penalties for corruption would also be necessary to "guard the guardians."

The symbolic monarch is perhaps the most controversial of Jiang's proposals, and here too he would have to compromise. In principle, a symbolic monarch may be a good idea: as Jiang points out, it is important to separate a symbolic ruler who can exert a pull on people's emotions from the real power holders who should be subject to more rational scrutiny.[45] But the conclusion that the monarch must be the direct descendant of Confucius is open to the obvious challenge that he or she may not be sufficiently talented or virtuous to exercise the job well.[46] Jiang's view that the monarch must be a direct descendant is derived on the basis of criteria for choosing the symbolic monarch that owe more to political considerations than to normative commitments, so he can be flexible about these criteria if they lead to potentially problematic outcomes. Perhaps the symbolic monarch can be chosen on merit from among a randomly selected group of descendants of Confucius (there are several thousand in Qufu) rather being the direct descendant of Confucius, thus minimizing the risk that he or she would lack basic talent or virtue.

The Way of the Humane Authority may be a worthy ideal,[47] but it is a work of political imagination. Hence, Jiang Qing should be open to the possibility of modifications of the ideal that can bring liberal Confucians and socialists on board (so long as they do not undermine his core normative commitments). One advantage is that there would be a widely shared standard for evaluating political progress in China. Instead of judging political progress simply by asking whether China is becoming more democratic, the new standard would provide a more comprehensive way of judging political progress (and regress). And there may be more reasons for optimism. In several years, for example, Chinese leaders are not likely to be chosen according to one person one vote, but if meritocratically chosen leaders do more for workers, farmers, and future generations, and if there is more political support for the protection of history and culture in China, then on balance different political forces could agree that China is moving in a more humane direction.

Another advantage of a "third best way" that can bring liberal Confucians and socialists on board is that the goal of "Confucianizing" society and politics may be easier (or less difficult) to realize. But even such modifications remain a long way from the political reality. Just as Kang Youwei's proposal for Confucian constitutionalism a century ago could come close to shaping China's political future only in the context of substantive parliamentary debates in a relatively open society, so Jiang Qing's proposals (even in modified form) are not likely to see light of day without more freedom of political speech that encourages open debate about substantial political reform.[48] But we can thank him for putting some strikingly original and thought-provoking proposals on the table. I do not know if they will have substantial political influence, but let me end with one prediction: we will still be debating Jiang Qing's ideas one hundred years from now, just as we are still debating Kang Youwei's ideas today.[49]

PART I

*A Confucian
Constitutional
Order*

CHAPTER I

....

The Way of the Humane Authority

THE THEORETICAL BASIS FOR CONFUCIAN CONSTITUTIONALISM
AND A TRICAMERAL PARLIAMENT

Jiang Qing

The way ahead for China's political development is the Way of the Humane Authority and not democracy.[1] This is the only way in which Chinese culture can respond to the challenge of Western culture. However, in recent years China's political development has begun to go astray. Every current of political thought in China assumes that democracy is the way ahead for China. This goes without saying for liberal democracy's Western-style "genuine democracy," or for the pursuit of a "socialist democracy" by socialism that is supposed to differ from "capitalist democracy." It even includes the neo-Confucians who exalt Chinese culture and make democracy the "new kingship" derived from the Confucian way of the sage.[2] A glance over China's current world of thought shows that Chinese people have already lost their ability to think independently about political questions. In other words, Chinese people are no longer able to use patterns of thought inherent in their own culture—Chinese culture—to think about China's current political development. This is a great tragedy for the world of Chinese thought! It is, therefore, necessary to go back to the inherent patterns of Chinese culture to ground the development of Chinese political thought, rather than simply following the Western trends and forgetting our own culture. By the "inherent pattern of Chinese culture" I refer to the "politics of the Way of the Humane Authority." The politics of the Way of the Humane Authority is the way ahead for China.

THE POLITICS OF THE WAY OF THE HUMANE AUTHORITY

At the heart of the Way of the Humane Authority lies the question of three forms of political legitimacy. Legitimacy is the deciding factor in determining whether a ruler has the right to rule. *The Gongyang Commentary* to the *Spring and Autumn Annals* says that to rule one must "share in the realms of heaven, earth and human beings," or that "the Way of the Humane Authority links three spheres," which means that political power must have three kinds of legitimacy, that of heaven, earth, and the human, for it to be legal and justified.[3] The legitimacy of "heaven" refers to transcendent, sacred legitimacy. In Chinese culture "heaven" has both the character of a ruling will, personal yet hidden, and a transcendent, sacred sense of natural morality. The legitimacy of "earth" refers to the legitimacy that comes from history and culture because cultures are formed through history in particular places. The legitimacy of the "human" refers to the legitimacy of the will of the people because conformity to the will of the people directly determines whether or not people will obey political authorities.

The State of Equilibrium and Harmony says, "He who attains to the sovereignty of all the kingdom attach due importance to three points." The first is "he sets (his institutions) up before heaven and earth, and there is nothing in them contrary (their mode of operation). He presents himself with them before Spiritual Beings, and no doubts about them arise." This refers to sacred legitimacy. The second is "he examines (his institutions) by comparison with those of the founders of the three dynasties,[4] and finds them without mistake. . . . He is prepared to wait for the rise of a sage a hundred ages hence, and has no misgivings." This refers to cultural legitimacy. The third is "rooted in his own character and conduct, and attested by the multitudes of the people."[5] This is the legitimacy of the popular will.

The politics of the Way of the Humane Authority states that legitimacy comes from recognition and representation of the Way of heaven, history, and the popular will. It can ensure that the ruler's authority and the people's obedience are seen, respectively, as right and duty. Should the political authority simultaneously lack legitimacy in the three spheres, it will be obliged to constantly make bargains and will never win the full loyalty and acknowledgment of the people. The result could easily be a crisis of political authority. Political order will constantly be on the brink of falling into chaos. Hence, the Way of the Humane Authority of Confucianism seeks to fully and wholly resolve the question of the legitimacy of political power, and to establish a political order that is stable and harmonious over a long time. As we say in Chinese, we want to found a political order that is stable and long-lasting and that is "in accordance with the Way, with reality, with law and with the present situation."

In the terminology of Chinese politics, the Way of the Humane Authority deals with "legitimizing the Way" (*zheng Dao*) and not with "implementing the Way" (zhi Dao).[6] By "legitimizing the Way" we mean the legitimacy of political power, while by "implementing the Way" we mean the way in which legitimate political power is implemented and exercised, as well as the methods and art of using legitimate power. Hence legitimizing the Way is superior, and prior to, implementing the Way. And the legitimacy of political power is the basis and goal of every political system, method, order, and art of politics. Without it, no political reality has any meaning or value.

In China today the biggest and most urgent question that politics faces is the legitimacy of the political order. If this question is not first dealt with, the lesser questions of implementation cannot be properly managed. Therefore, the mission of contemporary Confucianism is to establish a complete and integral legitimacy for the future of Chinese politics. The Way of the Humane Authority can lay the foundations for the legitimacy of China's political order and so repair the failure to resolve this question and make up for the deficit of legitimacy that has been around for the past hundred years.

The Way of the Humane Authority seeks not only to determine the three forms of legitimacy but also to ensure that the three are properly balanced. Western democracy is built on the separation of powers, but from the view of the Way of the Humane Authority, the separation of powers is a matter of implementation and not of legitimization. Western democratic legitimacy is based on the sovereignty of the people. This is said to be unique, supreme, absolute, exclusive, and inalienable. From a political point of view there is nothing that can keep it in check. The Way of the Humane Authority is different. It holds that equilibrium is an issue not only in implementation but also in legitimization. It is not only to be used in the structure and working of political power but also to be used in determining the basic meaning and legal structure of political legitimacy itself. In the Way of the Humane Authority, no one form of legitimacy should be allowed to become sovereign over the others, for this will lead to political bias and failings.

Should transcendent legitimacy be overemphasized, it will quench a correct expression of human needs and the popular will. Examples of this can be seen in the religious politics of Christianity in the Middle Ages in the West, or in that of Islamic fundamentalism today. On the other hand, if popular legitimacy is overemphasized, it will deny the value of the sacred and lead to extreme secularization and pandering to human desires. Contemporary Western democracy is an example of this. Thus, the best thing is that legitimacy be balanced, so that no one form of legitimacy excludes the others and they will work together in harmony. Each will have its own proper place, playing its own role and not interfering with the others.

But the equilibrium of the three forms of legitimacy is not one of mere equality. It is not a two-dimensional, flat equality but a three-dimensional one, a hierarchy. Heaven generates the myriad things from above, and the myriad things depend on the determination of heaven and earth. Their multiplicity comes from the one principle of heaven, as Cheng Yi says: "principle is one; its manifestations many." Thus, the sacred legitimacy of the way of heaven is prior to both the cultural legitimacy of the way of earth and that of the popular will of the human way. The basic relationship of heaven to earth and the human is given in the *Book of Changes* as the way of the *Qian* (heaven) hexagram, which is "great harmony are preserved in union" and "everything obtains it correct nature as appointed [by the mind of heaven]."[7] It is the sovereign, and so the three forms are not equal or on the same plane. Hence, the three forms of legitimacy have a three-dimensional relationship as well as having a horizontal relationship of distinctive identity. As a result, the harmony of the legitimacies of the Way of the Humane Authority is a three-dimensional rather than a flat harmony.

The reason why the Way of the Humane Authority stresses the three-dimensional harmony has to do with Chinese ways of thinking. The influence of the *Book of Changes* and of the *Spring and Autumn Annals* means that China does not think in terms of either one or the other. Rather, the world is seen three-dimensionally in a structure that embraces many ways of thinking. To look at the question of legitimacy from the point of view of the three elements of heaven, earth, and the human brings out the tri-dimensionality of legitimacy and the separation of its constituent parts. It is one whole but multiform; priority and equilibrium both have a place. The Western idea of sovereignty of the people is the product of a Western way of thinking in straight lines, rather like the "supreme being" of Greek philosophy, which does not allow for multiplicity. The current Western notion of sovereignty of the people is simply the result of a rejection of the medieval sovereignty of God. In the Christian Middle Ages political authority came from God. God was the ultimate source of the legitimacy of secular power. God is unique, absolute, self-sufficient, exclusive, and the supreme essence, and so was what derived from God. The only difference between the sovereignty of God and that of the people lies in the content itself. In both the form and the way in which legitimacy is thought of, the two are exactly alike. Both come from a tendency to think in terms of absolutes, and so neither can admit any other form of legitimacy. In fact, the sovereignty of the people is simply the secular equivalent of the sovereignty of God. In contemporary Western politics, the people play the role that God played in the Middle Ages. Precisely for this reason, democratic politics asserts the sole legitimacy of the will of the people and cannot imagine any other form of legitimacy.

THE WAY OF THE HUMANE AUTHORITY
IN THEORY AND HISTORY

The Way of the Humane Authority is the theoretical model by which Confucianism establishes a way of solving the question of legitimization on the basis of the historical archetype of the sage kings of the three dynasties (Xia/Shang/Zhou). Hence, the Way of the Humane Authority is grounded both in real history and in quasi-history. It is both an ideal and also an ideal that is not purely formal because it has been fashioned through history and is erected on a historical basis. This is very different from democratic politics. When faced with the question of legitimacy, democracy places its theoretical foundation in social contract theory. The idea of the social contract is one that uses reason or, better, concepts to posit the origin of the state and then to construct political legitimacy. The legitimacy of a democracy is a product of pure reason and speculation that lacks an authentic historical background.

The Way of the Humane Authority is a theoretical model constructed on the basis of historical facts. There are two features that determine the Way of the Humane Authority. Firstly, the Way of the Humane Authority was implemented in history, unlike the pure mystique that democracy is.[8] Secondly, the Way of the Humane Authority is an ideal model, which implies that in history it has only been gradually and partially realized. Its full implementation requires a long and slow historical process. In the course of Chinese history the Way of the Humane Authority has been implemented in only a fragmentary fashion; there is still a significant gap between the Way of the Humane Authority and the political realities of Chinese history.

The concrete way in which the Way of the Humane Authority has been implemented in Chinese history is that of monarchy. In the view of the Way of the Humane Authority, the legitimacy of the monarch is conditional upon benevolent and virtuous governance. Lack of benevolence and virtue entails a loss of legitimacy. Above we noted that the political order is part of "implementation" while "legitimization" is a theoretical model. Although "legitimization" appears in history, once it appears it is able to transcend concrete history and has everlasting value. "Implementation," on the other hand, is the concrete historical means by which legitimization is realized. Hence, for the Way of the Humane Authority, legitimization does not change, whereas implementation may. Monarchy is in the realm of implementation. It was the only natural choice in the long course of Chinese history and carries the necessity and rationality of history. Historically speaking, it is the legitimate form of politics in China.

Yet monarchy is not the sole, unwavering choice of Confucianism, nor is it the unchanging and fixed form in which the Way of the Humane Authority can exist. Changes in historical circumstances may necessitate changes in the form of rule. Hence, the given state of implementation of the legitimacy of the Way of the Humane Authority is valid only for that particular period in history. As an ideal, the three-dimensional harmony of the three forms of legitimacy is one that can be universalized. It is creative and transcendent and can go beyond monarchy to establish other forms of rule. The various forms of government that have appeared in history—monarchy, aristocracy, democracy—are limited and partial implementations of the values of the Way of the Humane Authority in history. But history has also shown that no historical form of government fully implements all the legitimacy we might expect from the Way of the Humane Authority. It should, then, be possible to bring together some of the ways in which human beings have imagined and created political systems into a new system and by this new system fully implement the threefold legitimacy of the Way of the Humane Authority. The way in which Confucius brought together the wisdom of the three dynasties is precisely the wisdom that we must study for the Way of the Humane Authority today. The sage kings have already established an unchanging standard of legitimization. Our task today is to use this standard of legitimization to construct a new policy of implementation. This mission is not incumbent only on contemporary Confucian scholars. It also falls to everyone who is concerned about the political future of China.

THE LEGITIMACY OF DEMOCRACY

In the *End of History*, Fukuyama says that since the end of the Cold War, democracy has become the only possible form of government.[9] The fundamental roots of democracy have already been planted. The political problems that contemporary human beings have to face are only a matter of unrealized or only partially realized democracy. The types and the principles of human politics cannot develop any further. Hence, human history has come to an end; there is no hope left for politics. We might ask if this is true. Fukuyama writes from the point of view of Western culture, a culture that has taken the road of democracy, a culture that is proud and self-centered. Naturally, he is unable to see that other cultures have their own political principles and contexts. It is certain that what Fukuyama says does not apply to China. Indeed, democracy itself already suffers from serious problems and is by no means the only formula for humanity. Democracy is merely part of Western culture. That democracy will not develop further does not mean that politics cannot develop further because democracy is not the final form of politics. Political history does not end just because democracy has come to an end. According to the *Book of Changes*, history never ends. Politics will certainly continue to develop, but that development need not be in democracy. Rather, it could be beyond, or above, democracy. It will develop into a superior form in a political civilization other than that of democracy. This is where the Way of the Humane Authority of Chinese culture comes into play. It is the new starting point for politics and the new hope for human history.

To appreciate the value of the Way of the Humane Authority, we must first of all understand the flaws of democracy. The major flaw of democracy is the uniqueness of the legitimacy of the popular will. The exaggerated importance given to the will of the people leads to extreme secularization, contractualism, utilitarianism, selfishness, commercialism, capitalization, vulgarization, hedonism, mediocritization, this-worldliness, lack of ecology, lack of history, and lack of morality. The legitimacy of the popular will has its proper place in dealing with the question of legitimization, but to use it exclusively is to exclude other forms of legitimacy and to leave it uncorrected by those other types of legitimacy. The result is that it is inflated without restraint, bringing about many political problems.

For instance, by only stressing the legitimacy of the popular will, we exclude sacred legitimacy. Even the balance of the separation of powers at the level of implementation is merely a tool at the service of a secular will or desire. Sacred values cannot enter into politics in a structural way. They can be involved only through personal belief or society's demands. They are neither necessary nor effective in politics. This means that the democratic system has no place for the restraint provided by sacred values. It makes a secularized popular will its only center. But since a secularized popular will is deeply rooted in worldly desires, democratic politics amounts to a politics of desire.[10] When people choose their representatives and there is a clash between partial interests and the common interest—the common interest is a matter of sacred legitimacy—they must choose representatives of partial interests rather than those representing the common interest. For a democracy to choose people who represent the common interest would mean contradicting the will of the electorate, and so the democracy would loose its legitimacy. Once legitimacy is lost, the authority of the ruling body is weakened and it will fall. Hence, in a democracy, political choices are always down to the desires and interests of the electorate.

For example, the U.S. government's ratification of the Kyoto Protocol depends on pressure from domestic popular opinion.[11] The reason is very simple. The U.S. government is formed by an election every few years. During that time most people think only of the immediate interests of those few years. They do not think of long-term interests or of the common interests of all mankind, in which they themselves will not share. For the U.S. government, it should always cleverly uphold the will of the American people—in reality, their desires and interests. The cause of this can be traced back to the singling out of the will of the people as the sole source of legitimacy and the lack of restraint that ought to be provided by sacred legitimacy.

Democracy has a further serious problem: it lacks morality. In a democratic system, the authority and legitimacy of the government are determined by a formal will but not a substantive will of the people. They concern majority opinion with no respect for the quality of the opinion. Suppose the will of the people goes against human morality; it is enough for a majority of the electorate to attain the legally required number to give rise to political authority and legality. This is why democratic electorates give rise to imperialism, fascism, and hegemonism. Democracy is a matter of head counting, and this means that there is no regard for morality. An immoral will of the people can produce a legitimate authority and government. The root problem is that at the level of legitimization, the will of the people is not restrained by sacred legitimacy or universal morality. Its historical and cultural origin lies in the split that occurred between church and state. In the West, the church stands for morality, and so the separation of church and state meant that the church (morality) departed from the political arena.

A stress on the will of the people as the sole source of legitimacy also means that in the running of a democracy there are no ideals. We know that the "people" seek, above all, their immediate interests. At the level of the state, this translates into wanting the basic commodities. As a result Carl J. Friedrich defines "democracy as the politics of the common man."[12] It cannot be denied that, as the politics of the ordinary person, the desires and interests of the populace do have a certain justification. Hence, an important part of political legitimacy has always been this grounding in the desires and interests of the people. But, in the recent era, Western culture has gone astray, leading to the separation of church and state. Human beings are the only source of political legitimacy; sacred values are relegated to beyond the pale of politics.

Since Western rationality does not allow for several kinds of legitimacy to exist together, there has been a tendency for the will of the people to be accorded unique status. As a result, in politics there is no great morality or high ideals. All that is left are bare desires and interests. There is no longer any room for lofty hopes and great vitality. In these circumstances, politics takes the road of vulgarization and pandering to desires; the government becomes a company with political leaders as the directors; political rule becomes a matter of signing contracts, and everything can be assessed in terms of financial interests. The ideals once pursued and the noble personalities of the past are no longer possible.

There are theoreticians in the West who hold that the emergence of an extreme left-wing or right-wing government is due to mediocrity because a democracy is incapable of proposing any moral ideals. An authoritarian government may, on the contrary, happen to propose moral ideals—though of course today it would seem to be illusory ones—but there can be no disputing that the mediocrity and lack of ideals brought about by the sole sovereignty of the popular will in democracy result in people despising, and getting tired of, democracy.

Since democracy makes the will of the people the sole source of legitimacy, it is unable to tackle environmental problems at the root. This is because environmental issues have to do with sacred legitimacy or, in Confucian terms, with the legitimacy of the Way of heaven. The Way of heaven can, at times, clash with the popular will. This is because the popular will is formed by human desire, and the only way to resolve conflicts between heaven and the people is to curb desire. But in a democracy the will of the people is a secularized form of God's will, and so it alone is sovereign, absolute, supreme, and sacred. There is no place for curbing human desires as this amounts to turning one's back on the sacred will of the people, which is politically illegitimate.

When the will of the people goes against the Way of heaven, that is, when desires and the environment clash, a democratic system can allow for only a certain degree of technical tinkering and no deep-rooted solution. The balance of a democracy is perpetually tilted in favor of desires because the will of the people accepts no restraint from sacred legitimacy. It holds unrivaled sway over the whole political field. The legitimacy of ecological values can have a place only if they attain some value at the level of the popular will and thereby enter the political process.

In fact, Western democracy is able to tinker with a few ecological issues only by interpreting these as a longer term, higher quality satisfaction of desires. It is not able to do so because it wants to obey the Way of heaven, or even less because it wants to assert the legitimacy of the Way of heaven itself. Hence, even when Western Green Parties are successful on the political stage, they can never fully implement their green ideals. Green Parties represent the legitimacy of the Way of heaven, while democratically elected representatives represent popular legitimacy. If Green Parties really wish to realize their ideals, what they need to do is to correct the flaw by which the will of the people is seen as the sole source of legitimacy. They should use sacred legitimacy to restrain popular legitimacy. But this is impossible in a democracy because it leaves no space to other forms of legitimacy. The very desires that democracy is built upon are the main political cause of ecological problems.

In non-Western countries, which have established democracies, the exaltation of the popular will as the sole form of legitimacy has led to an exclusion of the legitimacy provided by history and culture. This has led to a rupture between politics and a people's own tradition of history and culture. Politics fails to win the recognition and support of tradition. Even if popular opinion is willing to concede recognition and support to democracy, yet because democracy lacks roots in the culture and has no source in that tradition, it fails to win recognition and support from that people's cultural tradition and can never be wholly legitimate. The will of the people is simply endorsement by the current population of the state at a particular time and place, while the legitimacy of history and culture is the endorsement formed by many generations over hundreds and thousands of years.

A state is an organic, living body. It continues through history. Politics may not break with the historical continuity of a state, or else the organic life of the state will be smothered and we will see historical nihilism in politics. The state is the state of the past, of the present, and of the future. The role of the state today is to transmit the life of the past state to that of the future. The state is not the result of a rational choice or the will of the people. It is the fruit of historical continuity and traditional inheritance. It is this organic nature of the state that decides questions of legitimacy. Political authorities must gain recognition from history and culture. They must continue the life of the past state, and only then can they claim legitimacy.

Western democracies do not have the problem of historical and cultural legitimacy because democracy itself is a product of, and has deep roots in, Western history and culture. But in non-Western countries, which lack a tradition of democracy, states may have already established democracy and won popular recognition but lack recognition from their own history and culture. The legitimacy of this colonial implantation of Western-style democracy on non-Western states has to go through many twists and turns to win acceptance. Its reliance on the will of the people alone is a very weak form of imperfect legitimacy.

To summarize, we have seen that democracy is not, as Fukuyama thought, without fundamental problems. The political problem of the present time is not simply a matter of how to implement democracy. Indeed, as I see it, the problem is precisely the opposite. The political problem of today's world is that democracy itself presents a serious problem. So long as the will of the people is seen as the sole source of legitimacy, politics can never aim at implementing the good. Hence, the problem is not to implement democracy, as Fukuyama reckons, but how to change the basic principles of democracy and reestablish the principles of legitimacy. This is the most fundamental political issue facing humanity. In practice this means demoting popular legitimacy from its status as sole source of legitimacy and founding a new model of politics in which several kinds of legitimacy work together in equilibrium. This new form is precisely what the Way of the Humane Authority is about. History has not come to an end. The Way of the Humane Authority marks a new beginning in political history and a new hope for politics.

THE WAY OF THE HUMANE AUTHORITY: SURPASSING DEMOCRACY

The Way of the Humane Authority produces an equilibrium, that is, a balanced politics, by uniting the three forms of legitimacy. Sacred legitimacy (transcendent), cultural legitimacy (historical), and the will of the people (human-centered) restrain each other; no single form can be an unrestrained dominant force. Each form of legitimacy has its own intrinsic justification, and each contributes in its own way to the work of checks and balances, contributing to the whole through what is different in each. This is the Chinese spirit of each exercising its proper role so as to obtain harmony. Whenever any one form of legitimacy becomes dominant and exclusive in political history, problems arise.[13]

Acceptance of the Way of the Humane Authority does not amount to a complete rejection of democracy. The Way of the Humane Authority is not opposed to giving the will of the people a reasonable place. It accepts the will of the people as part of legitimacy and ensures it is protected at the structural level by providing a more perfect framework. The Way of the Humane Authority is superior to and better than democracy because it does not exclude the other two forms of legitimacy. History shows that the three forms of legitimacy must balance each other out if there is to be a perfect politics. In the history of politics, the Way of the Humane Authority is the only one that unites all three forms of legitimacy in equilibrium. Therefore, it is the perfect form of politics that we ought to seek.

Firstly, the Way of the Humane Authority includes sacred legitimacy, which can correct the flaws inherent in the recognition of the will of the people as the sole form of legitimacy. Sacred legitimacy can restrain popular legitimacy so that it does not get inflated. The will of the people is subject to the universal restraint of religious morality, which embodies the Way and principle of heaven. Thus, it may overcome the extreme secularization of democracy and the flaws inherent in human desires and to realize sacred values in political life.

Secondly, the Way of the Humane Authority is able to put morality into politics. This is because sacred legitimacy is itself practical morality. The Way of the Humane Authority is not interested only in the formal will of the people. It must also consider the practical will of the people, that is, morality. The Way of the Humane Authority can take sacred legitimacy as a standard to test the legitimacy of political power and, in this way, introduce morality into the exercise and process of politics. Should the formal will of the people attain a majority, yet go against sacred legitimacy, then it is against morality and judged illegitimate according to sacred legitimacy. Hence, the Way of the Humane Authority, unlike democracy, is not a matter of rule by a formal majority. It is, instead, a practical rule in conformity with morality. The people who rule in conformity with morality are concerned only with the morality of the ruler's will and not with the formal issue of majorities or minorities. Although the Way of the Humane Authority gives a place to the will of the people, this will must conform to morality. If the majority of wills do not conform to morality, then what they want is illegitimate according to the Way of the Humane Authority. We must criticize and oppose illegitimate politics, and the standard for doing so is that of sacred legitimacy.

Thirdly, the Way of the Humane Authority has high ideals because it shares in heaven, earth, and the human. Through these threefold legitimacies it is able to encompass all things and yet respect the integrity of each, showing how Chinese culture, which is also human culture, can maintain the nature proper to each while seeking the ideal of their harmony. The same ideal of harmony must also be accomplished in the personality of every politician. Politicians not only have a responsibility to carry out the will of the people but also have a duty to realize the sacred Way of heaven and to ensure that the wisdom of the ages endures forever. Politics is, then, an arena not only for implementing the secular interests before us but also for seeking the ideal of harmony, for realizing the Way of heaven and ensuring the life of cultural wisdom.

To be human is to hope. To be alive means to be prodded by the stimulus of searching for ideals. Without ideals or hope, political life brings about regression and a falling away from life itself. We fall into the unending gloom of the depths, where we can never escape from the power of darkness. So it is that the Royal Way can overcome the vulgarization of democracy brought about by capitalist consciousness and awaken people of today, whose stimulus has been extinguished by the end of the Cold War.

At the same time the politicians sought after by the Royal Way are not mere officials chosen on the basis of universal equality, but rather persons of *charisma*, sages who share in heaven, earth, and the human. This kind of sage is precisely the ideal type of person and model personality that humanity has always looked up to. In other words, the Way of the Humane Authority is the only form of politics by which a three-dimensional elevated model of personality can be brought into politics and overcome contemporary politics—democracy—with its formal equality of one person one vote and the leveling out that this brings to politicians. It alone can spur humanity on to seek great political ideals and elevated political personalities.

The Way of the Humane Authority includes the legitimacy of the Way of heaven (sacred legitimacy), which means that ecological values serve as the source for legal implementation. Any political system or conduct that goes against the Way of heaven will be deemed illegitimate. In other words, the Royal Way not only includes ecological values but also allows them to restrain the legitimacy of the popular will and so resolve ecological problems at the root. If the popular will is not against ecological values, it can be implemented in politics. Immediately the popular will is opposed to ecological values; the legitimacy of the way of heaven will restrain it so that it cannot exceed its bounds or bring about grave consequences. In this sense, we can say that the Way of the Humane Authority is a politics of ecology.

The Way of the Humane Authority includes cultural legitimacy, and it can thereby also help non-Western countries to develop politically without obliterating all their cultural tradition. We know that most non-Western countries, such as India, Japan, and Turkey, have followed the Western model of political development and have wholly embraced democracy.[14] Since democracy manifests the flaw of the sole sovereignty of popular legitimacy and excludes cultural legitimacy, the political development of these countries has turned its back on their own historical and cultural traditions. They have created a political system that is in rupture with their own tradition and without roots. This type of rootless system lacks the nourishing sustenance of the resources of the past millennia. In contrast, the Way of the Humane Authority can provide historical-cultural legitimacy, and so non-Western countries will be able to draw on their own rich resources for their political development. The legitimacy of their authority to rule will be reinforced, and it will be more stable and able to last longer.

The Way of the Humane Authority hence has brought together the values of monarchy and theocratic rule from ancient times, the democracy of the modern era, and contemporary ecology. It can also help non-Western countries to draw on historical-cultural legitimacy for their political development. Just as Confucius brought together the spirit of reform of the three dynasties and Aristotle said that a mixed form of government was the best, so too the Way of the Humane Authority has brought together the good models of human political history. The Way of the Humane Authority is the best form of politics. In today's world, politics has run into many difficulties, of which the most serious is the domination by one form of legitimacy alone. The Way of the Humane Authority requires the simultaneous operation of three forms of legitimacy, their mutual equilibrium and a refusal to allow any one to exclude the others or become unrestrained. Each one may exert its proper value only within the balance of all three. Equilibrium of legitimization is the means to resolve the tendency toward extremism in legitimacy of contemporary politics. In this sense the Way of the Humane Authority surpasses democracy. Contemporary politics will find in it an ideal and hope for political development.

IMPLEMENTATION OF THE WAY OF THE HUMANE AUTHORITY

The fundamental principle of the equilibrium of legitimacies of the Way of the Humane Authority has already been laid by the ancient Chinese sages. Yet the implementation of this equilibrium depends on, and adapts to, the concrete circumstances of each period of history. In practice, Chinese history has posited monarchy as the form of implementation, and so the equilibrium has been realized only under monarchy. Within this system, Confucian sages proposed a number of methods of implementation, such as establishing six offices modeled on heaven,[15] the three dukes,[16] the Bright Hall,[17] training of the crown princes by the Chief Tutors and court lectures on the classics,[18] the keeping of historical annals,[19] the performing of sacrifices at altars of state,[20] the presentation of popular opinion through poetry, choosing the worthy and capable, discussion by all ministers, petitions from the ministers of state, ruling according to the classics, making Confucianism the state religion.

Today historical circumstances have changed greatly. China's old system of government has collapsed, and a new system has not yet been established. History stands open. It is a time that calls for great political creativity. It is a time of trial for the creativity of Chinese culture. Every Chinese who is concerned for China's political development and the revival of her culture is faced with the problem of implementing the equilibrium of the three legitimacies entrusted to us by our sages. A new structure of implementation is a complicated, detailed affair, requiring much reflection and giving rise to controversy. This section tries to outline what should be done so as to encourage people to talk about it such that together we can all assist in the creative progress of Chinese culture.

Within a constitutional framework, the Way of the Humane Authority proposes a parliamentary system. The executive is produced by the parliament and is responsible to the parliament. The parliament has three houses, each one representing one of the three kinds of legitimacy. The three are the House of *Ru (Tongruyuan)*, which represents sacred legitimacy, the House of the People (*Shuminyuan*), which represents popular legitimacy, and the House of the Nation (*Guotiyuan*), which represents cultural legitimacy.[21] The Scholars (*Ru*) are chosen by recommendation and nomination. The People are chosen by universal suffrage and by election from functional constituencies. The members of the Nation are selected by hereditary criteria and by assignment.

The leader of the House of *Ru* is a great scholar proposed by the Confucian scholars. He serves for a long-term mandate of fifteen or twenty years. If unable to attend he may send a delegate to deal with affairs of the House. Members are recruited in two ways. The first is that scholars among the people propose candidates. The second is that the state establishes a Confucian Academy that prepares scholars conversant in the *Four Books* and the *Five Classics*. Following examinations in the relevant topics and after a trial period in administration, they will then be assessed on their learning, practice, ability, and knowledge and assigned to the parliaments at the levels of the state, the province, or the city or county. The norms for choosing them and the way of doing so may follow the examination or recommendation systems used in China in the past.

The members of the House of the People are chosen according to the norms and processes of Western democratic parliaments.

The leader of the House of the Nation is to be a direct descendant of Confucius.[22] If he is unable to be present he may also assign a deputy to chair the assembly.[23] He personally selects the members of the House from among the descendants of great sages of the past, descendants of the rulers, descendants of famous people, of patriots, university professors of Chinese history, retired top officials, judges, and diplomats, worthy people from society, as well as representatives of Daoism, Buddhism, Islam, Tibetan Buddhism, and Christianity.[24]

Each house has real parliamentary power, and a bill must pass all three, or at least two, of the houses to become law. The head of the executive and the chief justice must be chosen by the consensus of all three houses.

The House of *Ru* enjoys a permanent power of veto. A bill, such as one permitting homosexuals to found a family, that passes the House of the People but is against the Way of heaven will be vetoed by the House of *Ru*. Likewise, a bill that may be good for the Way of heaven and that passes the House of *Ru* will be only a weak bill if it fails to win the support of the People's House. If both the People and the House of the Nation are opposed, then the bill will not pass into law. Such bills are like those of Western Green Parties, which are too progressive and ahead of their time. If a bill passes in the People's House but fails in the House of the Nation, then it can become only a weak bill. Should both the Nation and the Ru oppose it, then it will not enter into law. Bills that will fail in this way are those asking for a referendum to change the name of the state, the national language or religion, and any separatist bills.

Since each of the houses has the power to pass laws and make decisions about the real powers of the head of the executive and the chief justice, the three forms of legitimacy realize the three-dimensional system of restraint at the level of implementation in their vertical interdependence and in their horizontal specificity. The priority of sacred legitimacy is expressed in the veto power exercised by the House of *Ru*, but each form of legitimacy, each house, has its own place and may not interfere in the running of the others or exalt itself at their expense. Hence the tricameral system enables each form of legitimacy to cooperate with the others and to restrain them when necessary. Each also wins the recognition of the others and does not interfere in their legitimate proceedings. For instance, even though the Scholars have veto power, if they propose a bill restricting religious freedom, the People and the Nation will oppose it and it cannot become law. This shows that the latter two houses exert their balancing and restraining role. Hence, the three-dimensional equilibrium ensures that the House of the Scholars has no priority among the houses such that it could dominate the legislative process.[25]

CONCLUSION

The Way of the Humane Authority provides three kinds of legitimacy and ensures that, in both legitimization and implementation, the three are combined in a three-dimensional format, which guarantees their individual distinction and yet maintains their mutual equilibrium. The Way of the Humane Authority is, therefore, superior and better than democracy or theocracy. China's ancient sages have already established the eternal and unchanging principle of legitimization. Our duty today is to put that eternally valid norm into practice at the level of implementation. This mission is out of the ordinary, difficult, and complicated and may require several generations to be accomplished. The Way of the Humane Authority is the best possible form of government that human beings have ever invented. Even though we have not yet been able to create a satisfactory system of implementation—it requires a long period of hard thinking and also the right historical conditions—we can categorically affirm that political development of China today must tend toward the Way of the Humane Authority. This will not only solve China's political problems but also give humanity a new ideal and open a new way ahead. This is a test of the creative wisdom and creative ability of the Chinese people and also a contribution that Chinese civilization has to offer to human civilization.

....

CHAPTER 2

The Supervisory System
of Confucian Constitutionalism

REFLECTIONS ON THE SUPERVISION OF THE STATE BY THE ACADEMY

Jiang Qing

STATING THE PROBLEM

For the last hundred years, China's political system has slipped into serious chaos and lack of order, attributable to the forceful invasion of the West and the collapse of the imperial system.[1] Within the country there have been continuous waves of political struggle, party struggle, and wars. People's life and possessions have suffered severe losses; as the saying goes, "Businesses languished; it was hard to eke out a living." Simultaneously many Chinese intellectuals, whether of the old or new school, sought to continue the moral ideal and religious zeal of the scholar-gentry who longed to save the people and strengthen the state. They dashed into the fray, even shedding their blood for the cause, in the hope that they could give China a stable political order and enable the state to grow strong and prosper. Among all these political demands there was none stronger than that calling for a constitution for China. In the late Qing there were demands to establish a constitution, once the Republic was established there were calls to draft one, and in our own days there were cries to rule by the constitution, all of which goes to show that Chinese intellectuals with their concern for governance (see *The Great Learning*) were fired by the constitutional dream and deeply attached to the constitutional project. Chinese intellectuals today are even more enamored of rule by the constitution than in the past, the reason being that while for the last hundred years the constitutional dream has never materialized, the intellectuals' hopes have continued to increase.

Looking back we can see that in their desire to save the world and strengthen the country, intellectuals in China did not consider their own insignificance. They drew up drafts of a constitution and hoped that these drafts would be realized so that China would be a constitutional China. For instance, in the early Republican era there were four private drafts of constitutions. Liang Qichao drafted a Draft Constitution of the Republic of China; Kang Youwei wrote a draft with a similar name and also composed a Law for the Election of Representatives to the National Assembly of the Republic of China. Wang Chonghui and Wu Guanyin both drafted constitutions. After this the famous drafts are those by Zhang Taiyan and Carsun Chang (Zhang Junmai) as well as that drawn up by the Nationalist Party (KMT) on the basis of Sun Yat-sen's Five Power Constitution. There are a whole array of drafts. Sixty years after the founding of the People's Republic of China, a group of Chinese liberals has composed the constitutional-like Charter 08.

Now the most surprising feature of these draft constitutions is that not one of them includes any place for China's own historical and cultural specificity in their basic ideas or in their constitutional format, with the exception on the latter point of the Five Power Constitution. Although the Five Power Constitution includes an Examination Yuan and a Control Yuan as part of Sun's five-part plan, this bow to Chinese tradition is only at the level of implementation. At the level of legitimization there is total acceptance of the Western idea that legitimacy comes only from the sovereignty of the people and popular consent. Thus, for all these draft constitutions, what Western scholars refer to as the "higher law background" or constitutional "transcendental values" are all Western. They depend solely on Western values and resources and make no allowance for Chinese cultural values to act as the supreme law.

The most objectionable thing is that even a traditionalist such as Zhang Taiyan recommends the Swiss system of committees with direct democracy, or the traditionalist Confucianist Kang Youwei recommends a constitution that combines the British cabinet and French presidential systems. The new Confucianist Zhang Junmai recommends a modified British cabinet system. These constitutions lack any Chinese contribution whatsoever. They fail to incarnate the Confucianist political idea and fundamental norm of the sacred transcendence of the Way of heaven. Their basic ideas and systems are, without exception, purely Western, and they express only the features of Western culture.

We can prove this by looking at a classic example. Kang Youwei, who hailed from the Protect the Emperor Party, established a National Assembly chosen by indirect elections as the most authoritative body. The constitution could be changed by an elected president. The revolutionary Sun Yat-sen also included the same features. In 1947 the National Assembly formally passed Zhang Junmai's draft, which drew on the principle of the cabinet system but also included Sun's Five Power Constitution. The 1947 constitution was billed as a combined cabinet-presidential system. Moreover, this constitution was very similar to that of Kang Youwei based on English and French models. Thus, though Sun and Kang differed in their political aims—one supported revolution, the other wished to keep the emperor—their constitutions were surprisingly alike. Moreover, this was the same for Zhang Junmai's version, though, unlike Kang, he had no sympathy for retaining the emperor.[2] This cannot but make us sit up and reflect, why is it that people of radically opposite political views hold similar views of the constitution?

The problem arises because all modern Chinese thinkers, of whatever political persuasion, take the transcendental values of Western constitutional law as their constitutional ideal and principle of explanation. They never criticize the ideal itself. In other words, they all swallow the Western presupposition without the slightest critical comment. For them the constitutional principle is the sovereignty of the people and popular consent. They hold this as a universal norm, the unchanging norm for all humanity. Since this norm is best expressed in the idea of direct elections to a National Assembly, this body is what they most favor and set as their goal. Hence, Chinese constitutionalists persist in adding layer to layer and setting up a National Assembly above the legislature. For instance, Kang Youwei has a National Assembly above his two-house legislature. Zhang Junmai's revision of the constitution of the Republic of China also has a National Assembly above the legislature. We can say that the Western ideal of the sovereignty of the people is constantly placed as the supreme norm of Chinese constitutions. This norm has dominated constitutional history over the past century and established a tradition that reaches up to our own time.

Our own era is different from that following the late nineteenth century with its search for a constitutional ideal. At that time concern over domestic order and foreign domination meant that the great people of the time concentrated on saving the nation and keeping it united and lacked the time to calmly reflect on the problem of China's constitution. Their task to save the country has been largely achieved, and so now we have the time to reflect on these matters. We have seen that Confucianists have been active promoters of a constitution for China, which is a sign of their traditional concern for governance and their wisdom and courage in getting things done. We must show them our highest respect and do all we can to imitate them.

However, we also cannot fail to see how Confucianists, such as Kang Youwei and Zhang Junmai, and even more non-Confucianists, were guilty of a mistake in trying to resolve constitutional problems according to the Western norm of sovereignty of the people. They should have been critical of the whole of Western constitutionalism at the level of legitimization, while remaining free to pick and choose from the West at the level of implementation. We should ensure that the issue of legitimacy of Chinese constitutional government is resolved on the basis of Chinese ideas and culture.[3] We need to bring Chinese constitutionalism back to the correct path, and to do so we need to establish a Confucian constitutionalism. This is what this chapter aims to do.

DEFINING CONFUCIAN CONSTITUTIONALISM

With the revival of traditional culture in recent years, there have been some, not many, papers discussing constitutionalism from a Confucian perspective. Within China, Qiu Feng, Du Gangjian, and Xiao Han have written on the topic, while in Korea Chaihark Hahm has. These authors all speak of Confucianist (*Rujia*) constitutionalism and never of Confucian (*Rujiao*) constitutionalism. The reason for this may be because of an ongoing discussion in China as to whether Confucianism is a religion and whether Confucianist and Confucian are equivalent. Actually the question of whether or not Confucianism is a religion is fundamentally meaningless, rather like asking if a particular theological school of Christianity is a religion or is Christianity itself.

Clearly a Confucianist school is not a religion or Confucian in the broader sense. It is a current of thought within Confucianism, what the *Bibliography of the Han History* refers to as "adapting to *yin* and *yang*, making teaching clear."[4] There is only one Confucianism, but there are many schools of Confucianist philosophy. In the past it was said that the Confucianists were split into eight groups, while later we talk about contemporary or past Confucianism and Confucianism of the Han or of the Song. The mistake arises only because, since the Han dynasty (from 206 BCE), the influence and power of Confucianism have been too strong, with the result that the term "Confucianist" has mistakenly been read as being identical to China's mainstream culture. As a consequence, Confucianist philosophy is understood to be mainstream Chinese culture or civilization. Confucianist culture is then contrasted with other cultures such as Buddhist or Christian culture. Confucius said that if a name is not correct then discourse does not flow smoothly (*Analects* 13.3), so we must distinguish narrow Confucianism and broad Confucianism, focusing particularly on a correct understanding of the latter term.

In my opinion, broad "Confucianism" (Confucian religion) is the only term that can apply to the specificity of China's civilization and culture, because from the time of Fu Xi to that of the Two Emperors and Three

Kings up to the Qin-Han empire and until 1911, a great religion has existed in China, namely, the Confucian religion (*Rujiao*). To talk of broad Confucianism (Confucian religion) is to refer to Chinese culture and civilization. This is the only term by which China can be compared to other cultures or civilizations. Indeed, the term itself was created in response to the influx of Indian Buddhism in the Jin dynasty (265–420). This shows that the term refers to the entirety of China's civilization in the face of another.[5] Thus, when we talk about Confucian constitutionalism today we are taking about Chinese constitutionalism. There is no other Chinese constitutionalism outside Confucian constitutionalism, bar Western constitutionalism. For Chinese constitutionalism to be Chinese, it must be Confucian and cannot be called by any other name.

THE KEY IDEAS OF CONFUCIAN CONSTITUTIONALISM

The basic feature of Confucian constitutionalism can be summed up in the phrase "the sovereignty of heaven." Sovereignty refers to an authority that is sacred, absolute, exclusive, and supreme. Such authority can belong only to heaven, not to the people. "The people" is a secularized, limited, and narrow collection of human desires. It is far from being sacred, exclusive, or supreme. Thus, the will of the people also lacks the features of sacred authority. Dong Zhongshu said, "The Way is great. Its origin is in Heaven. Heaven does not change, nor either does the Way."[6] Applied to Confucian constitutionalism, this means that heaven is the ultimate source of constitutional sovereignty. Confucian religion holds that the universe, and all it contains, comes from heaven, which is the origin of human life and culture. It determines that this constitutionalism is transcendent and sacred, that is, religious in nature. It assumes the will of heaven, not of the people, as its guide, norm, and vehicle of restraint. In a word, the sovereignty of heaven means that the origin of the legitimacy of the highest political authority comes from heaven, not from the people. Heaven is the higher law background of Confucian constitutionalism or its transcendental value. This feature has a religious dimension that is very unlike the current Western model of secular democracy.

At this stage we need to distinguish the will of heaven from the will of the people. Under the influence of Western democratic thought, many Chinese scholars—including many Confucianists—imagine that the will of the people is the will of heaven. In support, they often cite a line from the *Classic of History* (the *Shu King*): "Heaven sees as my people see; heaven hears as my people hear."[7] This is to seriously misunderstand the Confucianist view of the relationship between heaven and the human world.[8] In a Confucianist perspective, heaven is heaven and human is human. The union of heaven and the human is only a goal pursued by Confucianism and not something that can actually be realized in human life. Human beings are often acting against heaven, so that there is a constant and grave tension and separation between the two. Moral (*xin-xing*) Confucianism believes that serious practice is required to overcome oneself and return to the rites, an effort to know nature and to know heaven so as to restore human nature. Political Confucianism holds that the will of heaven can be read from natural disasters, and these teach us to change our conduct and appease heaven's wrath.

The Confucian classics have much to say about the tension and conflict between heaven and the human. The *Book of Odes* has several poems in which the author chides the whole country, or the people, for acting against heaven's will and bringing about corruption and the demise of the country or of society. Although the author of the *Classic of History* orders, "do not oppose the people's [wishes] to follow your own desires," the author also says, "do not go against what is right, to get the praise of the people."[9] From this it is clear that the Way and the people are not the same; to "get the praise of the people [the will of the people]" may be to go against what is right (the will of heaven).

Therefore, for Confucianism, the will of the people may, at times, be that of heaven and at times not. When the will of the people does not conform to the Way of heaven, it is against the will of heaven and is simply the individual will of an immoral person. For instance, when Western parliaments passed laws to invade and colonize other countries, these were an expression of the immoral will of the people. Heaven does not desire to destroy the country of other people or commit genocide. When today the people of the world overconsume and destroy the environment or develop destructive weapons, these are not the will of heaven because heaven loves to give rise to virtue and is endowed with limitless benevolence. It could not possibly want such destructive things.

Taking one step back, even if the will of the people does coincide with the will of heaven at times, it does so for the most part only by accident because according to Confucianist thought only the sage is attuned to heaven and able to naturally unite his will with that of heaven. The sage can attain to the sacred mind of heaven, that is, the life of the realm of the will of heaven. At the level of the ordinary people it is impossible that the will of the people could be the will of heaven. The main reason why Chinese scholars in recent times have so thoroughly misunderstood the relationship of the will of the people to that of heaven is that they have used Western humanism and the Enlightenment to interpret the relationship and so resolutely turned against a comprehensive understanding of the basic Confucianist idea that the will of the people is the will of heaven.

The heaven to which sovereignty belongs is, according to Confucian religion, a metaphysical, sacred, and personal heaven. The personality of heaven is not simply modeled on that of human beings. It is expressed by the creativity, lordship, will and nature of heaven. Cheng Yi thinks that there is no difference between "heaven" and "God" (*shang-di*). Both names have a common reference: "heaven" refers to the form while "God" speaks of the lordship. "Speaking of its mysterious acting it is 'spirit,' of its nature it is *Qian*."[10] The "mysterious acting" is what we now call "heaven," and it includes all that exists; the "lordship" implies that heaven has a sacred will. "Mysterious acting" refers to heaven's creative omnipotence; "nature" refers to its transcendent principle (the principle of heaven). In *Mao's Commentary to the Book of Odes* we learn that "what is honoured as lord is called August Heaven (that is Heaven is a Lord with a will); whilst the vast extent of original *qi* is called Vast Heaven (Heaven includes all that is and is without limit or boundary). 'Benevolence covering all under its mercy' is called Merciful Heaven (Heaven has a benevolent and merciful nature). 'What comes from above and is sent below' is called High Heaven (Heaven can send down disasters and warn humanity by portents)."[11] From this it is clear that in Confucian religion the various names for heaven express different aspects but that there is indeed only one heaven, which Dong Zhongshu described as the "Great Prince over the hundred spirits." In metaphysical language this heaven is the complete unity of all under one principle.

It is from the transcendence of the one principle that we speak of heaven as the one principle. However, from the physical world, from the creativity by which heaven enters into history and culture this one heaven cannot but separate, constructing different worlds. Thus, the separation engendered by heaven gives rise to the inequality of things in the physical world, including in the human world and the world of politics.

So when Confucian constitutionalism speaks of sovereignty as lying with heaven, this is because it is here speaking of an ultimate metaphysical reality. But in the world of politics, politics must embody, exhibit, and realize the oneness of heaven at different levels. The Way of the Humane Authority of Confucian constitutionalism is the way in which this differentiated heaven is expressed politically. It links heaven, earth, and the human as the three united forms of sacred, cultural, and popular legitimacy, together which are heaven's embodiment in politics. We must note, however, that this separation is not a flat two-dimensional differentiation because "heaven" has a higher status. We can call this a three-dimensional separation or a differentiated separation. In practical terms the sacred legitimacy of heaven in the Way of the Humane Authority is prior to the cultural legitimacy of earth or the popular will of the human.[12]

The threefold separation of legitimacy in the Confucian constitutional-ism is the support for its tricameral parliament. Each house represents one strand of legitimacy, whereas in Western parliaments both houses together represent one form of legitimacy, that of the people. In the Confucian tri-cameral system the three houses exist in a differentiated and not in a flat relationship, as determined by the legitimacy of heaven.[13]

Politics is a human activity. To be implemented and made visible, sover-eignty must be exercised by human beings. Otherwise it is merely a concept of political thought, a philosophical idea. It is worth asking what kind of person can engage in political activity and embody this sovereignty. This is the political problem of delegation of sovereignty. In Confucianism the sage king is the one to whom sovereignty is delegated.

The sage king is a sage because he is the mediator between heaven and the human. The *Explanation of Words* glosses the word sage by "communi-cates with," that is, the sage communicates with heaven and humanity. He knows the will of heaven above and communicates this to human beings below. In the oracle bone script, the character for "sage" is composed of an ear, which listens to the voice of heaven, and a mouth, which transmits the will of heaven. Likewise the *Analects* says that someone spoke of Confucius, "Heaven uses your master like a wooden mallet to strike a bell" (*Analects* 3.24). The *Record of Rites of the Elder Dai* notes the same: "[T]he sage knows and communicates with the great Way and responds and changes without end." The "great Way" here is the Way of heaven. These texts all speak of the transcendent, sacred nature of the sage, who is united in life and virtue to heaven. In him heaven and the human are one.

Moreover, the *Gongyang Commentary* says that the sage king is someone who can link heaven, earth, and the human. Through his kingly mind and sagely personality, the sage king represents and embodies the threefold legitimacy. Only the sage king can embody the will of heaven, the decree of heaven, the way heaven sees, the Way of heaven, the order of heaven, the norm of heaven, and the principle of heaven and only he can really understand the wrath of heaven, the awe of heaven, the mirror of heaven, the warning of heaven, and the punishment of heaven. Thus, in the realm of politics, it is he alone who is qualified to embody the sacred and eternal value of heaven and to stand in place of heaven and direct political affairs—representing heaven in carrying out government. Moreover, this applies both in the case of the unity of principle and in its separation.

Hence, heaven entrusts sovereignty to the sage king, and he rules according to his sagely personality as heaven's representative. Conse-quently, in Confucian constitutionalism the form of representation is that sovereignty lies with the sage, not with the people, who lack the heavenly qualifications of transcendence, sacredness, and eternity. After the passing of the three founding kings, the world awaits the birth of a new sage king. Those sage kings have left the classics to posterity, but in political terms the sages have indeed disappeared, and sovereignty has found no one to represent it. Hence, the sovereignty once delegated to the sage kings has to be further delegated to the scholar-officials. They hold the classics of the sage kings and so exercise administration on behalf of the sage kings. Hence, the sovereignty that lies with heaven must be delegated and subdelegated, first to the sage kings and then from them to the scholar-officials.

Like Western constitutionalism, Confucian constitutionalism is also a form of delegated governance, but the way in which that delegation is carried out is different. In Confucian constitutionalism heaven delegates to the sage kings; in contemporary Western constitutionalism the people delegate to the people. The former is a delegation that is both a matter of silent spiritual belief and a historical tradition of the ruling by the Way; the latter is expressed openly in a will and is a delegation that is a matter of law and due process.[14]

In Confucian constitutionalism, sovereignty and political legitimacy are expressed in two ways: through persons and through institutions. That sovereignty lies with the sages or with the scholar-officials is an expression of the personal aspect of sovereignty, while that it lies with the Academy and in the tricameral parliament is the institutional aspect of sovereignty.

There is one further, major, difference between Western and Confucian understandings of sovereignty. In Confucian understanding, the main purpose of sovereignty is to implement religious and moral values, using transcendent and sacred goodness to regulate sovereignty and guide it toward the good. Consequently, the fundamental purpose of Confucian constitutionalism is to regulate and educate the holders of supreme power in the state so that they will realize the transcendent values of China's Confucian culture. A state order in conformity with Confucian ideas encourages the political authorities to implement the goodness of the Way of heaven.

Here we come up against the issue of how constitutionalism should be understood. The Confucian and Western understandings are very different and cannot easily be reconciled. My definition of constitutionalism is as follows:

> Constitutionalism is to take the most effective manner, written or unwritten, of regulating the basic political order of the exercise of state power and the running of state activities. With regard to authority, con-

stitutionalism does not only use the basic order of the state to prevent authority from doing wrong, it also impels it to do good. With regard to the people, constitutionalism does not only use the basic order of the state to protect civil rights, it also promotes their morality.

The unwritten ways in which constitutionalism acts are the rites of Confucian civilization. These state rights are what regulate politics, and they are always moral and religious in nature. The written ways refer to modern constitutions. Furthermore, the term "regulate" in the definition is much broader in meaning than that of "prevent." To regulate implies using the political order to both limit power and also impel it to do good. In Western constitutionalism, however, the emphasis is only put on limiting power and the stress falls on controlling state power.

We know that currently in the West there is an emphasis on demoralization, which is shown in the way Western constitutions make the protection of rights their basic aim. Here we must clarify an important issue: rights and morality are not the same. Nowadays people who talk about Western constitutionalism fail to see the difference and equate rights with morality. The result is that rights become the transcendent moral foundation of Western constitutionalism. Common sense tells us that morality demands that a person has a responsibility to do good to others and to society, whereas rights demand that others or society have a duty to do good to me. In Dong Zhongshu's words, morality is to "use justice to correct myself";[15] rights are "to use justice to correct others." Hence rights are very selfish and very lowdown. They are to protect my own self-interests, which certainly is not done by morality. Rights, then, can only be a matter for the law or legal demands.

Rights as the moral basis of the constitution is only a recent phenomenon in the West. In the past, religious morality was the basis of Western constitutions and religious morality regulated state authorities so that they would do good. This is to be found in the works of various authors. For instance, Cicero stresses that God's natural law should be used to regulate the Roman constitution. Aquinas emphasizes that God's eternal law should regulate the Christian constitutions of the Middle Ages. Even the sixteenth-century French legal scholar Jean Bodin (1530–96), in his work on sovereignty, holds that the highest sovereignty, which is above the law of the land, must be limited by God's norms and be answerable to God. But with Hobbes, Locke, and Rousseau, Western thought took a great, false turn backward. By means of the social contract, the goal of political power was shifted from morality to rights, from implementing the good to protecting rights. So constitutionalism no longer made the goodness of sacred morality the basis of its legitimacy. In its place came a selfish, secularist, legal power masquerading as sacred values. Leo Strauss has already noted this aspect of modernity, by which morality becomes rights, and holds that it is a point of great rupture in Western political thought. In the face of this change, Confucian constitutionalism argues from a traditional perspective and criticizes this substitution of morality by rights. In criticizing modern rights-based constitutionalism, we want to appropriately and creatively reconstruct the ancient tradition of morality-based constitutionalism.

In fact, it is not wrong to use political power to protect rights because, by protecting the rights of others and of society, power is then at the service of morality. Yet rights and morality are very different, though they do overlap to some degree. For example, authorities have a moral obligation to protect rights to life, liberty, property, and the like. But this kind of morality does not include the whole of morality, or even many important aspects of morality such as benevolence, justice, loyalty, filial piety, sincerity, fidelity, honesty, temperance, moderation, harmony, humility, and deference. The morality that authorities have to respect far outweighs the rights they must protect. In other words rights can be included as part of moral governance, but the protection of rights cannot include all of moral governance. Thus, we can see that the problem with modern Western constitutional government is not that it emphasizes protection of rights but that it makes rights the only purpose of a constitution, and thereby excludes much of ordinary morality that has been in human society for hundreds and thousands of years. Morality is no longer to be implemented or protected by the constitution. American conservatives are critical of the "Naked Public Square" at the heart of political society, its lack of moral values.[16]

The basic purpose of Confucian constitutionalism is, then, not to protect rights but to implement morality, though in so doing it naturally includes protection of rights in its remit. Protection of rights is simply the bottom line of the political order. There are far many superior religious and ethical values that authorities must implement. Here Confucian constitutionalism is not against the protection of rights per se but making this protection the sole aim of a constitution. Confucian constitutionalism does not eliminate the moral nature and moral role of power by reducing power to an exclusive fixation on protecting individual rights alone.

Now we turn to the limitation of power. We may ask if Confucian constitutionalism wants to limit power. The answer is naturally yes, though it does so in a way that is different from that of the West. As well as emphasizing structural limitations of power, Confucian constitutionalism also stresses the religious and ethical limitations of power. In practice, power's realization of morality and morality's limitation of power are two sides of the same coin. To ask power to realize morality is, in practice, to use morality to limit power so that power does good and not evil. Morality in its broadest sense is the higher law background or transcendental values of constitutionalism at the level of the constitution, while at the political level it is legitimacy. In the *Spring and Autumn Annals*, this is called its "law." Hence, Confucian constitutionalism stresses limitations on power so as to put into practice its own aim of using power to implement morality.[17]

We might say that since the three dynasties (i.e., after 221 BCE), throughout the whole of China's Confucian political history, the Confucian classics have been used as constitutional law books to limit the power of the state. The supreme religious and moral standards of these Confucian books are the sacred values of the Way of heaven. Throughout this time, this to a great extent has already been systematized. Hence, Confucian constitutionalism limits power by the use of religious morality, the classics of the sage kings, and Confucian principles and their corresponding structures. It is not, as some have said recently, an untrammeled power or dark despotism.

THE STRUCTURES OF CONFUCIAN CONSTITUTIONALISM

With the ending of the three dynasties, Chinese politics went from rule by sage kings to rule by monarchs. Under the monarchs, Confucian constitutionalism could not directly relate to the monarchical system by relying on the monarch to implement the ideals of the sage kings. It could not use the sacred legitimacy of heaven found in the Confucian classics and in religious or ethical principles to limit power and impel the authorities to the best of their ability to do good. Even though in implementing its own political ideals Confucian constitutionalism went through many trials, even reversals, the body of scholar-officials never gave up in their effort to realize the Confucian ideal. Now that China has ended monarchical rule and begun republican rule, Confucian constitutionalism must create a new structure adapted to the times. The Confucian values must be put into practice in new historical circumstances. As I see it, there are three main parts to a Confucian constitutional structure: the Academy to supervise the state, the tricameral parliament, and symbolic monarch republicanism. This chapter focuses on the first and touches briefly on the second. The third will be left to the following chapter.

The Supervisory Role of the Academy

Traditionally China's government is carried out by scholars. This form of government is generally traced back to Emperor Shun, who instructed the music master Kui to teach his children. It existed during the three dynasties (twenty-first to third centuries BCE), reaching perfection under the Western Zhou (eleventh century to 771 BCE). By scholarship we mean that the state founded a special school to train scholars in religious, moral, political, historical, and literary knowledge. Administration was put into the hands of these specially prepared scholars.[18] Later this kind of special school began to be politicized and gradually took on the functions of a parliament, executive, supervisory body, judicial body, and religious rites body. This state-sponsored school is called the Academy (*Tai Xue*). The Academy continued China's tradition and spirit of rule by scholarship.

In *Waiting for the Dawn*, Huang Zongxi (1610–95) discusses the Academy's role in forming scholar-officials. He notes that the first role of the Academy is to form scholars, but that is not its only role: "Only if the [Academy] produced all the instrumentalities for governing all-under-Heaven would they fulfil their purpose in being created."[19] Hence, the Academy also had a role in governing the state and exercising political power. Secondly, the Academy performed various functions such as attendance at court, publishing decrees, looking after the elderly, caring for orphans, and celebrating victories. Even more importantly, "conferring with generals and officials on the occasion of great military reviews, meeting with officials and people during great judicial proceedings, and making offerings to the first ancestors at great sacrifices."[20] Huang describes the nature of the Academy by saying that the rights and wrongs of public matters would be aired in the Academy and not left up to the Son of Heaven to decide by himself. In other words, the Academy was the highest organ for discussion of state politics. It could appraise and adjudicate the rights and wrongs of the administrative policies of the highest ruler. In today's language, the Academy had the power to train people fit to rule the state, to execute state government, and to carry out discussion of state affairs, state's juridical function, military functions, and state rites and ceremonies. In his notes to the *Zhou Rites*, the Tang dynasty scholar Jia Gongyan (fl. 650) points out that "the Zhou established the Academy to the east of the palace to serve as a corrective so that it could correct and inspect the king's business." Hence, the Academy also has a supervisory function as the highest form of control. Clearly, the Academy had virtually all the highest powers of the state, and thus it is best suited to embodying the tradition of scholarship in government.

If the Academy is strictly speaking the highest body in the state, then all political activity should emanate from it. The highest ruler, the Son of Heaven, can exercise his authority only within the norms and limits set by the Academy. So the Academy is particularly appropriate to the spirit of Confucian constitutionalism, which aims to use the sacred values inherent in the classics of the sage kings to limit power. These values can be learned only through the texts, teaching, and practice of a specialized school. We can say that the ancient Academy was the most comprehensive and most complete model of Confucian constitutionalism. It is the highest political ideal of Confucianism and its ultimate goal.

However, this most comprehensive and most complete form of Confucian constitutionalism comes in an outdated model, and times have now changed. We now live in a republican era, in which rule is no longer by inheritance. State power has been split into a number of different bodies. It is no longer possible to return to the unified model of power present in the Academy of old. That model can serve only as an ideal. In refounding the Academy today as part of Confucian constitutionalism, we need to make an Academy adapted to the present. In short, in establishing the supervisory role of the Academy we need to pick and choose from among its ancient functions, while insisting on the basic spirit of rule by scholarship and supervision of the state.

In modern politics, discussion of policy already has its own specialized body, the parliament. Executive functions are performed by the executive, judicial functions by the judiciary, supervision by disciplinary bodies, and military affairs by specialized military bodies. Hence, there is no need, nor would it be possible, to retain the Academy's traditional discursive, executive, judicial, supervisory, and military roles. The roles that should be retained, as I see it, and the new tasks that are to be added are six in number. The Academy should be the highest supervisory body in the state, the highest body training and examining scholars, and the highest body for ceremonial and ritual. These are three traditional functions, to which should be added three new ones: the highest powers of recall, of mediation, and of upholding religion.

The Supervisory Power of the Academy

Possession of the highest supervisory power in the state is determined by the nature, purpose, and role of the Academy. The Academy regulates politics by embodying the Way of heaven and uses a sacred, religious-ethical principle to limit state power. It is the highest forum for discussion and supervision in the state and has the authority to appraise and adjudicate the rightness of any policy. It exercises this function over all the state bodies, including the legislature, the executive, the judiciary, the disciplinary body, and the military. This is the Academy's ancient function of correction and inspection of the king's business. The aim is to ensure that the state authorities do not infringe Confucian values and to guarantee that they act according to sacred, moral values. It is also what Huang Zongxi talks about when he says, "If there is anything wrong with the administration of the country, the Libationer should speak without reserve."[21]

Here it should be pointed out that the Academy's state supervisory power is not the same as the disciplinary functions of the state. The former is a constitutional power while the latter is an executive power. The Academy has the constitutional authority to supervise all state institutions, while the disciplinary bodies supervise only the executive institutions, as in the case of China's Prosecutorial Department today. The Academy's supervision of the state is also not the same as Sun Yat-sen's Control Yuan, which is on an equal footing with four other Yuan and not above them all like the Academy. The Academy is not subject to any other state body, unlike the Control Yuan.[22]

The Academy's supervisory function is also evident in its setting up a Modern Historical Records Office.[23] The purpose of the Records Office is to help in the Academy's work of supervision. By means of a special constitutional method, power is obliged to be open and transparent, and all forms of secret, unsupervised government are stopped. At the same time, the various forms of pressure exerted by this method ensure that the use of power by the highest state bodies (especially the executive organs), and the words and actions of the highest decision makers are answerable to their own time, to history, and to future generations.

In ancient China, the historians were ministers subordinate to the emperor and to the government and had no independent power over and above that of the emperor or government, hence the Historical Records Office was unable to exert its full supervisory function. But in the Confucian constitutionalist system, the Academy is legally established as independent and superior to all state bodies, hence the modern Historical Records Office can fully attain to its constitutional function of supervision and restriction of the operations of the highest state bodies. It can truly incarnate the spirit of China's traditional politics in which historians supervise the state. Ban Gu (32–92) says, "In the times of the old kings, there were historians. Every action of the ruler was to be written down. He then had to be cautious in word and deed and act according to laws and standards."[24] The Historical Records Office of the Academy is the successor to its ancient counterpart and enables the Academy to fulfill its constitutional role of supreme supervisory board.

We may also consider the establishment of a Modern System of Posthumous Titles by the Academy. The discussion and determination of posthumous titles for state leaders at provincial level or above is to be made according to their career and virtuous living as prescribed by the traditional Law of Posthumous Titles. The state archivists are to use these to write history. State leaders will act with circumspection knowing that they will be judged after death. In this way, history can supervise the exercise of power. The *Record of Rites* states, "on hearing their posthumous designations, we know what had been [the character of] their conduct."[25] As for other supervisory functions, it will be necessary to reflect more on them.

The Educational and Examination Powers of the Academy

To educate scholar-officials is to prepare persons and ensure that the state has persons capable of ruling. Examinations guarantee that they have the basic qualifications for governing. The Academy both trains such persons itself and chooses them by statewide, open, and fair examinations. These examinations are not much like the former imperial examinations, since the Academy examinations prepare people for all state institutions whereas the imperial examinations were largely geared to the executive organs alone. The imperial system also did not train its own scholars. The Academy examinations are for choosing top administrative officials of the first class such as legislators, provincial-level administrators, and judicial officials. The imperial exams chose only the ordinary people for the first class level of administration as in the modern civil service exams. The imperial system did allow for selection outside the triennial examinations, by court and palace examinations,[26] but this was not the main form of recruitment.

In practice, within the framework of Confucian constitutionalism and its three houses, some of the parliamentarians in the House of *Ru* should be trained by the Academy. The top officials of the executive, judiciary, prosecutor's office, and disciplinary board must pass the examinations of the Academy and obtain a relevant qualification.[27]

Furthermore, the Academy can found a modern Chair of Classical Studies as follows. At regular intervals, such as once a month, the Chief Libationer or an Academician of the Academy should give a lecture to the highest state leaders on the Confucian classics: the *Five Classics* and *Four Books*.[28] Under the old system of Lectures on Classics, this is how Confucian constitutionalism uses the transcendental values of Chinese culture and the classical tradition to regulate and educate political leaders, who are later to be tested on what they have learned by reiterating the lectures to the Chief Libationer or Academician. In *Waiting for the Dawn*, Huang Zongxi describes it thus: "The Chief Libationer should face south and conduct the discussion, while the Son of Heaven too sits among the rank of the students."[29]

In terms of modern politics, the Chair of Classical Studies performs three roles. It is a form of state education carried out according to the constitution that regulates and educates the political power holders. Secondly, it uses a solemn and repeated method of education that will restrain their minds and actions. Finally, it institutionalizes the sacred meaning of the classics of the sage kings by according them a place in the constitution, in state ceremonial and at the highest level of authority. In these ways it ensures that power holders will act according to the classics and be answerable to the values inherent in them. Hence, the Chair of Classical Studies is a contemporary modification of the old lecture system and should become a basic component of state ritual.[30]

The Ceremonial and Ritual Powers of the Academy

Modern states still retain many state celebrations of a religious nature, such as sacrifices to Great Heaven to demonstrate sacred legitimacy (at the Altar of Heaven), to the progenitor of the nation to express historical legitimacy, for example, to the Yellow Emperor, to the sages and worthy people of the past to indicate cultural legitimacy,[31] to the earth, mountains, rivers, sun, moon, planets, and stars as an expression of gratitude to nature and prayers for blessings on the people, for example, sacrifices to the land, to the Five Mountains, and to the Six Honored Ones.[32] There are also ceremonies when state leaders take office, ceremonies in times of natural disasters, ceremonies to pray for the dead when the state suffers great loss of life or disasters, as well as remembrance services for those who have given themselves for the nation. All of these require the uppermost level of state ceremony.

Previously all of these rites would have been presided over by the monarch because he was held to be the Son of Heaven and endowed with a certain sacred character. But nowadays, as Weber has observed, state institutions have already been wholly rationalized and secularized, "disenchanted." State leaders are merely the representatives of secular, rationalized institutions and have no sacred character to speak of. Yet the state, by its very nature, cannot be wholly rationalized or secularized because the state is not the same as the government. The state is a sacred, organic living body, endowed with sacred, mysterious, and continuing existence. Hence, even in today's states, secular leaders represent secular state institutions in performing state ceremonials of a religious nature, which, even if they do not match old rituals, nonetheless are not purely rationalized. The institutions and their leaders, who officiate at these state ceremonies, should have a degree of sacred honor, a certain mystique about them. Since the institutions and their leaders no longer have this mystique, all the above ceremonies should be presided over by the symbolic monarch, who is a descendant of the founder of the state.

According to Confucian constitutionalism, the symbolic monarch represents the nation, that is, he represents the historical continuity of the state and the state as such. Hence, ceremonies of state should not be carried out by elected, secular state, or government leaders, who are in office only for a period of time.[33] Among the state religious ceremonies there are some which, while carried out nationwide, do not implicate the state as such but refer to God, to the origin of cultural values or to natural features. These are presided over by the Academy. Thus, the Academy and the symbolic monarch share in the role of carrying out ceremonies.

In general, the Academy is responsible for sacrifices to heaven, to sages of the past, to mountains and rivers, and to the sun, moon, and stars, while the symbolic monarch is responsible for sacrifices to the Yellow Emperor, to the land of the state, to the past emperors and kings, and to past heroes. Ceremonies to mountains, rivers, and earth may be presided at by the Academy or by the symbolic monarch, but with varying significance. The Academy treats heaven as the natural heaven, as the symbol of nature, what the *Classic of History* describes as "looking up to [i.e., 'sacrificing to'] mountains and rivers." The symbolic monarch deals with elements of particular geographical significance within the country to symbolize that the state exists in a given territory, as the old ritual says, "the feudal lords offer sacrifices to the famous mountains and great rivers within their allotted territory." Likewise, when the country suffers great disasters such as earthquakes, drought, flooding, and plagues, either the Academy or the symbolic monarch may pray for the dead and for the survivors, but the Academy does so as a representative of heaven and Confucian religion, while the symbolic monarch represents the state and himself personally in performing the same functions.

The Academy alone presides at the investiture of a new head of state because the Academy represents the Way of the Humane Authority. As president of the investiture, the Academy confers this legitimacy on the incumbent, and so the symbolic monarch is not required. The Academy confers the three kinds of legitimacy on the incumbent. The state leader thus acquires the authority to rule from heaven, history, and the people. The Confucian religious ceremony transforms political power into a right to rule and thus guarantees that the people will willingly accept and obey the leader. In performing these rites it is the highest spiritual leader of the Academy who acts on behalf of the Academy, the Chief Libationer.

The Academy and the symbolic monarch perform different functions when persons are appointed to office. According to the constitution, the parliament and government recommend persons to serve as top officials. They are confirmed in office by the symbolic monarch while the Academy presides over their investiture. The Academy should carry out this role in its own seat of learning, the Bright Hall, according to a solemn and sacred Confucian ceremony of informing the spirits, that is informing heaven and earth, the ancestors, and the sages and worthy people.[34] Only in this way will it be possible to confer sacred, historical, and popular legitimacy on secular power and thus ensure long-lasting and stable authority and order.

In China's political tradition, only the Academy and its intellectual and spiritual leader, the Chief Libationer, enjoy the sacred legitimacy of the sovereignty of heaven and the sage kings, or, in other words, Confucian legitimacy. The Libationer possesses an honored, elevated, and sacred status, the mystique of charisma. Hence the Academy is the only body qualified to represent the state in being responsible for, and in presiding at, state ceremonies of a religious nature. In performing this function the Academy demonstrates its sacred and religious nature. In so doing, one can avoid the undignified spectacle of young ladies from secular, commercial companies presiding at state ceremonies such as that to Confucius. It will also prevent the modern wholly secularized state institutions and their leaders presiding at sacred ceremonies in order to dereligionize them (as in enrollment or military graduation ceremonies).[35]

The Academy's Power of Recall

The people, parliament, or the Academy itself may recommend any top leaders of state institutions to be removed from office for serious matters pertaining to morality, ability, performance, or legality. The Academy may then dismiss them without recourse to parliament or any other state bodies. This power of impeachment covers the parliament, the government, the supreme court, the chief prosecutor, and the state disciplinary board. The Academy may also discuss appointments with the parliament and ask it to withdraw any candidate and nominate another one instead. The significance of this procedure is that it ensures that the state leaders are subject to the religious authority of the Academy and thus invested with the three forms of legitimacy. In case of dereliction of duty, the Academy has the authority to withdraw the legitimacy it granted because the Academy is the institutionalized representation of the sovereignty. In contrast, in a democracy the power of recall lies with the people since democratic sovereignty lies with them.[36]

The Academy's Power of Mediation

In modern Western democracies when state institutions come into serious conflict with each other, the parliament may pass a vote of no confidence in the government or the people may go to the polls or the government may dismiss the parliament. These doings all create massive constitutional crises and even political unrest. This is because, in contemporary Western constitutions, all state bodies are on an equal plane, and there is no one supreme institution, and so clearly it is impossible to properly resolve serious conflict between state institutions on a structural basis. The ultimate appeal is to the will of the people (by a general referendum). Now, the will of the people is the very source of political chaos and violence because it will be whipped up by interested politicians or by violent, ambitious dictators. The Academy's supervision of the state ensures that, in a Confucian constitutional framework, this will not happen.

Constitutionally, the Academy is the highest holder of legitimacy in the state. Functionally, it is a place of scholarship and training, which means that it does not exercise any concrete political power of responsibility. It does not interfere in the day-to-day running of state institutions. However, when serious conflicts among the state bodies occur and it is not possible to resolve them through consultation or discussion, the Academy has the power to undertake mediation of the conflict. The verdict of this mediation is final, and the parties involved must accept the ruling. The reason for this arrangement is that being an academic body above all social interests and political and party infighting, the Academy is answerable only to the way of the sage kings. It is not subject to the many interests in society nor to the influence of a secular, popular will that easily cause political instability. It is independent, transcendent, and stable. This is why the Academy has the ultimate power of mediation and can ensure that the political process of the state is stable and legal, in conformity with the threefold legitimacy of the Way of the Humane Authority. This prevents the state from descending into anarchy as a result of a constitutional crisis brought about by serious political conflict.

The Academy's Power to Uphold Religion

During the three dynasties, society's practice of religion was excellent and the level of morality was high. Everywhere "virtue reigned and the footprints of the unicorn were seen."[37] As a result the Academy did not then have the authority to uphold religion since this happened as a matter of course. Today the situation is very different. Society is now secularized and prey to many interests. Moreover, under the powerful influence of political modernity, states of all political persuasions (*cuius regio eius religio*) all want separation of church and state. There is a grave tendency in politics to exclude religion and morality. Indeed, modern politics itself has become a secularizing force that destroys religion and morality. As a countermeasure, it is essential that there be a transcendent, constitutionally established force, that is powerful, not subject to the influence of secular society or politics, which can maintain religion in society and morality in politics and prevent society, politics, and the economy from plunging into corruption and ensure an environment in which a moral and good society can exist. To perform this function there must be a constitutionally established structure, which is religious and moral in nature, that is the Academy.

In Chinese society, any important matter that touches on religion or morality, any important issue that is contrary to the way and principle of heaven or universal human morality may either be investigated by the Academy itself or handed over to the judiciary.[38] The Academy is responsible for ensuring that these issues are dealt with under the full power of the state. Only in this way can society uphold its morality and religion and guarantee that China does not become what Mencius portrayed as a land where people are well fed and housed but unlettered like birds and beasts (*Mencius* 3A:4).

The Academy supervises but does not run the state. Subordinate bodies exercise their own authority according to the principle of balance of powers and independence. Although the Academy has the highest supervisory power in the state to ensure that the other state powers are separate in their functions, its restraining power is thus limited to the constitutional level. The Academy does not carry out daily affairs, or perform legislative, executive, or judicial acts.[39]

Thus, although the Academy is above all other state institutions and does not interfere in their actual tasks, yet both in terms of the legitimacy that comes from sovereignty and in its constitutional significance, it has the highest power in the state. This is precisely the kind of ideal political system that Chinese scholar-officials, such as Huang Zongxi, sought. This is the most important structural part of Confucian constitutionalism and the most outstanding feature of Chinese constitutional government. Naturally, this political ideal is also what China's scholar-officials of past, present, and to come tirelessly labored for. In this sense state supervision by the Academy is the basic feature of Confucian constitutionalism or, one might say, of Academic constitutionalism. Academic constitutionalism embodies the tradition and spirit of rule by scholarship, which is the unique feature of Chinese political culture.[40]

The above sets out one aspect of the structure of Confucian constitutionalism, the supervision of the state by the Academy. Below we discuss another aspect of the same, the tricameral parliament. Since I have presented this aspect on numerous other occasions, I outline only the main features here.

The Tricameral Parliament

The parliament is a product of both Western constitutional culture and Chinese rule by scholarship. More precisely, the tricameral parliamentary system has absorbed the Western provision of sovereignty lying with the parliament, or rather the priority of the legislature. The parliament represents and embodies political legitimacy and is the source of all legitimate political authority. As the national parliament, the tricameral parliament is related to other state institutions in much the same way as Western-style parliaments are to their respective state institutions. However, there is a distinction since the Academy is above the parliament, while in democracies the people are above the parliament. The Academy and the parliament are not mutually balanced.

The tricameral system draws on Western models but is integrated into a Way of the Humane Authority. Each of the three houses represents one form of legitimacy As explained, the houses exist in a three-dimensional relationship owing to the priority accorded to heaven and hence to the Scholars. The priority of the House of *Ru* is an indication of the traditional Chinese spirit of rule by scholarship. The tricameral system hence has both the Chinese features of rule by scholarship and the Western features of parliamentary sovereignty and balance of powers. The term "Confucian constitutionalism" itself is also a union of Chinese and Western features: "Confucian" being Chinese and "constitutionalism" Western. The union of Chinese and Western elements articulates the ancient spirit of Confucian civilization that "the times matter most." In other words tradition is conserved alongside creativity.

However, the union is not a haphazard, mechanical, or equal placing of the two in a relationship of substance and use (*ti-yong*). Rather, it is on the basis of the development of values inherent in Chinese culture that these are then combined with the constitutional system. The tricameral parliament is the outcome of this development. The Western elements that are absorbed exist in an organic, rational, and intimate relationship, with the basic substance drawn from Chinese culture. There is thus no intrinsic conflict with the basic Chinese values. This is very different from a mechanical-style substance-use relationship since in our system "substance" and "use" are synthesized in an intriguing, dialectical way. We have thus avoided the substance-use relationship derided by Yan Fu (1853–1921) as "an ox used as a horse."

We have not gone against the basic values of Confucianism; rather, we have achieved a use that springs from a Chinese substance. The Way of the Humane Authority is the Chinese "substance" and the tricameral parliament is the Chinese "use" to which it gives rise. But at the level of "use," Western elements that are not contrary to the Chinese substance are also adopted and, together with the Chinese substance, give rise to a Chinese "use." Confucian constitutionalism is a Chinese-style constitutionalism that has absorbed certain reasonable elements of Western constitutionalism. The tricameral system is thus and even more so is the Academy's supervision of the state. However, this is a difficult matter, and we will leave it for another occasion.[41]

THE LEGAL FOUNDATION
OF CONFUCIAN CONSTITUTIONALISM

There are answers to two fundamental questions in politics and for constitutional government: (1) By what authority does the state govern? and (2) Who is invested with that authority? The answer to the first question involves issues of sovereignty and legitimacy, which we have treated above. Here we will look at the second question, the person or persons who represent, or officiate on behalf of, authority. Above we noted that sovereignty lies initially with heaven, that it was delegated to the sage kings and further subdelegated to the scholar-officials. Hence in a Confucian system, the key persons who exercise rule today are the scholar-officials.

There is, then, a basic difference with regard to sovereignty and legitimacy, between Confucian and Western constitutionalism. Western constitutionalism is rule by the ordinary people, the masses, what the American political scholar Carl J. Friedrich calls "government by ordinary people." A Confucian system is elite rule by scholar-officials, what Qian Mu described as "rule by scholar-official." The former illustrates the Western democratic tradition, the latter China's tradition of rule by scholars and by learning.

Besides being Chinese as such, Confucian constitutionalism is postulated on jurisprudential grounds as a result of reflection on Western constitutionalism. In Western constitutionalism, legitimacy faces a grave problem. Ever since the legitimacy of the will of the people has assumed priority in Western politics, it has led to secularization, modernization, mediocrity, pandering to desires, vulgarization, an exclusion of morality, history, and ecology, and a host of other problems. Confucian constitutionalism thus does not accept the sole dominance of this form of legitimacy. The cultural education derived from the sacred values in the classics of the sage kings restrains, instructs, educates, and thereby purifies the will of the people so that it is freed from lowly, vulgar pursuit of self-interest. In other words, the purpose of drawing up Confucian constitutionalism is to achieve a constitutional order that is directed by elite scholar-officials imbued with the spirit of rule by learning who will then enable the will of the people, indeed even their very nature, to rise to more lofty heights of perfection. This is the "kingly government" of the *Gongyang* commentators of the Han dynasty, by which the values of the sage kings are institutionalized so as to educate the people so that they tend toward the good. So it would seem that the Chineseness of Confucian constitutionalism touches indeed on its universality because the flaws of the popular will are a universal phenomenon, which requires the promotion of universal moral values as a remedy.

In Confucian political thought, that the way of heaven is a transcendent, absolute value is indisputable; however, the demands rising from secular interests are open for discussion. Since secular opinions are not absolute and so may be discussed, the parliament may be split into three houses that do enter into discussion. In other words, the Academy stands for the one principle of heaven, while the parliament stands for the multiplicity, which derives from heaven.

I am, though, quite well aware that in China today Confucian constitutionalism is a high-flying political ideal, very far removed from China's current situation. At least three conditions must be met if its realization is even to begin to be considered. Firstly, there must be a complete revival in society of a Confucian-centered Chinese culture. Secondly, within the country there should be the spontaneous formation of a substantial body of scholars in China who keep to Confucian beliefs and practices. Thirdly, the way of Yao, Shun, Confucius, and Mencius must be added to the constitution. Unless these three conditions are all met, Confucian constitutionalism will remain only an ideal.

However, it is not impossible that one day they should all be realized. China has already left behind a hundred years of cultural self-mutilation. The beginnings of a Confucian cultural revival are to be seen among the people and in the government. Coupled with the rise of China, this movement will continue to progress and be unstoppable. Secondly, within the country there are already many kinds of groups of Confucian belief mushrooming, such as Internet sites, halls of learning, academies, societies, research bodies, foundations, and reading circles. While they may still be only quite small, scattered, and with few resources or personnel, they are full of vitality. Their future growth cannot be restricted, and perhaps they may join forces with the revival of Confucian culture in forming a conscious, large, united, and sufficiently resourced body of scholars.

Finally, it should be noted that the constitution is not an unchanging fixed document. Every state can alter its constitution, and China is no exception. In the sixteen years from 1988 to 2004 the Chinese constitution was altered four times. The alterations were largely due to the success of China's liberal-democratic factions. Their demands have already been written into the constitution. The four demands were for private ownership in the economy, a market economy, private ownership of property, and human rights. While these demands do show a certain degree of overlapping consensus with Confucian values, they were the most important and most forceful political demands of the liberal-democratic factions. All were thus written into the constitution and became China's most fundamental political principles, guaranteed by the constitution, even if China's political situation today is still a very long way from fully implementing them. This step would have been unthinkable under China's Marxist-Leninist-directed socialism before the movement of reform and opening up. The revolutionary ideal of Marxist-Leninism is precisely the complete suppression of the system of private property and free employment and a thorough eradication of a commercial and market economy. Yet by means of constitutional amendments, the unthinkable happened in socialist China. Surely, this was a miraculous reversal of history!

Now, given that these principles—private property, market economy, and "bourgeois" human rights, which are contrary to socialism—could yet enter the constitution, why could the way of Yao, Shun, Confucius, and Mencius that expresses the sacred values of Chinese culture not also enter the Chinese constitution? Constitutional changes usually reflect changes in society. Once the revival of Confucianism has become strong enough to influence the whole country, once the scholars have grown in numbers and weight and arrived at a political consensus and constitutional demand for a "Palace" School, then the day for inscribing the way of Yao, Shun, Confucius, and Mencius into the constitution will have arrived. I believe that there will be another such miraculous reversal of history in China. It is only a matter of time. When the above three conditions have been met, we can await the establishment of Confucian constitutionalism.

CONCLUSION: ESTABLISHING CONFUCIAN CONSTITUTIONALISM IS TO REESTABLISH CHINA'S CONFUCIAN CIVILIZATION

To establish Confucian constitutionalism is to accomplish the great task of reestablishing China's Confucian civilization at the level of politics. Currently Confucian civilization is at a low ebb, unable to respond to the challenges of Western culture or to modernity. This inability is most obvious in the political sphere. In the past century of China's constitutional history, Sun Yat-sen's Five Power Constitution was the only case in which Confucian civilization was considered, albeit only at the instrumental level of implementation. All other constitutional drafts, uncritically and unthinkingly, copied Western constitutional models. There were even Confucianists among these copycats. Today we can see that the biggest problem facing China as regards a constitution is the failure to produce a plan for a constitution that reflects China's own political civilization and that gives room to basic Confucian ideas at the level of legitimization. Over the past century the most serious Westernization has happened in politics, such that politics has become China's disaster zone, a cultural dead end. Is it any wonder that many Confucianists today sigh and say, "it is not that we did not think of founding a political system that would be inherently Chinese, but looking over the world today, and noting the problems of democracy, we could still find no other choice"? We can say in amazement that this shows how much Chinese intellectuals lack courage, wisdom, and ability. If the world can offer no better alternatives, why do we not then rely on our own civilization to overcome the defects of Western politics and create a better political system?

Confucian constitutionalism aims to accomplish precisely this task. Our reestablishment of Confucian constitutionalism is to prove to the world that the Confucian civilization is able to create a political structure that has rich resources, great vitality, and creativity. At the same time we are demonstrating to the world that contemporary Chinese intellectuals, relying on Zhang Zai's Four Sentence Doctrine, have the courage, wisdom, and ability to create a bright political system for humanity. This is the common historical mission, cultural responsibility, and sacred task of contemporary intellectuals in China, and it requires that we all take a share in it and create it together.

The ideal state of Confucian constitutionalism was during the three dynasties. In Huang Zongxi's view, after the three dynasties, rule by sage kings took a false turn and became monarchical rule. This led to a massive setback for Confucian constitutionalism in that the highest power in the land switched from the Academy to the monarch, who became the embodiment and representative of sovereignty, leading to the great evil of one man allowing his own private interests to poison the whole country for over two thousand years. While this view of Huang is a bit far-fetched and imbued with historical nihilism given that over those two millennia only very few monarchs were brutal or evil, yet Huang's observations do point out a historical fact, namely that there is great tension and conflict between monarchical rule and Confucian constitutionalism. While the monarchy did allow a certain degree of rule by scholarship, it gave rise to two centers of sovereignty, one located in the sage kings and the other in the monarch. Although Confucian constitutionalism holds that rule by virtue takes precedence over rule be politics, there is no ruling out that, in practice, there was frequent tension and conflict between the two centers. Worldly monarchs constantly sought to usurp the sovereignty of the sage kings and present themselves as sages. Hence, it is clear that monarchy could neither fully realize the rule by scholarship of Academy constitutionalism nor fully implement the values of this kind of rule in a Confucian constitutional system. This is the historical restriction that monarchical sovereignty has led to.

Today the days of the monarchy are over. China has entered into a republican era based on law. Republican rule is much better adapted to realizing Confucian values than monarchy is because it lays an emphasis on separation of powers and no longer has one person at the top who can claim to arrogate sovereignty to himself—in the case of sovereignty lying with the people the "people" are not a given person. Given that Confucian constitutionalism allows for the separation of powers at the level of implementation, among the various state institutions, and even more at the level of legitimization by the separation of the three forms of legitimacy, the republican era has prepared a good opportunity for the establishment of Confucian constitutionalism.

We should take this opportunity as our rightful duty and establish an inherently Chinese, Confucian constitutionalism and so refound China's Confucian civilization. This will be a beautiful case of rule by morality, the guarantee and implementation of a system in which the ideal of the morally transforming power of ethics can be realized through the sacred values of the Way of the Humane Authority for all humanity. In my opinion, this alone is a genuine constitutionalism that has noble values and historical depth. If today we can reestablish Confucian constitutionalism and make our contribution to this task, then we will have accomplished the greatest sagely enterprise available to humanity. By participating in this great creation of history and culture, we shall attain limitless joy. How noble the task is; let all who are concerned for the future of China's constitution work for it together.

CHAPTER 3

A Confucian Constitutionalist State

THE CONSTITUTIONAL ROLE AND CONTEMPORARY SIGNIFICANCE OF REPUBLICANISM UNDER A SYMBOLIC MONARCH

Jiang Qing

The special features of Confucian constitutionalism are the unique system of supervision, the parliament, and the type of state.[1] The type of the state is a republic under a symbolic monarch. Having already discussed the first two features, this chapter looks at the third.

TYPES OF STATE

The first question to be addressed is what one means by types of state, which presupposes that we first understand what the state is itself. The Chinese term "body or essence of the state" refers to the basic character of the state that makes it different from all other forms of human organization.[2] The basic nature of a state is described variously according to one's theory of the state. For instance, Marxism takes class as the basic nature of the state and hence adopts class dictatorship as the essence of the state. Liberal democracy is based on contracts and so assumes that the essence of the state is to uphold rights. Carl Schmitt (1888–1985) makes political exceptionalism the nature of the state and so sees the state's power to make exceptions to the rule of law as the essence of the state. Meiji Japan was a constitutionalism under the emperor and so saw imperial sovereignty as the essence of the state.

Confucianism locates the basic nature of the state in its historical identity. National history is sacred, mysterious, whole, awe-inspiring, and enduring because the state is not the artificial creation of one generation or one group of people.[3] The state is formed naturally and reasonably over a long period of history owing to the cooperation of heaven, earth, and the human element.[4] Therefore, Confucianism holds that the historical nature of the state is its essence.

From the point of view of political theory, the history of the state is its historical legitimacy. The essence of the state is then embodied in national historical legitimacy. The state derives its right and authority to rule from historical legitimacy, and from acceptance of this history the state obtains the voluntary acknowledgment and long-term obedience of the people.[5]

We now turn to explaining the types of state. The type is the way in which the essence of the state is expressed in political form. For instance, a state based on protection of rights may be a constitutional monarchy, a cabinet, or a presidential or committee system. In a class dictatorship, there could be two houses of parliament under the People's Congress as in the former Soviet Union or one as in China. So in today's world different types of state can exist alongside different state essences. In other words, the political form of the state must correspond to its essence. In that way the body politic is also the national or state body.

In Confucianism historical legitimacy must be part of Confucian constitutionalism. If national history cannot be embodied in politics, the state will lack historical legitimacy. Therefore, Confucian and Chinese constitutionalism demand that the body politic in China embody the national history and historical legitimacy. Republicanism under a symbolic monarch is the type of state that Confucian constitutionalism leads to.

In China today, republicanism under a symbolic monarch is the only way in which historical identity of the state and national historical legitimacy can be united. No other way is possible. Western political types such as republicanism under a president or a chairman are not faithful to China's history and so cannot embody the nation in China. Below we will discuss the format of this type of government.

Here we need to clarify what the historical nature of the state is. Firstly, it is something that cannot be wholly analyzed or grasped by reason. It is sacred, mysterious, whole, and awe-inspiring. To try to rely only on reason to understand it would be to "exorcize" it, which would amount to destroying it and making it into the temporary creation of humanity of limited rational ability. Secondly, it cannot be completely grasped by the will either. Western political thought has been influenced by Roman civil law, which uses the will to understand the state on the basis of consent to a contract. The state is made into the product of the will. Human will and human reason are both limited and temporary in nature. Even if this limited and temporary will can provide the basis for contracts between people today, it cannot do so with people of the past or of the future. So even if there were a social contract, it would be binding only on the present generation. But the state is not only the state of the present generation. It belongs also to past and future generations. A contract decided today cannot change the historical nature of the state. Therefore, will is insufficient as a means of understanding the historical nature of the state.

Furthermore, interest and desire are even less apt for grasping the historical nature of the state. Ever since Machiavelli, modern theories of the state have relied on secular interests to understand the state. Hobbes went one step further in holding that the state should be understood as deriving from the desire to protect one's own life. The result is the utilitarian view of the state as upholding interests and desires. But the state is not a deliberately constructed public service body dedicated to providing for human needs (a legal person). Still less is it an interest group (a company) formed to obtain secular interests. Rather, the state is lofty and spiritual, transcending the secular interests and selfish desires of a given time. It is a mysterious body from a distant past. Hence, the historical nature of the state cannot be understood on the basis of desires or interests.

Finally, the concept of rights cannot be used to understand the historical nature of the state. Western constitutionalism defines the purpose of the state as the protection of rights. Now, "rights" is a universal, abstract, metaphysical concept that does not belong to the category of history. Likewise it is subject to the limitations of reason and so cannot grasp the historical nature of the state. That nature may be intuited only in sincere tones of cultural warmth and in a spirit of respect for history. In other words, it must be wholly and loyally believed in, with a quasi-religious sincere faith and humble morality. Thus, reason, will, interest, desire, and rights have no place in understanding the basic nature of the state, its historical identity, though they should not be excluded from an understanding of some aspects of its functions.

Now the historical nature of the state is formed over a long period of time through many twists and turns of rational historical events or chance happenings. It is composed of both reasonable and fortuitous factors that have coalesced into a definite history. The long process of formation will finally settle down and once settled will not go in reverse.[6] This irreversibility of history is determined by the strength exercised by the length of time and by historical rationality and by many chance factors. There is no one standard for all cases. The real reason for this is that the state is an organic living body. Once the body is born, it changes in history and becomes a historical reality.

In the course of formation of a state there are constantly people who come and go, but over a long period of intermingling a definite type of state will be shaped and, on the basis of this type, the historical identity of the state will be formed. This historical identity is not an absolute, static concept but one formed in relation to history. However, once formed it is stable and continuous over a long period of time, and so it creates a stable national character and an unchanging national essence; that is the basic characteristic of the state.[7] The historical identity of the state is a complicated, dialectical concept of stability that has grown up and been formed. It cannot be thought of in terms of simple reason.

While the historical nature of the state may be expressed in the form of the state, its most basic and vital embodiment is in the highest ruler of the state, in the person of the ruler. In traditional monarchies the person of the monarch is the embodiment of the state's historical identity as well as the embodiment of political ruling authority. The monarch represents the state and runs the government. In the person of the monarch, the state's historical identity and political authority are united. In modern times the two have come apart. The nation is represented by the king, president, or chairman, while the government is in the hands of the parliament or government. In Confucian constitutionalism, the two are also distinct: the ruler of the state embodies the nation and the historical identity of the state, while the parliament and head of government hold the power to govern. The ruler in Confucian constitutionalism is the symbolic monarch. He is a head of state, who descends from a noble and ancient lineage.

STATE AND GOVERNMENT: DIFFERENCES, STRUCTURE, AND REPRESENTATIVE ROLE

Under the influence of Western constitutional theory, today state and government are frequently confused, to the point of seeing them as one and the same, with the result that the state is constitutionally and representatively disorganized and chaotic, to the point of abolishing its existence altogether. In Confucian constitutionalism, state and government are separate, and both have their own independent sphere. They run according to different norms and have both different systems of organization and of representation. In detail, the differences are as below.

State and Government Differ in Nature

According to the Confucian historical view, the state is the product of an autonomous long evolution of history and culture. It is a spiritual, organic, and living body that has a spiritual life that runs through past, present, and future and forever. The spiritual life of the state will not be cut short or destroyed by the rational choices or deliberate decisions of a group of people at any given time. This is what the *Spring and Autumn Annals* refers to as one body of the state that endures through the centuries.[8] This means that the state is one body with the nation and not with the people.

The nation refers to a historically enduring idea that transcends the present period, whereas the people refers to a defined contemporary group and is a modern political idea. The living spirit of the state is inherited and passed on by each generation of the nation.[9] The spiritual life of the state embodies the spiritual life of the nation. Through the spiritual life of the nation, the spiritual life of the state is received from the ancestors and handed down to their descendants forever and ever.

In Confucian language, it is the decree of heaven that gives rise to, and maintains, the state, and so the spiritual life of the state is also a result of that decree. Under the guidance of the decree of heaven, politics is led through history to form a state. Therefore, the state itself can be embodied and explained only by the decree of heaven working in history. In contrast, the Western contract theory cannot explain the rise or continuity of the state or its nature because contemporary interests cannot determine the nature of this spiritual body, nor can the reason of individuals comprehend its nature, nor can the will of the people determine its life or death.

We now turn to the government. The government is very different from the state. It is not the product of an autonomous long evolution of history and culture but the product of a particular generation or particular group of persons motivated by interests, desires, and rights and relying on reason or the will. For instance, the ancient monarchs themselves managed affairs outside the court or delegated them to a prime minister. Nowadays, one party may monopolize the government and propose a government for one term, or the people may choose a government by general elections at legally determined intervals, or a government may be formed by violence and revolution.

In this sense the state can be said to be a transcendent sacred existence, while the government is this-worldly secular existence. Moreover, the government is one with the people and not with the nation because it is chosen and supported explicitly or implicitly by the people of that generation without the need for the consent of the ancestors or of generations yet to come. The government is the presence of the people not of history. The state, by contrast, is produced by the will of heaven and is the presence of history.

Furthermore, what the government monopolizes is executive power, which is not the same as the power of the state. This executive power is entrusted by the people to the government, which governs in their name. It is a highly institutionalized, structured, hierarchical, universalized, monopolized, secularized, this-worldly, violent, and substantive form of power. If power has a purpose, then executive power is to prevent people's various rights from being abused and to ensure they can be exercised. This is because it is a form of political power that derives its legitimacy from the people. In contrast, the power of the state is far more often symbolic and spiritual in nature. It is religious, historical, continuing, and national and expresses the values of the state's historical legitimacy. The purpose of state power is to protect the state as an organic, living body, to ensure its continuity, and to guarantee that the nation's historical identity is not destroyed. In practice, the daily running of political power is executive power, while state power is the power of the national leader. The government's executive power is in the hands of the head of the government, while the state power is in the hands of the leader of the state. It is thus clear that both in their origins and in their nature state and government are very different. The two may not be confused.

Structural Differences between State and Government

Firstly, one may consider traditional governments, especially monarchy. In ancient times monarchies allowed the emperors and kings to represent the state and the prime ministers to represent the government, as in traditional China. Yet since in monarchies all legal power is in the hands of the monarch, there is frequently little real distinction between the emperors and the prime ministers. In practice the monarch can represent both state and government, which means that the structure of the state and that of the government are confused and not very clearly separated.

Yet precisely for this reason, monarchy is better able than other forms of rule to manifest the distinction between the state and the government. The historical identity of the state is better embodied in a unique political institution, monarchy itself.[10] Given that monarchy is hereditary, there is a sense that the state lasts forever. Hence monarchy, rather than any other form of rule, is better able to bring it about that the national leader is made conscious of his sacred duty to uphold the decree of heaven in continuing the organic life of the state and its historical continuity.

We now turn to contemporary politics, which expresses political modernity. The main form is democracy, which in practice means constitutional monarchy, a republic headed by a president or a state under a chairman.[11] Constitutional monarchy clearly distinguishes between the government and the state: the monarch represents the state and the cabinet represents the government. Although today most constitutional monarchies have a democratic parliament and cabinet, since this kind of monarch inherits the ancient monarchy, monarchy still represents the tradition of the nation. Hence, this form of polity can best express the foundation of the state on the sacred political tradition of history, and best show that the state as an organic, living body inherits and continues the undying spirit of the nation, and also best reveals that the distinction between state and government is that the former is the presence of historical continuity.

Although in republicanism the president is not a hereditary monarch, he or she does take on the monarch's role as representative of the spirit of the nation. Normally the president represents the state and the premier the government, but there are republics in which the president represents both state and government, the classic example being that of the United States. The president's role in the state is usually set out in the constitution. He can conclude treaties with other countries in the name of the state; he can proclaim the law. He can send and receive ambassadors; he can grant amnesties, name officials to civil and military posts, give out honors and awards, and preside at state ceremonies. All of these tasks were traditionally performed by monarchs.

Even in countries, such as France, where the president holds power over both state and government, the presidential office still represents the state. The constitution of the Fifth Republic accords the president many executive powers that properly belong to the government. It also grants the president quasi-monarchical powers traditionally reserved to one who represents the state, so the president represents both state and government. The most outstanding feature of this constitution is to be found in Article Five, which describes the president as guaranteeing the continuity of the state.[12] Charles de Gaulle (1890–1970) understood this clause as serving to ensure the unbroken continuity of the government. He thought that the president should be above party politics and should represent the state. Furthermore, de Gaulle believed that the premier stood for the temporary and changeable nature of the government, not the continuity of the state. The president alone, the head of the country, was qualified to embody the continuity of the state. Hence, even in a country like France, where there is no clear distinction between state and government, one cannot deny that the historical nature of the state must be embodied and represented by the head of state. The head of government cannot represent this historical nature because of the temporary and changeable nature of the government itself.[13]

However, it is highly problematic to have an elected president replace a hereditary monarch in guaranteeing the continuity of the state and upholding its historical nature. This is because the president is elected by a rational process dependent on the periodic expression of the will of the people and thus is temporary and subject to change. A president is thereby not up to representing the historical nature of the state and lacks sufficient legitimacy to ensure the continuity of the state. Representing continuity demands that legitimacy is accorded by the historical nature of the state. This is the legitimacy required if the people are to permanently and willingly recognize, and sincerely obey, state authority, according to their awareness of the state as an organic, living body with a continuing history and their sense of loyalty. Heads of state chosen by periodic elections do not have the sacred nature that transcends the present that the title of head of state demands, nor do they have the mysterious aura created by the state, nor the authority that has developed of itself by the state throughout a long history, nor the nobility of the blood of the founding father of the state, nor the loyalty of the citizens to their state and the state's role in binding them together.

Moreover, to elect the head of state by the consent of the people's will is to look at the state as the product of a contract. The election of a head of state is equivalent to a political contract drawn up between each citizen and the head of state, granting him or her rule for a limited period of time. A state like that is just like a company. It is a rationalized, contractualized secular organization. The head of state becomes the general manager of a secular company. The only difference from any other company is that the product produced is different. The company is formed by the individual wills of the people present, and the manager is the legal representative of the will of the shareholders. Once the state is turned into a company, the election of the head of state is rather as if by the consent of each individual, the head's right to rule is entrusted to the head of state by means of a law, the constitution, and a contract for a number of years is signed entrusting the power of running the state to one person. The result is that the historical nature of the state no longer exists. This is a considerable devaluation of the state.

Truly performing these functions necessitates that the head of state not be chosen by universal suffrage. Inheritance alone is demanded. For only a hereditary head of state can represent this historicity for he alone has the requisite noble blood, sacred and august personage, and unique exalted status that can compare with the characteristic of the state and its essence and that can ensure the transcendent, mysterious, and historical nature of authority combined with noble lineage and exalted status as well as commanding the loyalty of citizens and the state's role in binding them together. No other way thus ensures that the state is not reduced to being a temporary company.[14]

Representation in State and Government

Above we set out how the heads of state and government have different representative roles. To make the point clearer we will continue to develop our argument. The state is an organic body founded on the sacred recognition and historical sense of loyalty among the people. These sentiments arise from the citizens' intuitive awareness of the will of heaven acting in the state and their profound sense that history will continue. It is these two feelings that constitute the historical legitimacy of the state, by virtue of which the state earns a long-lasting and continuing stability and the authority of legitimate rule. No matter how much the government, or the imperial court in the past, changes, rises, or falls, this cannot influence the continuing existence in history of the organic and sacred nature of the state.

To achieve this, the essence of the state must correspond to the state's own historical continuity, and hence can be nothing else but hereditary. Inheritance alone bears the hallmarks of status and tradition demanded by the continuity of the state. In all forms of government invented by humans up to now, a hereditary head of state is closest to the nature of the state itself and therefore can represent it in respect of historicity and continuity. Governments, on the other hand, may be of many types, such as prime ministerial, presidential, with a premier or a committee, oligarchy, or dictatorship. Thus, there cannot be only one best form of government, unlike in the case of the state. Many options are possible. In practice governments can be democracies or dictatorships, with separation or centralization of powers, based on elections or on nomination, civilian or military, but there can only be one best form of representation of the state: hereditary succession.

SYMBOLIC MONARCH REPUBLICANISM

Now we must ask how a hereditary head of state can be introduced to represent the state in China today. I believe that a republic under a symbolic monarch is the answer to that question for it can ensure the historicity and historical legitimacy of the state within the constitution.

Today we propose republicanism under a symbolic monarch because of the challenges that China faces in establishing her own type of constitution in face of the political modernity spread by globalization.[15] We want to look for a constitutional format that is true to the specifics of China's history and culture. As I see it, republicanism under a symbolic monarch is the only way forward for history in the search for a polity within the context of republicanism, one that will embody the state in its historicity and continuity with a hereditary head of state—a symbolic monarch—who will represent the form of the state today.[16]

By a symbolic monarch, we mean that he does not hold actual political power either legislative like the parliament or executive as in the government. He exercises state power only by virtue of his ancient and noble lineage and serves as the head of state, whom the citizens look up to with respect. Hence "symbolic" refers to not holding the political power that belongs to the parliament or government. It is not really "nothing" though. State powers such as signing and concluding international treaties, proclaiming the law, naming civil and military officials, proclaiming amnesties and pardons, distributing honors, and the like, while their symbolic significance is greater than their real power, nonetheless really exist and are powers with a widespread influence.[17] Hence, the significance of the symbolic monarch is to establish a clear distinction between the head of state and the head of the government. To say that the head of state exerts no political power but holds only state power is not quite like the really purely symbolic statue that Kang Youwei thought the symbolic monarch should be.

Moreover, when the symbolic monarch is a hereditary head of state, the symbolism has even greater meaning. It means that the head of state is not appointed following abdication or by election, nomination, canvassing, force, a change of politics, revolution, or assassination but according to inheritance, the tradition of a lineage. This form of creating a head of state is very simple and can also be called "symbolic."

The symbolic monarch must have a long and noble blood lineage and also be a hereditary head of state. In today's China the symbolic monarch will have to meet five conditions to be acceptable: (1) the monarch must have a noble and ancient blood lineage; (2) this lineage must be political in nature; (3) it must be clearly shown that the lineage is direct and unbroken; (4) the lineage must be so unique as to exclude competition from any other lineages; and (5) the citizens must universally respect and accept the person with this noble political lineage.

According to these five conditions, the symbolic monarch must be a descendant of one of the Chinese dynasties because only their lineages are political in nature. Such lineage is both noble and capable of winning universal respect from the citizens. However, it is not so easy to find a suitable candidate among the descendants of the dynasties. This is partly because the ancient kings ruled a long time ago and there are no clear genealogies preserved. People may claim to be descended from past dynasties, but this is merely on the basis of deduction. There is no trustworthy proof.

Moreover, even if it were provable, the descendants of the past dynasties have split into too many branches such that it would be impossible to prove direct descent. Without direct descent, the blood line would be neither pure nor close, in which case the candidature would be contested and it would be hard to make a choice. Since the question of the symbolic monarch involves power and honor, his election could provoke competition unless there were only one possible candidate. Otherwise, competition would be virtually unavoidable. Secondly, China has had too many dynasties. It is difficult to know which particular dynasty should give rise to the symbolic monarch.

In Japan the imperial line has never been broken, so the emperor is of pure blood, from one family, and there can only be one possible candidate. China cannot present such a political trump card. It is also impossible to draw up a standard to adjudicate in the matter. Hence, the choice of the descendant of any of China's dynasties would provoke only competition and render the choice of symbolic monarch impossible.[18]

Thus, it would seem that the five conditions can not be met. We need to ask, then, if there is not some other way of finding a candidate to be symbolic monarch and thereby realize the form of state present in symbolic monarch republicanism. The answer is yes, and that person is the direct heir of Confucius.

THE HEIR OF CONFUCIUS AS SYMBOLIC MONARCH IN CHINA

The heir of Confucius has three forms of identity: political, cultural, and personal. Although they are united in the one person, they remain quite distinct in nature and illustrate the various historical-cultural duties and political-social roles the heir enjoys.

The cultural identity of the heir is his identity as the descendant of the sage and hence as the symbolic representation of Confucian culture. This cultural identity is exercised in the heir's presiding at rites to Confucius and the other Chinese sages at Confucius's side. The heir holds this role by virtue of blood and not by virtue of learning itself. The tradition of learning is passed down by the great Confucians among the people and by the Chief Libationer of the Academy. However, that the heir holds this cultural identity is a fact that has never been contested. The personal identity of the heir is an internal matter for the family of Confucius since as the direct descendant of the sage, the heir is head of the family and performs rites to Confucius as a member of the family. Both the cultural and personal identities of the heir are clear and have always been so. There is no need to add anything more.

Yet in this chapter we have noted that the post of symbolic monarch is a political matter. The heir's cultural and personal identities do not directly touch on politics and so are not discussed any further. However, their very prominence throughout history has led to concealing a very important political identity, namely that the heir of Confucius is also the descendant of the early kings. The heir inherits the lineage of the Shang kings from before Confucius.[19] Since we are interested in the political status of the symbolic monarch, we do need to deal with this political status of the heir in more detail and examine its significance for republicanism under a symbolic monarch.

According to the *Han History*, in the reign of Emperor Yuan of the Han (49–33 BCE), the new emperor wanted to honor the kings of the Zhou and Yin dynasties. The *Spring and Autumn Annals* prescribed investing a surviving relative of the previous dynasty with the duty of continuing to offer rites to his ancestors as a way of indicating that the empire did not belong to one family and as a mark of respect for the previous kings. Since the founding of the Han came shortly after the collapse of the Zhou, it was not difficult to find a direct descendant of the Zhou kings. Very soon into the reign of Emperor Wu of the Han (141–87 BCE), a descendant of the Zhou, who had been honored as the Zhou South Prince, was honored with the rank as Zhou Successor Marquis-in-Waiting.[20]

But eight hundred years had elapsed since the fall of the Yin, and when the first Han Emperor sent officials and scholars to find a descendant, they reported that the descendants were scattered among over ten family names, all of whom were known to be descendants of the Yin kings, but it was impossible to identify the direct descendant of the kings. At the time the prime minister, Kuang Heng, suggested selecting one of the families as the descendants of the Yin and asking them to inherit the mantle of the first kings of the Yin and perform the rites to King Tang, founder of the Yin. He noted that in the *Record of Rites*, Confucius said he was a man of Yin and so his descendants should be chosen as "First Prince" in place of Qi, Viscount of Wei,[21] who had first been appointed to this role, and since it could be shown that Confucius was a direct descendant of King Tang, his descendants would then be able to perform the rituals to King Tang from generation to generation. At the time the emperor judged Kuang Heng's suggestion as failing to conform to the classics and so did not follow it. Later, under Emperor Cheng (33–7 BCE), the *Spring and Autumn Annals* specialist Mei Fu sent in a memorandum asking that Confucius's descendants should be granted the honor of offering rites to Tang. The emperor accepted the suggestion and so the *Han History* notes, "In the first year of Sui-he, Kong Ji was honored as Meritorious Marquis: Successor to the Yin. In the third month he was ennobled as a duke."[22] When the search for a direct descendant by primogeniture had failed to yield any results, Kuang Heng and Mei Fu both suggested that the direct male lineage of Confucius was in the line of King Tang and so Confucius's heir was honored as Meritorious Duke: Successor to the Yin.[23]

From the above history we can see that Confucius's heir is not only the heir of the sage Confucius but also the heir of the sage king Tang of the Shang. His blood not only represents the "Uncrowned King" Confucius; it also, and even more importantly, represents the founding King Tang of the Shang. Tang of the Shang is one of the three royal dynasties of old and one

of the lines of Chinese rulers. As heir of the kings, Confucius's heir embodies a political identity that qualifies him to take part in the basic structure of
the state because in the ancient rituals to the Zhou and Shang monarchs,
what is touched on is the basic structure of the state.

Today we wish to establish a Chinese-style Confucian constitutionalism
and want to make Confucius's heir the symbolic monarch in the Republic.
It is in his political capacity as successor of the Shang dynasty that the heir
takes his place in China's present state structure as a part of the Chinese
constitutional setup. This political participation of the heir is not something thought up today but something that has been around from the past.
It is just that it has been obscured in recent times owing to the emphasis on
the heir's personal and cultural identities. Since Confucius's heir is of royal
descent, he can represent the rule of the kings and emperors, and with this
political qualification he can embody the unity of China's history and take
part in the public and political arena in China. He is the most authoritative representative of both the national spiritual and living body of China
and the continuity of her history. In this way the constitutional order of
China will be able to manifest the unity of the three dynasties and the fact
that China does not belong to only one family while also honoring the early
kings. It is the hereditary status of the heir that enables him to embody history and represent the state as such.

Confucius's heirs were ennobled as dukes in both the Han and the Song,
but the significance of these actions was not the same. The Han ennoblement as Meritorious Duke: Successor to the Yin brought out the political
significance of the unity of the three dynasties. The Song ennoblement as
Duke: Successor to the Sage was an acknowledgment of their personal role
as head of the family clan. What is surprising is that everyone remembers the
second title but forgets the first. Just as Emperor Yuan of the Han thought
that the title was unclassical, so too many people today consider it unthinkable that Confucius's heirs have a political identity. This is why I have gone
back to the sources to prove that Confucius's heir is the descendant of the
Shang kings, that he has a political status and thus can embody the essence
of the state, namely its historical nature, and so show that his appointment
as symbolic monarch is based not only on scholarship but also on history.

Having discussed the history we now turn to explaining why Confucius's
heir is best qualified to be the symbolic monarch and why he is the best candidate for an hereditary head of state. We will use the above five conditions
and show how Confucius's heir fits them all.

Nobility and antiquity of lineage is not a problem for Confucius's heir
because he not only inherits Confucius's blood but also inherits the blood
of King Tang of the Shang. Confucius was a sage and King Tang was a sage

king. The blood of a sage and that of a sage king are what merit the most respect from Chinese people throughout our long history. Compared with other historical, political, or cultural personalities, the lineage of Confucius's heir is best suited to matching this condition to be the symbolic monarch. Confucius lived over 2,500 years ago and King Tang over 3,600 years ago, so Confucius's heir has inherited blood lines of 2,500 and 3,600 years. This may be said to be the most ancient lineage in human history. There must be practically nobody who can claim a more ancient pedigree.

The second condition is that the lineage must be political in nature. As the descendant of the sage kings, Confucius's heir embodies the unity of the three dynasties, which is the basic concept of Chinese political theory. By virtue of the political nature of his lineage, the heir represents the unbroken essence of the state and can guarantee the continuity of the state. This political identity held true in the past and continues to do so today.[24]

The third condition is that the lineage is direct and unbroken. Over the past two millennia Confucius's family tree has constantly been revised and added to. It is the longest, most detailed, most complete, and most systematic family tree in human history. Hence, as a descendant of a sage, Confucius's heir's credentials are well established. As a descendant of the sage kings, the picture is more complicated. There are no unbroken records of direct descent from the other kings such as the Xia and Zhou kings.[25] Given that by the time of the Han the direct lineage of King Tang of the Shang was no longer clear, at least we know Confucius was of that lineage and the direct descent from Confucius onward is clear because of the father-son succession. It is then no problem to present Confucius's heir as representing the direct descendants of the sage kings. This has been resolved by the ennoblement of Kong Ji as Meritorious Duke by Emperor Cheng of the Han. Given the lack of any clear direct descendants of the sage kings, the claims of Confucius's heir are unparalleled. That means that today Confucius's heir is the only person whose lineage can clearly affirm that he is the heir of an unbroken lineage from the sage kings. Apart from Confucius's heir, no other person in China can claim a direct, unbroken lineage from the sage kings. Hence, Confucius's heir is best qualified to represent the rule of the ancient kings.

The fourth condition is that the lineage must be so unique as to exclude competition from any other lineages. Firstly, Confucius's heir lineage is no problem in terms of antiquity, political significance, or direct descent. Furthermore, the lineage of other personages in Chinese history is either not as noble as his or, though ancient, is not political in nature, or is both ancient and political but we cannot determine direct descent. Hence, no one else in Chinese history can be superior to Confucius's heir.

The fifth condition is that the citizens must universally respect and accept the person with this noble political lineage. Since his lineage goes back over several thousand years to people whom the Chinese universally honor and look up to, no Chinese person has a lineage more reputable than this. Furthermore, the political nature of this lineage has been recognized since ancient times. The *Gongyang* school of the *Spring and Autumn Annals* acknowledges Confucius as king. Sima Qian in his biography of Confucius's family in the *Historical Records* also held Confucius to be king. That Confucius had a political status means that his descendants also do. That is self-evident. Hence, since ancient times Chinese people have maintained an attitude of approval for the political identity of Confucius's heir.

From the above we can see not only that Confucius's heir meets the five conditions. He meets them best of all, which shows that he is the most suitable person in China for the post of symbolic monarch.

PRACTICAL ARRANGEMENTS FOR THE SYMBOLIC MONARCH

Before discussing how Confucius's heir can be the symbolic monarch, we must first clarify his title as Duke. In ancient China protocol required that those who followed the king were named dukes, and so Confucius's heirs were ennobled as dukes. After the Republic of China was founded, the Nationalist Party government of Chiang Kai-shek believed that it was now a republic and so hereditary titles no longer existed. To continue to call Confucius's heir Duke: Successor to the Sage was deemed to harm the republic, and so the heirs were forced to abandon a title they had held for over two thousand years and exchange it for the common office of Sacrificial Official of the Highly Accomplished, Most Sagely, First Teacher. I do not recognize this change of title because it fundamentally destroys China's Confucian tradition and historical culture.[26]

However, the title of heir to Confucius is not an issue of ordinary state honors, nor is it a personal honor. Rather, it affects the whole basis of the state. And it will also change in accordance with the times. The symbolic monarch represents the state constitutionally, internationally, and by virtue of his title. It is somewhat unbecoming that Confucius's heir, as head of state, is known only as a duke. The *Record of Rites* says that ceremonies can be modified as common sense demands.[27] The constitution is the ceremony of the state, and so it too can be changed. To overcome the inadequate title of duke assigned to the head of state, he should be promoted in accordance with Confucian theory.[28] I think promotion by one degree to the rank of king is sufficient, and he should be called King: Successor of the Sage. My reasons are given below.[29]

There are three meanings of the title "king," which match the three identities of Confucius's heir. Firstly, the title "king" implies reference to the first sage kings. These kings of the first three dynasties were the highest rulers of ancient China and of political significance. The royal title assigned to Confucius's heir shows that he continues the rule of the sage kings and manifests his political significance. Secondly, the title "king" appears in the ascriptions "Uncrowned King" and "King of Perfected Culture" that were granted to Confucius, not for his actual political rule but for his maintaining the virtue of the sage kings and their culture. He was the highest ruler of China in a cultural sense and hence was called King Who Proclaims Culture. This testifies to the cultural identity of Confucius. His heir symbolically represents the cultural reign of Confucius. It should be noted that the actual representation of this rule of culture lies with the academies throughout the country and with the National Academy. At any rate, the heir's qualification to be called a king in a cultural sense is in accord with his cultural identity. Thirdly, Confucius can be called a king in that he is the ancestor of all the Confucius's family, and so he may be hailed as their king in a broad sense. The title thus fits the personal identity of Confucius's heir.

The actual arrangement of republicanism under a symbolic monarch is not complicated. Constitutional monarchies such as those of Great Britain, Japan, and other countries in which the monarch is within a constitution are the basic models for the position and functions of the hereditary head of state in republicanism under a symbolic monarch. The King Successor of the Sage is the permanent representative of the Chinese state, and republicanism with him as its core is China's national form. In practice this means that the King Successor of the Sage as hereditary head of state is not a post that is the object of political party competition. Hence, it can effectively uphold the stability, continuity, and eternal nature of the state. He is thus not influenced by any party political disputes.[30]

THE CONSTITUTIONAL ROLE OF REPUBLICANISM UNDER A SYMBOLIC MONARCH

Those who discuss constitutionalism in China today are stuck in the narrow constitutional thought and models of the modern West. They merely see the constitution as a matter of the separation and balance of powers in the political arena and overlook the separation and balance of power between the body of the state and the body politic.

Locke thoroughly idealized the state making it the product of will and something created by people drawing up a contract. In so doing he demolished the state, removing it from the purview of the constitution. All that was left were the parliament, law courts, and government. This was because Locke was a rationalist; it is impossible to grasp the sacred, spiritual, historical, organic living nature of the state. Locke did not know that the sacred and historical nature of the state can be grasped only by a transcendent faith and intuitive life. It is no surprise, then, that the first part of Locke's *Treatise on Government* begins with a criticism of the divine power of kings. Locke's rationalist viewpoint blinded him to this reality of the state, and his grounding in the social contract led him even further to ignore the nature of the state. In Locke's eyes, the state was lifeless, unhistorical, lacking in self-identity or special characteristics and, even more, in power. So Locke's theory can be considered only as political theory and not as a theory of the state. What is surprising is that people later took it as a theory of the state, resulting in a lot of confusion over the matter of the state. This confusion persists in our own time.

We now turn to Montesquieu. Although Montesquieu held that the king could hold executive power, like Locke, he divided state power into three. The government represents the state with the result that the state has no character of its own and no power. In politics anyone can represent the state, even if they are not a hereditary monarch. In my view this kind of narrow Western constitutional thought and model is problematic.

Hence, when I talk about constitutionalism today, I want to go beyond the narrow Western thought and model of modern times, speaking of a separation and balance of powers not only at the political level but also at the state level, the separation and balance of the body of the state and the body politic. In practice this means talking about constitutionalism on the basis of the symbolic monarch as restrained by parliament and government. It is only by addressing the issue at both the level of the body politic and the body of the state that one can fully discuss constitutionalism in all its depth.

The symbolic monarch holds a state power that is purely symbolic. Although this power entails no substantive control at the political level or in practical life, this symbolic power is still substantive in nature in the life of the nation, influencing and determining actual life at the level of the state. Although the carrying out of his functions may depend on decisions or recommendations of the government, the people know in their hearts that the power belongs to the state. Unless the functions are carried out by the symbolic monarch, they lack the state's historical legitimacy. The state power implies endorsement by the people, which is deeply rooted in the historical legitimacy of the state. Although endorsement by the people is the basic factor in Western constitutional legitimacy, grounded on limited reason and the temporary will, parliament and government cannot embody the endorsement of the people deeply rooted in the historical legitimacy of the state.

Hence, the symbolic monarch provides a form of check on the parliament and government, limiting them by the exercise of the authority of the state on the basis of its historical nature. By this check, the spirit of separation of powers and political justice is achieved. This acts as a check on parliament or government encroaching on state power in respect of legitimacy.

At this point we need to say more about the relationship and difference between state power and political power and how parliament and government decide the powers ascribed to the head of state. These powers include the practical details of alliances concluded with other countries, the details of the constitution or laws, and the persons who should be appointed to civilian or military posts and declare states of emergency or rallies for the whole people. Since the content of these powers touches on state affairs, they are not purely political matters like maintaining security, protecting human rights, developing the economy, increasing well-being, and collecting taxes. A body that specifically represents the state is the only one constitutionally qualified to carry out these functions—albeit after the requisite decisions made on the political level by parliament and government. Political powers that affect the state require a constitutionally appointed body at the state level to ensure that these functions themselves are elevated to state level. By this means they are endowed with the legitimacy of the body of the state, and their abstract nature as state functions is rendered visible by being carried out by a state-level body. That body is the symbolic monarch. Hence, we may say that state power is the political power that touches on state affairs. In addition, neither parliament nor government may decide the content of the state power that is religious and cultural in nature; even less may they ever exercise it.

Of course sacred state power may also not encroach on, or seize, secular political power and unite both in one monopoly of power. There has been a failure to distinguish the boundaries, leading to situations opposed to the constitution such as parliamentary dictatorship, executive dictatorship, or party dictatorship. The extremes of these abuses can be seen in the left- and right-wing governments of the last century in which secular political power encroached on, and replaced, sacred state power to swallow up all sacred space and the historical nature of the state in a totalitarian regime.[31]

The symbolic monarch has a further power: the nomination of the head and members of the House of the Nation. The symbolic monarch should appoint the leader and members of the House of the Nation because both, in constitutionally different ways, represent the historical nature of the state. At the same time, this is a challenge to the idea that sovereignty lies solely with the people. Part of the legitimacy must come from the historical nature of the state. This mechanism effectively prevents parliamentary dictatorship.

It is clear that republicanism under a symbolic monarch is a new form of constitutional arrangement, one that is rooted in history. It has been rooted since ancient times in the historical nature of the state, which has been represented by the monarch.[32] To say that republicanism under a symbolic monarch is new refers to the fact that, under modern constitutions, the traditional monarchy no longer represents the historical nature of the state. This traditional role is reintroduced into a modern constitution.

Thus, symbolic monarch republicanism is not a matter of restoring the monarchy or reviving the past.[33] Rather, it maintains the basic spirit of constitutional checks on power within new historical circumstances and establishes a more perfect and complex constitutional setup. The purpose is that, by using the state to restrict the parliament and government, all three will attain to a level of harmony and balance.

THE PRESENT SIGNIFICANCE OF REPUBLICANISM UNDER A SYMBOLIC MONARCH

Over the past several hundred years, one wave after another of modernity has swept in, establishing an unprecedented political modernity. In my view, political modernity is precisely the chief cause of political problems. The most serious problems wrought by political modernity in the state are as set out below. I will also explain how republicanism under a symbolic monarch can be a remedy for the losses.

Loss of Historical Nature, Continuity, and National Spirit

The state has a historical nature because it is an organic entity that continues to exist in unbroken succession. It differs from other forms of organizations by virtue of having a self with national spirit. Yet political modernity looks on the state as a secular product of contract, limited reason, and temporary will that are constantly subject to change by a given group of persons at some given time, rather than a spiritual self.

Loss of Sacredness, Prestige, and Value

As political modernity reduces the state to a mere product of a secular contract, the state no longer has the sacred nature and prestige derived from the will of heaven. In the absence of a religious atmosphere of awe and devotion, people no longer obey the state out of sacred duty or reverence but simply out of their own temporary will and worldly interests.

Moreover, since the value of the state as the universal and moral good originates from its sacred nature, the loss of one would also entail the loss of the other.

Loss of Loyalty

By loyalty we mean the sacred, single-minded, profound, enduring fervent call arising from an irrepressible, heartfelt moral sense of belonging. This heartfelt sense of belonging is not a commonplace feeling. Rather, it is a religious and moral sense. It is the profound psychological element from which political duty and the right to rule are born. This religious and moral sense arises by bringing together the spirit, historical nature, continuity, sacredness, and value of the state. It is the psychological feeling that is at the basis of the unity and stability of the state.

Moreover, loyalty to the state cannot be treated as it is in Western theories of legitimacy, in which religious and moral feelings are excluded and may be embodied only under a rational framework of constitutional and legal arrangements established by the citizens. It is imperative that loyalty is embodied in living people and personalities. Perhaps for a very few philosophers, such as Socrates, loyalty can be a rational thing that adapts to a lifeless objective legal order, but that will not work for most citizens. For them, what really matters is that the sacred personality of the ruler should embody or call forth the binding loyalty of the citizens to their state, or what Weber called his "charisma," which is the characteristic of the head of state, by which his person becomes the object of citizens' loyalty. This loyalty can then be loyalty to the state and realize the kind of sentiment that the continuity and stability of the state requires.

In modern rationalized politics, however, the head of state is chosen by the citizens' calculation of their own interests. The subjects will brazenly expect that the head of state should be no different from anyone else. All are simple citizens or commoners. The head of state lacks the sacred, historical, lofty, and eternal mysterious power of attraction and transcendent great magic in his person. The people will obey him for his acts for a time and give him a loyalty that does not last. He can never hope to gain the quasi-religious moral loyalty of a long-lasting and fervent heartfelt service rooted deep in the hearts of the citizens. Hence, in modern states, when the head of state is assassinated, dies in office, or dies in an accident, there can no longer be the ancient custom of loyal servants sacrificing their lives for the monarch. China's "loyal ministers" will never be seen again.[34] This is because a loyal minister expresses his loyalty to the state in his loyalty to the person of the monarch, but contemporary heads of state produced by rational elections are not worthy of the loyalty of the citizens for they are contracted, entrusted, exchanged, temporary, secular, and vulgar.

Nonetheless, republicanism under a symbolic monarch can be a remedy for the above losses. First of all, given his exalted identities and hereditary status, a symbolic monarch can restore the historical nature, continuity, sacredness, and spiritual self of the state. The people will hold the state in awe and relate to her with a profound sense of loyalty since the relationship of citizens and state will once again be founded on a religious and moral sentiment. This will ensure the cohesiveness and stability of the state and restore the state to its religious and moral foundations. Furthermore, as China's unique unity of state and religion is made clear, the state can recover its value and prestige by restoring religious and moral aims, as opposed to mere satisfaction of the selfish desires, as its goal.

OTHER ISSUES INVOLVING SYMBOLIC MONARCH REPUBLICANISM

Symbolic monarch republicanism is the most political aspect of Confucian constitutionalism. The widespread influence of political modernity will lead many people to look askance at it, but there are also other complicated issues that it gives rise to, and so it is necessary to say something about these issues. This section raises a number of topics in a piecemeal fashion, but overall aims are to provide a better understanding of republicanism under a symbolic monarch.

The Place of Symbolic Monarch Republicanism in Confucian Constitutionalism

Confucian constitutionalism is structured according to the three forms of legitimacy. Symbolic monarch republicanism represents historical-cultural legitimacy. Monarchy has formed a very important historical and cultural nature of China. One could say that without the monarchy there would be no Chinese national historicity. Hence, in constructing a constitutionalism with Chinese historical and cultural characteristics, it is important to acknowledge the monarchy as an important constitutive part in Confucian constitutionalism.[35]

Today China has already become a republic; it is no longer possible to completely restore the monarchy. Yet in China republicanism cannot represent historical legitimacy. The only way to resolve this problem, while recognizing the principle that the times decide, is to use a dual way: to keep the basic spirit of the traditional monarchy by having a symbolic monarch and to maintain the basic constitutional framework of a republic. Thus, symbolic monarch republicanism respects the political reality of China today, while also finding a new format to express the historical legitimacy. It produces a harmonious balance and so truly realizes the constitutional ideal of equilibrium through checks and balances. This is not like postrevolutionary France, the Soviet Union, or China where republicanism and monarchy were viewed like fire and water, unable to mix, and there was total opposition to the basic spirit of harmonious equilibrium that the constitution should bring about in the state.

Comparison of Symbolic Monarch Republicanism with the House of the Nation and Supervision by the Academy

Firstly, both symbolic monarch republicanism and the House of the Nation represent historical legitimacy. Yet symbolic monarch republicanism does this at the level of the state and has no substantive political power. In contrast, the House of the Nation is political in nature and holds real political power. Furthermore, symbolic monarch republicanism is a form of the state that combines tradition and modernity, while the House of the Nation is fundamentally part of a modern constitutional framework.

Symbolic monarch republicanism is also different from the Academy. While both are in the realm of the sacred and of values, the Academy is so in a substantive way and the symbolic monarch in a purely formal way. The Academy engages in practical supervision of all forms of state and political power and enjoys a higher status in the constitution than any other body.

Symbolic Monarch Republicanism and the Ecological Crisis

There are many causes of the world's present ecological crisis. In politics, democracy is certainly the root cause because its deepest foundations lie in the ever-increasing material demands of the present generation of people. This has a malevolent influence on the environment. The long-term interests of the environment can never be satisfied in democracy.

In contrast, the symbolic monarch is a hereditary head of state, and so he is answerable not only to the present generation but also ancestors and generations yet to come. He can provide a check on the political power that destroys the environment for the worldly interests of a given group of people. He can use state power to give advice, question, encourage, and warn people in the various important areas of national life and suggest to the political authorities that they cannot use ecological destruction to run counter to the continuing and enduring nature of the state. He can prevent political power from engaging in transitory behavior based on selfishness motivated by elections that would harm the interests of future generations and the long-term interests of the state and in this way succeed in protecting the environment.[36]

Symbolic Monarch Republicanism and National Stability

From the point of view of human psychology, we know that a human being is not only a being with interests, reason, and will. He is also a being of feeling, not only in daily life but also in the context of the state. There are three kinds of feeling that are relevant to the life of the state: moral feelings, religious feelings, and psychological feelings. By moral feelings we refer to the citizens' feeling of loyalty to the state. By religious feelings we refer to the citizens' feeling of dependence on the state. By psychological feelings we refer to the citizens' feeling of loving admiration for the state. These three feelings all exist in human life, and if they can develop normally in the life of the state, they will enhance the cohesiveness of the state and further its stability. The reasons for this are given below.

When citizens have a feeling of loyalty to the state, both state and citizens will be of one mind and heart. Even when the state is beset by great internal difficulties or external oppression or even when it faces invasion from an enemy state, the citizens will not feel like deserting their state. The highest proof of this loyalty is to die for the state when it faces great danger. It is not necessary to describe this loyalty in detail. It is clear that it can increase the cohesiveness of the state and forward stability.

Secondly, the religious feeling of dependence can bring about a more intimate relationship between the citizens and the state and raise it to the level of a transcendent, sacred dependence. Human existence is limited and very fragile. Life is short and full of worries, and so people are often troubled at heart and need comfort and consolation from outside. In the life of the state, citizens place their worries and anxieties over their limited existence into the enduring life of the state, which is sacred and transcendent in form, and so there will be a belief in the state that is religious in nature. In this way the religious nature of the state can comfort the citizens in their worries and cares and console their feelings of hardship and trouble. State and citizens will thereby be bound in inseparable bonds of intimacy and the state will give rise to great forces of cohesiveness that result in ensuring the stability of the state.

The psychological feeling of loving admiration comes from one's love for one's parents. We know that from an early age there is a love for one's parents and this love lasts into adulthood and accompanies one to the end. This love is born from the depths of an individual's loneliness. This loneliness means that the heart is always in a state of emptiness and helpless suffering and by oneself alone one cannot overcome this deep sense of loneliness. So people can only long for a force from the outside that will relieve this loneliness, which force is parental love. The great feeling of love of the older generation enables a person to not feel alone. All people, then, long for the external force of the great and tender love of elders. The difference is that when young this feeling of admiring love is focused on the parents, and when one is older it is the state or religion. Therefore, people have a desire that the state will show a strong and tender feeling toward them in their loneliness, and they in turn will feel a deep love for their country rather like the love for one's parents. Since the state embodies the transcendent sacred will of heaven, it is able to resolve the innate feeling of loneliness of the citizens and become the object of their loving admiration, thereby effectively forward the stability of the state.

CONCLUSION

Monarchy is the most natural and most ancient form of political governance in human history. It must then have a reasonable core, or else it would not have existed throughout history, nor would it have enjoyed the support of countless scholars and sages both in the past and in the present, in China and abroad, people such as Plato and Burke in the West and Confucius in China. In my opinion the reasonable core of monarchy is that a hereditary head of state has a noble and ancient lineage, an honorable and respected status, and the mystical charisma of his person is such that he can embody the historicity and continuity of the state and thereby increase its cohesiveness and stability. What this reasonable core embodies is the basic spirit of monarchy. In contrast, monarchical autocracy, when the monarch is exclusive and subject to no checks and alone holds and exercise political power, is not the basic spirit of monarchy. It is merely a special form of holding onto and using power in which the monarchy has expressed itself in particular historical conditions. Thus, it is not of universal significance or long-lasting value.

In fact, the autocracy of prime ministers, presidents, or party cabals in the modern democratic form of dictatorship of political parties is certainly just as bad as monarchical autocracy. To criticize monarchical autocracy in the name of democracy is but a form of democratic ideology, a demonizing of all forms of politics that are not democratic and a means of democracy blasting its own trumpet. Therefore, the basic spirit of monarchy may be continued without change, though the form in which it is expressed must be changed. However, in recent times, political modernity, that is, republicanism, has so thoroughly demonized and denigrated monarchy that people are no longer able to see its reasonable core. In establishing a state structure they reject this basic spirit and universal value of monarchy, resulting in the head of state in a republic not being able to represent the historicity and continuity of the state in a way that is long-lasting or effective.

Based on these observations, when today we seek to establish a Chinese-style constitutionalism with Chinese historical and cultural characteristics, we must sort the wheat from the tares and acknowledge the reasonable core of monarchy and return to its original face, inheriting its basic spirit and rejecting its external form—that is, rejecting its dictatorial hold of substantive political power. In this way, the ancient tradition of monarchy, in the context of today's Chinese constitution, can attain a reasonable, proper, and positive constructive role. Symbolic monarch republicanism is a criticism of political modernity's demonization of monarchy and a corrective to republicanism's utter denial of monarchy. Symbolic monarch republicanism, then, inherits the virtues of monarchy, while avoiding its disadvantages of autocratic hold on political power.

Again, symbolic monarch republicanism also avoids the disadvantages of republicanism, that an elected head of state is incapable of representing the state, while inheriting its virtue, a constitution with separation and balance of powers. In this sense, we have every reason to say that for the establishment of a constitution for China today, symbolic monarch republicanism is truly an appropriate use of the past in the present, a use of what is Western in China, a rejection of what is out of date and creation of something new, a constitutional arrangement that is both critical and traditional. It is not an undigested restoration of the past, or wishful thinking, or a return to imperial rule or opposition to the Revolutions of 1911 and 1949.

In China today, political modernity has expanded to such an extent as to oppress and destroy political traditionalism. China is an even worse case than other countries. In the realm of the state, wave after wave of revolutions has utterly eradicated the traditional nature of the state. In this respect, China is the most modern state in the world. On the practical political front, China's current political setup is the most marked by modernity in the whole world because the People's Congress, which is based on the principle of sovereignty of the people, legally speaking, is more democratic and more republican than any other form of representative parliamentary system. While there is a gap between political realities and the constitutional norms of sovereignty of the people in China, this gap is one of failure to put into practice and not one of lack of legitimacy. In fact, in terms of legitimacy China's constitution today is basically no different from that of Western countries. Indeed, it is perhaps even more democratic. There is, therefore, no denying that China's current constitutional order very clearly embodies political modernity. It is just that this political modernity today has not yet acquired the protection of due process and rational law. China's mainstream thinking is concerned to remedy this defect and to follow international guidelines, the supposedly political civilization of humanity.

To propose symbolic monarch republicanism is not nostalgia for the past, putting the clock back, or wanting to restore the emperor. Rather, it goes beyond the divide into left and right and postmodernity's criticism of modernity and seeks to take a new road by using traditionalism to criticize modernity. The aim is to arrive at a constitutional model or constitutional road that is in accord both with China's historical and cultural tradition and with the development of modern politics. The result should be to overcome the complete rejection of tradition in China's recent past by which the state itself is left without any form of representation.

This duty is onerous and great and not something one person can solve alone or something that can be achieved in a short space of time, but I propose this framework of Confucian constitutionalism in the hope that the Chinese people do not allow the great economic success of China to lead them to neglect thinking about what kind of constitutional arrangement would be best for China and whether or not China should establish a constitution with Chinese historical and cultural characteristics. If the answer is in the affirmative and can be resolved within the theoretical path of Confucian constitutionalism, then there is hope yet for a revival of Chinese civilization. China will no longer be subject to the loss of her own cultural identity under the influence of thorough Westernization. The establishment of a Chinese constitution need no longer entail a rejection of her own self in order to follow the international line. The renewal of China's political civilization will no longer have to be carried out under the banner of humanity's political civilization. Instead, it will be done on the basis of China's own civilization, having absorbed and digested the positive values in Western civilization, to create a new Chinese civilization that embodies features of Chinese civilization. No longer will the cry that democracy is a good thing be heard in China, that naïve cry that implies the loss of national identity and a lack of critical reflection on the deficiencies of Western political thought.[37]

PART II

Comments

CHAPTER 4

On the Legitimacy
of Confucian Constitutionalism

Joseph Chan

INTRODUCTION

Confucianism began life more than twenty-five hundred years ago.[1] What preoccupied Confucius and other classical thinkers was the decay of social norms and disintegration of orders in their times. However, these thinkers believed that the norms, rituals, and institutions developed in the Zhou dynasty had been fundamentally sound, and the problem was only that they lost grip on the corrupted elites who lacked ethical cultivation and discipline. In response, they developed a set of relatively abstract ideas such as *ren* (benevolence, as commonly translated) and *yi* (righteousness), which, they hoped, could bring fresh insights and attractiveness into what was already a settled and perfected set social vision developed in the ancient time. As a result of this backward-looking perspective, the substantive content of what they proposed did not depart much from the current norms of the kind of society in which they lived— norms that are required for the successful functioning of a traditional small-scale peasant economy, a patriarchic family system, and a monarchic political order.

Today, the forces of modernization have demolished these main pillars of traditional Chinese society, and so Confucianism faces a challenge never occurred before. Confucians today cannot respond to the problem of disintegration of orders in the same way their classical masters did. They cannot simply try to revitalize the traditional values once cherished by people, without considering if these values are socially relevant at all in modern society. So the first challenge to Confucianism posed by the disintegration of traditional society and politics is whether Confucian values (ethical and political) are still relevant to modern people today.

Ther e are a few responses to this question. The first is one of pessimism.[2] It argues that it is extremely hard for Confucianism to find institutional expression in modern society. On the one hand, it is not merely a philosophy that can satisfy itself within the confines of universities; on the other, it is not an organized religion that can be anchored at churches and seminaries. It is rather a praxis, a practical philosophy aiming at translating thought into action, transforming people's moral lives, and building a harmonious and orderly society. But Confucianism cannot take effect in the world if it is not supported by institutions, and hence cannot fulfill its central mission as a praxis, however insightful and sophisticated it may be as a reconstructed modern *philosophy*. Confucianism today is merely a "wandering disembodied spirit" in modern society.

The second response is a bit more positive.[3] It admits that it is not easy to find institutions to embody Confucian values. It admits too that modern social and political institutions are not simple institutional extensions of Confucian ethics but are based on a different set of values and operate with a different logic. In this sense, Confucianism does not have its own institutional expression in modern society. But this second response maintains that modernity and its institutions should be subject to substantive ethical evaluation, without which they are likely to evolve into excessive instrumentalism, individualism, materialism, and democratic populism. In this context, what Confucianism can perform is a critical role, challenging the excessive tendencies of modernity and reminding people of the insights of traditional wisdom. The praxis of Confucianism lies in the practice of social critique, rather than that of social engineering according to a settled vision of ethics and society.

I favor a third response, which goes beyond the second one in the affirmation of the potential presence of Confucianism in modern society. According to this third response, there is no reason why Confucianism as a praxis is limited to the role of social critique, for any effective critique must point to a direction of change, or better still, an alternative to the object being criticized, be it a value, a policy, or an institution. Furthermore, if one believes that some major Confucian values still have relevance in modern times, it would be difficult to maintain at the same time that these values have no implications regarding institutional or policy issues. In addition, the values and practices of liberal democracy as we understand it today are neither a settled vision requiring no further development nor free of difficulties requiring no revision. In fact, liberal democracy as a set of institutions allows different justifications, and its concrete forms vary according to different historical circumstances and ideological inclinations. Ideologies such as conservatism, liberalism, libertarianism, communitarianism, and egalitarianism have shaped the forms of liberal democracy in one way or another. If one follows the approach of critical transformation, one would hope that a suitably reconstructed and transformed Confucianism, like other ideologies, not only can mesh with liberal democracy but also can contribute to its further development and revision. It may even seek to supplement liberal-democratic institutions with Confucian-inspired, non-liberal-democratic institutions.

So Confucianism's contribution to modern politics should go beyond its negative role to positively shape political institutions, legislation, and policy making. In a sense, this can be regarded as a version of "Confucian constitution." But what form should Confucian constitution take? This chapter distinguishes two kinds of Confucian constitution: (1) promotion of Confucianism as a comprehensive doctrine to design and regulate the constitutional order and (2) piecemeal promotion of Confucian values and perspectives through the strategies of what I call "moderate perfectionism." Jiang Qing's idea of "Confucian constitutional order" is an instance of the first kind. I argue that it is undesirable to promote and enforce Confucianism as a comprehensive doctrine in the political sphere, while the way of moderate perfectionism is the best we can do given the pluralistic nature of modern society.

TWO KINDS OF CONFUCIAN CONSTITUTION

Confucianism is a philosophy of politics as well as of life. Classical Confucians in the pre-Qin period believed that virtues, society, and politics were inseparable from one another. The role of political leaders was to guarantee good order in society and promote moral development of people. In the terminology of modern political philosophy, Confucianism can be considered as a kind of political perfectionism, in the sense that a central task of the state is to provide conditions for people to live the good life. We should, however, distinguish between two kinds of political perfectionism, and hence two ways of promoting Confucianism in the political sphere. Extreme perfectionism says that the state should adopt a comprehensive doctrine of the good life as the basis of state constitution, legislation, and policy. Following John Rawls, by "comprehensive doctrines" I mean those conceptions of the good life that involve systematic theorization about human life: they explain why certain things are good to human life, rank those goods into a certain hierarchy, specify concrete ways to realize those goods, and tie them to a tradition of thought that is distinct from, and in conflict with, other traditions.[4] Traditional Confucianism did contain a comprehensive conception of the good life understood in this sense. Moderate perfectionism, however, says that the state may appeal only to specific judgments about the good life, not comprehensive doctrines. The state may promote specific valuable goods such as the arts, knowledge, family life, and other valuable social relationships, and basic human virtues such as benevolence, courage, and practical wisdom. Moderate perfectionism does not seek to make fine-grained comparative judgments on many different ways of life. It looks at the broad social trends and environments that undermine or promote human goods and considers if any state action is necessary to create conditions conducive to the pursuit of these goods.[5]

Given this distinction between extreme and moderate perfectionism, we may distinguish two ways of promoting Confucianism. One way is to promote Confucianism as a comprehensive doctrine of the good and try to implement it as a comprehensive package. The other is to promote the Confucian conception of the good life in manners consistent with moderate perfectionism. Let me elaborate on this second way. Although as a moral or religious philosophy Confucianism may develop its conception of the good life as comprehensively and rigorously as possible, as a normative basis of political action it should present a noncomprehensive conception of the good life that contains only specific judgments about virtues and desirable goods, without trying to rank them into a hierarchy or tie them with metaphysical or religious doctrines. For example, it should offer a list of items that constitute the good life and the good social order, such as filial piety and familial relationships, practical wisdom and learning, sincerity, harmony, social and political trust and trustworthiness, and so on and so forth, and explore their implications on social and political arrangements.

UNDESIRABILITY OF PROMOTING CONFUCIANISM AS COMPREHENSIVE DOCTRINE

Civility and Pluralistic Society

Promoting Confucianism as a comprehensive doctrine is undesirable in the main because it damages civility. In modern society, citizens live according to various ways of life and beliefs, including different religions. For a pluralistic society, civility is of crucial importance. Civility is a certain kind of attitude toward fellow citizens of a society. It is marked by a concern for the *common bond* among citizens despite their differing opinions or conflicts of interest. Civility tries to diminish conflicts by seeking a *common ground* that underlies conflicting opinions and a *common good* that transcends partisan interests. To seek a common ground and a common good, civility requires citizens to be open-minded, to give reasons that others can share in justifying one's views, to pursue the economy of moral disagreement, and to be willing to make compromises if full agreement cannot be achieved. Civility is against "ideological politics" based on comprehensive doctrines. As Edward Shils observes, ideological politics is "obsessed with totality." Those who practice it believe that "they alone have the truth about the right ordering of life—of life as a whole, and not just of political life," and that "sound politics require a doctrine which comprehends every event in the universe, not only in space but in time." "Ideological politics are the politics of 'friend-foe,' 'we-they,' 'who-whom.' Those who are not on the side of the ideological politician are, according to the ideologist, against him." Ideological politics destroys the common bond of citizens and rejects civility.[6]

Promoting Confucianism as a comprehensive doctrine is a kind of ideological politics that has to be rejected if we regard civility as an important virtue. In an open society, the promulgation of comprehensive doctrines is not only protected by law but actively supported by civil society, resulting in a vibrant but at times volatile marketplace of ideas. Quite inevitably, conflicts and struggles will arise from the free exchange of views and free pursuit of (legitimate) interests. To maintain civic concord among free and equal citizens, it is important that citizens exercise a great deal of self-constraint and not let one group impose its own worldview and system of values on others in a winner-take-all fashion through democratic politics.[7]

To further illustrate the issue of comprehensive doctrine, we can begin our discussion concerning Jiang's idea of a Confucian constitutional order. His "Confucian constitutional order" refers to a constitutional order that "represent[s] Chinese culture and civilization in its entirety."[8] He emphasizes that "in past, present and future, Confucianism is destined to be practiced; it has to establish its principles, justify its order, materialize its ideal, and finally build a ritual-political system that manifests the nature and principles of the way of heaven, so that the kingly way and kingly heart of Confucius can be materialized in the world."[9] To implement this constitutional order, Jiang proposed a set of political institutions, including the Academy and a tricameral parliament.[10] Jiang also wants to turn China to a kind of constitutional monarchy, as the descendant of Confucius would be made the symbolic monarch of China. Wielding no political powers, the monarch would be the symbolic figure for China.[11] Through building China's political institution based on the Confucian classics, Jiang's proposal is a version of comprehensive doctrine.

Jiang's proposal is undoubtedly a kind of ideological politics, aiming at providing Confucianism with a hegemonic ruling position. Modern China, however, is already a pluralistic society in which citizens have different views about lifestyle, beliefs, religions, and ideologies. Therefore, civility is of crucial importance to Chinese society; it demands both the government and the people to be open-minded, to seek economy of disagreement, and to compromise when formulating policies. On the contrary, Jiang's Confucian constitutional order demands that the constitutional order be grounded on the worldview of Confucianism, which implies a total rejection of liberalism, socialism, Buddhism, or Christianity as possible grounds for the constitutional order. Implementation of this proposal harms civility as it deviates from the social reality.

To be fair, Jiang is not entirely unaware of the constraints of reality. He admits that there is a great distance between the current situation of China's society and the conditions necessary for implementing his Confucian constitutional order; therefore, he proposes three conditions for his ideal to be implemented: (1) "a complete revival in society of a Confucian-centered Chinese culture," (2) "within the country there should be the spontaneous formation of a substantial body of scholars in China who keep to Confucian beliefs and practices," and (3) "the way of Yao, Shun, Confucius, and Mencius must be added to the constitution." Jiang believes that these three conditions are not impossible to be attained because Confucianism has been undergoing a revival in contemporary China, while the Chinese constitution is modifiable, as can be seen by the fact that the PRC constitution has undergone multiple instances of modification already, including the introduction of groundbreaking clauses such as protection of private property. However, I find the conditions proposed by Jiang to be very improbable. Chinese society is getting increasingly diversified; although Confucianism has received much and increasing attention in recent years, it is unlikely to be revived completely. Even though Confucianism contains certain values that can influence the development of constitutionalism, it is still unlikely for the way of Yao, Shun, Confucius, and Mencius to be included in the constitution. Including the way of Yao, Shun, Confucius, and Mencius in the constitution is very different from including the clause of "protecting private property"; the latter is only one principle that goes hand in hand with a market economy, while the former is a comprehensive thought that comprises many values and principles.

More importantly, it is questionable whether we should try to attain these three conditions at all. Jiang admits that these conditions cannot be brought forth by civil society alone. Instead, it requires the cooperation of the political realm. Yet if there is a great distance between the conditions suitable for this Confucian constitutional order and social reality, how can we expect the government to promote Confucianism in the first place? What reasons do we have to accept the state using public authority to promote the three conditions necessary for Confucian constitutional order?

Jiang's reply is that Confucianism is the truth and the core of Chinese culture, so the people must support the state promoting Confucianism. The next section is devoted to discuss the validity of this point of view.

Epistemological and Historical Status of Confucianism

Because of the important value of civility in modern pluralistic society, Confucianism should not be promoted as a comprehensive doctrine, whether or not it is completely correct and true. But of course there is no reason to consider Confucianism as completely correct, and so promoting Confucianism as a comprehensive doctrine becomes even more objectionable. As a matter of fact, given all the great minds in history around the world, there has never been anyone whose thoughts have not been questioned and criticized. No matter how brilliant Confucian scholars in the past might have been, their thoughts could not have been flawless. This does not mean that we have to deny their insights and contributions, but being a complex system of thoughts which runs through a wide range of issues concerning life, politics, society, and economy, Confucianism cannot possibly be infallible and timelessly relevant. To illustrate this point, we may consider Confucianism's views on filial piety. In classical Confucianism, filial piety was generally understood to consist of three major moral requirements: respect for one's parents, honoring (or not disgracing) them, and supporting them financially. In traditional China, one main expression of "respect" for parents was to obey parental wishes. This is perhaps the single feature in filial piety that is incompatible with personal autonomy—the other two features are still valuable to many people today and consistent with autonomy. I have argued elsewhere that the significance of obedience as an element of "respect" was based on the social and economic structure of traditional Chinese society.[12] Once the social conditions changed, this element lost its social importance and attractiveness. Also, practicing this norm of obedience is not conducive to the long-term well-being of children in modern society. Modern Confucians need a new norm to express the more fundamental moral requirement of "respect for one's parents." For example, seeking advice from parents when one makes important choices could be seen as respecting one's parents. And there are other attitudes of respect that can and should remain, such as an attitude of reverence. A contemporary version of filial piety could therefore retain the three traditional requirements, respecting, honoring, and supporting one's parents, although the concrete expression of the first requirement would change. As not all Confucian values and rituals are attractive and suitable for our time, we should not promote it as a comprehensive doctrine.

Some may argue that the arguments above are insufficient to question the truth of Confucianism since it is based on the transcendental "way of heaven." Jiang has pointed out, "in Confucianism's metaphysical beliefs, the ultimate being of the universe could be called heaven, . . . or way of heaven."[13] And a fundamental tenet in Confucianism is the notion of "the sovereignty of heaven." Jiang has repeatedly emphasized that the will of people is not always moral; only the "way of heaven" can offer legitimacy to political power. One can agree with Jiang that there can be flaws in the people's views, societal traditions, and cultural systems, but this does not mean that we should therefore believe in the existence of any transcendental truth serving as our moral standard. Even if such truth exists, it cannot be held as self-evident. Instead of seeking moral truth in the metaphysical world, many scholars believe that the ways to improve humanity and social and moral norms can be found only in trying out our own human, and no doubt fallible, systems of thought and ways of life. In any case, any claims to the discovery of transcendental truth must be critically examined in just the same manner as nontranscendental views of truth and morality; yet Jiang asserts that the "way of heaven" is beyond the grasp of human rationality. Only sages like Confucius himself can possibly get hold of the "sacred transcendental way of heaven, therefore people must accept the 'way of heaven' so as to sanctify their secular life." However, why should we think that Confucius has grasped the "way of heaven"? Jiang agrees that humans make mistakes; even if Confucius is truly a sage, and that the "way of heaven" truly exists, it is more likely than possible that Confucius has made mistakes concerning the "way of heaven" due to the limitation of his personal and historical circumstances. Nowadays, thanks to the demythification of Confucius, his thoughts finally can be evaluated objectively. It seems unwise to once again hold Confucius as a demigod who possessed the truth and to assert that Chinese people should forever respect Confucianism as the "Palace" School in ancient China.

Supporters of Jiang may argue that Confucianism has to be promoted as a comprehensive doctrine despite the objections provided above because the legitimacy of political authority in China can only be grounded on Confucianism. As Jiang points out, "Political authorities must . . . continue the life of the past state, and only then can they claim legitimacy." Yet why is it so? This point is not self-evident. If "continuation of the state's life" refers to continuing the long-existing ideology and its corresponding policies, then such "continuation" can be highly immoral. History is not short of such examples; for instance, slavery in ancient times and the racial segregation policy of South Africa have been policies or systems based on some long-standing ideologies. One may complain that such comparison is unfair and argue that Confucianism not only is moral but also has been deeply respected by the people of China for a long time. These kinds of complaints, however, are misplaced, since they do not explain why only the continuation of Confucianism's old political status can provide legitimacy to political authority. Although Confucianism was generally respected in the history of China, it does not follow that everyone has accepted Confucianism as truth, or accepted its hegemonic position, especially when the dominant position of Confucianism has relied much on the coercive power of politics, including ideological manipulation. Moreover, even if we agree that Confucianism has revealed a great deal of truth, we still need not accept Confucianism as entirely correct. If we have no reason to believe Confucianism to be flawless, we have no reason to insist that the legitimacy of political authority in China must be based on the comprehensive doctrine of Confucianism.

The Human Embodies the Way

Finally, whether Jiang's Confucian constitutional order can be regarded as an appropriate interpretation of Confucianism is also debatable.[14] Due to limitations of space, I only discuss the part concerning relation between "heaven" and "humans" in Jiang's understanding. Jiang proposes that there are three kinds of legitimacy for political authority: "legitimacy of the way of heaven," "legitimacy based on history and culture," and "popular legitimacy." These three kinds of legitimacy supposedly correspond to the three "ways": of "heaven," "earth," and "human." Jiang suggests that these three kinds of legitimacy should be institutionalized into a tricameral parliament. Yet this threefold division of political institution seems to have deviated from the traditional stance of Confucianism, which holds that the three ways of heaven, earth, and human should be all subsumed under humanity. The ways of heaven, earth, and human should be considered as three different aspects/facets of one single Way, rather than three independent components entrusted in the hands of different groups of people. Establishing three houses so as to symbolize the ways of heaven, earth, and human separately would in effect be placing humans outside of the way of heaven. Jiang seems to be aiming at exactly that. He believes that the way of heaven is beyond the touch of the people; he insists that "the popular will is formed by human desire, and the only way to resolve conflicts between heaven and the people is to curb desire." No matter whether this view is sensible or not, it seems to have deviated from the Confucian tradition that "the Way is embodied by the Human."[15] Confucians have never viewed the commoners as alienated from the way of heaven. As suggested by the *Zhou*

Book of Change, "A benevolent man who finds similarity between the Way and benevolence calls the way benevolence, a wise man who finds similarity between the Way and wisdom calls it wisdom, common people are not aware of the Way but make use of it in their daily life, therefore, few understand the Way in full as superior men do."[16] This statement suggests that the commoners do possess the Way; it is just that they "are not aware of the Way but make use of it in their daily life." Although the commoners cannot fully understand the Way and hence not many can become superior men (*junzi*), their daily life is usually in accord with the Way even though they may not be aware of it. Explaining this claim from the *Book of Change*, Confucian scholar Zheng Xuecheng in Qing dynasty suggests that "learning from the sage, one becomes a worthy man; learning from the worthy, one becomes a gentleman; learning from the commoners, one becomes a sage."[17] The sage needs to learn from the commoners. This learning, of course, does not refer to whatever the people happen to want or do. Instead, Zheng suggests that one should observe the people's daily life so as to understand the "Way." As Zheng points out, "when the sage seeks the Way, he finds that the Way cannot be seen; so the sage can only see the Way through the people's viable way of life of which the people do not understand themselves."[18] Confucianism believes that the "Way" cannot be directly observed because it is metaphysical (i.e., "above the material"[19]); therefore, it can be perceived and conceived only through the perspective of humanity. It is in this light that *The State of Equilibrium and Harmony* suggests, "The path is not far from man. When men try to pursue a path which is far from what their nature suggests, it should not be considered the Path."[20] These kinds of views frequently appear in various Confucian classics; for instance, the *Book of History* suggests "heaven sees as my people see; heaven hears as my people hear";[21] Mencius also argues that the will of heaven can be manifested only through the flourishing of humans according to their own nature.[22] Seeing the people's will as sheer human desires, that is, as something separated from the way of heaven, almost amounts to seeing the people as "nonhuman."

Undoubtedly, Confucians have long agreed that the requirements of the Way are seldom fulfilled. After all, even Confucius feels sorry that the number of people who can fulfill the Way is as few as those "who can distinguish flavors" of food and drinks.[23] Confucian scholar Dong Zhongshu of the Han dynasty also insists that "the nature of the people is that they cannot restrain their own desires."[24] Confucian scholar Wang Fuzhi of the Ming dynasty even argues that the evil of the commoners is greater than that of the "petty people."[25] Although Confucianism has long been pessimistic about the quality of the commoners, it has never claimed that the way of heaven is separated from the people. Confucianism holds the principle that "the Way is embodied by the Human." In this light Confucius claims that "it is Man who is capable of broadening the Way. It is not the Way that is capable of broadening Man" (*Analects* 15.29) and that "I never enlighten anyone who has not been driven to distraction by trying to understand a difficulty or who has not got into a frenzy trying to put his ideas into words" (*Analects* 7.8). Since the Way can be manifested only through human effort, Confucianism has considered different ways to encourage humans to do so; yet the measures usually aim at encouraging voluntary effort in flourishing, rather than coercing the people to follow a certain notion of the Way that is separated from the people. In other words, although Confucianism agrees that it takes a long and slow (sometimes failing) process for the people to be in accord with the way of heaven, such a process is possible only because the way of heaven is rooted in humanity. In his constitutional designs, however, Jiang sees only some people as the "bearer of the way of heaven," while the people's will is regarded as separated from the way of heaven. This view seems to have deviated from the long-standing position of Confucianism.

MODERATE PERFECTIONISM AND PROMOTION OF CONFUCIAN VALUES

Civility is very important to an open, pluralistic society, and it is unreasonable to think of Confucianism as infallible. These two judgments are mutually reinforcing reasons for not promoting Confucianism as a comprehensive doctrine in the political realm of society. Nonetheless, I believe there is another kind of Confucian constitution that is worth our consideration: moderate perfectionism for Confucian values. I first elaborate on the notion of moderate perfectionism, explaining why the arguments against comprehensive doctrines are not applicable to moderate perfectionism; and then I further elaborate on the characteristics of moderate perfectionism.

As pointed out above, promoting Confucian values moderately can be considered as a version of moderate perfectionism. Moderate perfectionism suggests that Confucian values concerning the good life (e.g., Confucian views concerning family, wisdom, or virtuous character) and concerning the social and political order (e.g., trust and trustworthiness, fairness, harmony, support for the poor, mutual care) can be invoked in a piecemeal manner during the legislative process. Moderate perfectionism is a political principle contradicting that of state neutralism because the latter insists that the state should not invoke any political principle that is based on any particular notion of the good life. Many contemporary liberals (such as John Rawls) hold civility to be a major reason supporting state neutralism; they point out that any comprehensive doctrine (like Confucianism) can be reasonably rejected; hence, civility will inevitably be damaged if the state promotes any comprehensive doctrine. I argue, however, that even if we treasure civility, we still need not support state neutralism and refrain from adopting Confucian values as the basis of constitution or legislation. Many arguments for state neutralism have been grounded on a false assumption that we can choose between only state neutralism and comprehensive doctrines. Moderate perfectionism steers a middle way between Rawlsian state neutrality that rejects any appeal to nonpolitical values and extreme perfectionism that promotes full-blown comprehensive doctrines.

For Rawls, comprehensive doctrines cannot serve as the foundation for principles governing the basic structure of society because they are objects of reasonable disagreement and because state promotion of particular doctrines would easily lead to sectarian division and hostility. So the only workable option is to restrict us to values found in the political domain. Rawls writes,

> Since there is no reasonable religious, philosophical, or moral doctrine affirmed by all citizens, the conception of justice affirmed in a well-ordered democratic society *must be* a conception limited to what I shall call "the domain of the political" and its values.[26]

But the inference in this passage is invalid, for it ignores a possibility that lies between comprehensive doctrines and public reason (as political values), namely, piecemeal and specific judgments about goods and ways of life. Arguments that reject comprehensive doctrines do not necessarily reject these specific judgments, and hence what rejects comprehensive doctrines does not necessarily lead to public reason. The chief reason for this is that moderate perfectionism has none of the features of Rawls's notion of comprehensive doctrines. Moderate perfectionism appeals to specific valuable goods such as the arts, family life, and basic human virtues such as benevolence, courage, and practical wisdom. These goods are generally regarded as desirable for their own sake, and they can be found in many valuable ways of life. Moreover, moderate perfectionism does not seek to give a consistent ranking of them or assign them relative weight. None of them is regarded as primary or ultimate. More important, *the acceptance of these goods need not presuppose any particular comprehensive doctrine*. Rather, they are compatible with a great many such doctrines and are widely accepted by many people in modern society.[27]

Moderate perfectionism is compatible with civility. Civility does not require citizens to abandon their values or attachments or refrain from appealing to them in politics. In Shils's view, "civility is compatible with other attachments to class, to religion, to profession, but it regulates them out of respect for the common good."[28] Similarly, we can say that civility is compatible with our attachments to values and moral principles, and it asks us only to judge these things on their own merits, and to regulate disagreements with mutual respect and a readiness to find common ground, and to limit the area of disagreements by making specific rather than comprehensive judgments. The last point is significant—because moderate perfectionism is specific and piecemeal, the contest between citizens over individual legislation or public policy is also specific and piecemeal. Unlike ideological politics that is obsessed with the totality of truth, moderate perfectionism does not fashion a winner-take-all politics based on clashes of comprehensive doctrines, and the gain of winners and the loss of losers are limited and their positions can be reversed in different policy domains.

Promoting Confucian values moderately can enjoy the features and advantages of moderate perfectionism discussed above. Indeed, to promote Confucian values moderately, these values are likely to be reconstructed or even revised to suit the modern society. Moreover, values in Confucianism such as virtues, human ethical relations, the principle of meritocracy, the principle of benevolent politics, and fair rewards and punishments in the political system can in fact be accepted or understood by the citizens without adopting Confucianism as a comprehensive doctrine. In certain concrete legislative or policy issues, one may analyze step-by-step the insights of relevant Confucian values so as to compare and incorporate them with other values outside Confucianism. In the process of promoting Confucian values, we must engage discussion in a language and manner that citizens of the modern world can understand and accept. Supporting moderate perfectionism not only does not require ideological control by the state but in fact demands a high level of freedom of speech, so that the citizens can freely assess Confucianism and discuss policy in a rational manner. This process will decide which Confucian values to be promoted or adopted as the ground for legislation. Moreover, if social discussion and political procedure are conducted fairly, people opposing Confucianism will still have the chance to regain political victory in the future. In this light, moderate promotion of Confucian values does not contradict with civility. Instead, it will preserve civility among citizen in the pluralistic society.

One may wonder, "If we adopt moderate perfectionism in legislative and policy making process, to what extent can these policies be considered as 'Confucian'?" To inquiries of this sort, there is no one single answer because the actual extent of Confucian influence on each occasion will be decided by the processes of social discussion and policy making. If this process is free, fair, and open, then different beliefs and views can all influence the final outcome in a just manner.

CONCLUSION

Confucianism as a life philosophy is still very much relevant to our modern society, but to refit it as a relevant political ideal in the modern society is an immensely difficult task. If Confucianism is to shape sociopolitical development, it should be formulated as a set of reasons or values supporting certain kinds of institutions, legislation, and policy. Nevertheless, I have tried to argue that this set of reasons should not take the form of a comprehensive doctrine but a loose set of individual reasons or values understood in light of the idea of moderate perfectionism. Yet, even if we accept moderate perfectionism, many questions still remain. For instance, which Confucian values should be promoted? Are some Confucian values already obsolete? How should moderate promotion be materialized? Nothing short of a critical philosophical reconstruction can restore the viability of Confucianism in our times.[29]

CHAPTER 5

An Old Mandate for a New State

ON JIANG QING'S POLITICAL CONFUCIANISM

Bai Tongdong

RADICALS VERSUS CONSERVATIVES: CONFUCIANISM AS A MORAL METAPHYSICS VERSUS CONFUCIANISM AS A POLITICAL PHILOSOPHY

From the middle of nineteenth century on, under the attack of Western gunships and ideas, many Chinese intellectuals lost their confidence first in material things and the theories behind them that traditional China offered, and then in the traditional political structures; instead, they were convinced of the universality of Western science and democracy. The "radicals" among them even came to the belief that the traditional culture in China, in particular Confucianism, was in conflict with the culture underlying democracy. Thus, for democracy to take hold in China, traditional culture had to be eliminated. Contrary to this belief, the so-called "cultural conservatives"—the "New Confucians" being their chief representatives in the latter half of the twentieth century—wish to "conserve" and defend traditional Chinese culture. But like the radicals, they, too, bow down to Western science and democracy, embracing them as universal values. The difference between them and the radicals is that they still wish to defend traditional culture on the moral metaphysical level (the "heart-mind" level). Here lies their "conservative" side, and their bottom line in defending the Chinese tradition.

The problems with this conservative position, in my view, are twofold: on the one hand, the conservatives wish to conserve or defend too much and, on the other, they wish to defend too little. What they wish to defend is in fact a moral metaphysics, or, in a Rawlsian term, a comprehensive doctrine that defines the good for each individual. It is impossible for a people to adopt one moral metaphysics anymore in a fundamentally pluralistic world unless we resort to sheer oppression. At the same time, what they defend is too little. They yield to Western science and democracy without careful, critical reflection on them. On the latter point, Jiang Qing and I are in agreement with each other.[1] As Jiang points out, like the "liberals" in China (those who fully endorse Western values), New Confucians, too, fully embrace liberal democracy and take it as the mainstream values everyone has to embrace. Their brand of Confucianism, the so-called *xinxing* Confucianism (a kind of moral metaphysics), is a depoliticized Confucianism.[2] Contrary to this brand of Confucianism, Jiang introduces "political Confucianism," wishing to establish a Way of the Humane Authority of doing politics (Way of the Humane Authority being a technical term in Confucianism and not necessarily associated with monarchism) that is different from liberal democracy and has Chinese characteristics. These ideas of his have attracted a lot of attention among Chinese intellectuals, including those who cherish, promote, or practice the Chinese traditions, as well as the "liberals" who often are hostile to the former group. From the chapters of Jiang's works that are collected in this volume and the introductory chapter, we have already seen what Jiang wishes to construct. I thus give only a brief introduction to his latest work in the following.

JIANG'S WAY OF THE HUMANE AUTHORITY

Embodied in Fukuyama's *The End of History and the Last Man* is a belief common to many that Western-style liberal democracy is the only viable path for all states.[3] Taking this belief as a target, Jiang introduces Confucian constitutionalism. This kind of Chinese politics does not simply resist the West, or completely ignore the merits of Western civilization. Rather, it joins the world civilizations with the Chinese Way of the Humane Authority of doing politics that emphasizes winning people over by virtue. In international politics, the Way of the Humane Authority will change the hegemonic politics—another technical term in Confucianism that might be translated as *Realpolitik*—that resorts to force alone to settle all international disputes. In domestic politics, the Way of the Humane Authority will change the dominance of popular votes on all political matters. In Jiang's view, this dominance is the root cause of many political problems.[4]

According to Jiang, the "Confucian" in "Confucian constitutionalism" refers to Confucianism as a form of state religion (*ru jiao*), and not Confucianism as a school of philosophy (*ru jia*).[5] The motive behind this idea seems to be an attempt to defend Chinese culture, making it an equal to Christianity as transcendent and sacred beliefs and values.

In Jiang's view, the Way of the Humane Authority of doing politics is merely the ideal of Confucian politics in the real world and in human history and embodies the good politics at the imperfect stage of harmony.[6] The aim of a realistic ideal is to realize the rule of the Confucian elite.[7]

To understand the ruling structure of the Confucian elite, we need to understand first Jiang's "Explanation of the Way of the Humane Authority." This theory is intended to explain the relation among heaven, earth, and the human.[8] In Jiang's view, in theocracy or totalitarianism, the relation is defined as the absolute control of heaven over earth and the human. He calls this relation "the one principle without differentiations." In today's equal and pluralistic society, the three kinds of sovereignty are completely separated from each other. According to the Explanation of the Way of the Humane Authority, however, there should be both oneness of heaven and differentiations among the three kinds of legitimacy. Moreover, there is an order and a balance of power among the three.[9]

According to the Explanation of the Way of the Humane Authority, the legitimacy of today's regimes should be expressed through the threefold legitimacy of heaven, earth, and the human.[10] In a parliamentary system, this form of legitimacy is embodied by a tricameral system.[11] In addition to the tricameral structure, Jiang develops a republicanism under a symbolic monarch to keep the nation's historical continuity.[12] He also further introduces the institution of the Academy that supervises the state.[13]

There seem to be a few points of overlap in Jiang's institutional designs, and he offers some clarifications that explain the different Confucian concerns these designs try to address.[14] What he does not make explicit, in my view, is that the Academy, the symbolic monarch, and the three houses represent the relations among heaven, earth, and the human at a higher order than what is represented by the three houses.

Interestingly, Jiang claims that he once "was a radical liberal, and a radical westernizer, highly valuing western culture."[15] His recent works can be considered a radical break from his own past. But we can also say that Jiang has never changed and has remained a radical throughout his life. For even to those who are sympathetic to the above institutional designs, they appear to be extremely unrealistic. To this charge, Jiang's response is that what he is proposing is based upon principles, and the concern with practicality is about the right circumstances or opportunities. What he is doing is to understand the principles and wait for the right circumstances and use the principles to change the circumstances in the right directions.[16] Indeed, a political philosopher is a political philosopher and not a politician precisely because what he or she designs is idealistic and even utopic. But if this ideal regime has no realistic basis or no potential to be actualized, the political philosopher will not be different from an idle daydreamer. In Rawls's language, the regime a political philosopher designs has to be a "realistic utopia."[17] In Jiang's terms, the circumstances the principles are waiting for and are meant to change have to be realizable. He acknowledges the fact that today's China lacks the cultural soil demanded by his institutional designs. But he hopes to realize what he is hoping for by "Confucianizing today's China's political orders" (the upper route) and by "reestablishing Confucianism [the religion] in the civil society" (the lower route).[18]

AN OLD MANDATE FOR A NEW STATE

A New Mission/Mandate for an Old State or an Old Mandate/Mission for a New State?

I have been focusing on developing the political philosophical dimension of the classical (pre-Qin) Confucian philosophy, in which, among other things, I express my worry about the dominance of popular will in political matters in today's democracies and try to correct the excesses from the resources of Confucian political philosophy.[19] This has some resonance with Jiang's work. I, too, believe that we should not take democracy as something holy and sacred and accept it without any careful examinations. A possible source of the vitality of Confucian political philosophy is precisely for Confucianism to offer ideas different from liberal-democratic theories and show their merits.[20]

Moreover, in modern and today's China (as well as in the West), there have been way too many people who simply misunderstand, have contempt for, or are hostile toward the Chinese traditions. Against this background, I cannot help but have sympathy to the defenders of Confucianism. Recently, there has been an apparent Confucian revival in China. But one cause of this revival—though absolutely not the only cause, as some arrogant Westerners and "guilty" Chinese intellectuals like to put it—is the exploitation by the power in China. The danger of this exploitation lies in the possibility that the circumstances (the political conveniences and needs) will distort the principles, and thus leads to a failure to change the circumstances with principles, which is what Jiang and other Confucian sympathizers are hoping for. Some others, either due to lack of clear understanding of Confucianism or due to the desire to be the "emperor's teacher" (the "consigliere" for the emperor), introduce ideas such as "unifying the three traditions," including the Maoist tradition, the Deng Xiaoping tradition, and the Confucian tradition. On these political exploitations and distortions, Jiang maintains his integrity and clear-headedness as a Confucian. For example, he points out that the "socialism" in Gan Yang's idea of "Confucian socialism" is refereed to the radical equality in Mao's ideas. Not only does it violate the Confucian hierarchical ideal of the rule by the scholarly person, but it paradoxically creates a new (and worse?) form of hierarchy.[21] Moreover, there are creative ideas in Jiang's political designs that might be useful to our reflections on the issue of the best regime for humans.

However, there are many differences between how I understand the contemporary relevance of Confucian political philosophy and Jiang's political Confucianism. I understand Confucianism as a form of political philosophy. To take it as a political philosophy, in my view, means that it has eternal values to us because it deals with problems eternal to human beings. But these problems always express themselves at a special time, in a special place, and in a special form. The responses to these problems are thus contextual as well. When facing with these contextual responses, what we political philosophers need to do is to strip off the particular and contextual expressions, generalize the ideas beneath, or go to the spirit of this tradition (its "old state"), and then recontextualize them in today's context in order to deal with the perennial problems expressed in this new context, thus achieving the goal of "interpreting the 'old state' and give it a new mission/mandate."

Contrary to this, Jiang seems to take a contextual expression of Confucianism (the Han *Gongyang* interpretation of Confucianism) as the fundamental teaching of Confucianism, making it a dogma and a sacred teaching and imposing it on today's world. This is to impose an "old mandate" (a particular, historical interpretation of Confucianism) on a "new state" (new political reality). Jiang often proudly views himself as a Confucian fundamentalist. But if we take Confucianism as a form of political philosophy, Jiang actually violates the spirit of Confucianism, and those who try to interpret the old in order for it to deal with the new are the faithful followers (the "fundamentalists") of Confucianism.

Confucianism as a Philosophy or as a Religion?

Of course, what Jiang wishes to revive is Confucian constitutionalism where "Confucian" means a form of religion, not a form of philosophy. Confucianism as a religion refers to a transcendent, sacred, religious, and metaphysical system. Therefore, although Jiang is opposed to New Confucianism for its full embrace of Western liberal democracy and its neglect for the political philosophical dimension of Confucianism, both Jiang and New Confucians understand Confucianism as an a priori system, which is why Jiang also supports the revival of Confucianism as a moral metaphysics (*xin-xing* Confucianism).²² But at a time when pluralism is inevitable, such a system cannot be universally adopted by everyone. Therefore, Confucian constitutionalism (the religious kind) cannot even be a constitutionalism for all Chinese, but only for a cult that follows a particular reading of Confucianism. Contrary to this, if we can develop a Confucian political philosophy that is free from an a priori metaphysical system and offer political arrangements on the basis of this philosophy, they may become a universal political system. For pluralism is the pluralism of a priori systems, but those who adopt different a priori systems may have a common share of political problems and common political needs. What I develop in the first part of my work *A New Mission of an Old State*, in my view, is precisely such a "thin" yet universal system.

A possible motive for Jiang to construct an a priori system is to resist Christianity. In the past a hundred years or so of Chinese history, many Chinese have come to the belief that a key problem with traditional Chinese political system and culture is the lack of sacredness and transcendence that is offered by Christianity. For example, a popular writer and intellectual, Liu Xiaofeng, in his early years vehemently attacked on Chinese traditions precisely on this ground (which I find is based upon a shallow understanding of both Chinese traditions and Christianity). Jiang once collaborated with Liu in introducing works of Christian philosophy and theology into China. Following a similar premise that transcendence is essential to a moral and political system, but being more sympathetic to the Chinese tradition, Jiang may have felt a need to construct the transcendence of Chinese traditions that will help counter the aggression of Christianity in China. Related to the aforementioned understanding of the relations between Christianity and modern Western political regimes, many come to the conviction that the transcendence of Christianity is the basis of Western liberal democracy. Jiang, too, seems to believe the close connection between the two.²³ But he then concludes that since Christianity belongs to the Western culture, while China is (or was and should be) a Confucian state, Chinese should not embrace democracy that is rooted in Christianity, but should adopt instead the Confucian Way of the Humane Authority.

In constructing his system, Jiang may have had another worry. That is, for him, politics must have an a priori foundation. Otherwise, it will fall prey to relativism and nihilism. He seems to believe that pluralism in modern societies must imply the denunciation of truth and the Good, and must lead to nihilism. This echoes well with a key point Chinese Straussians have made.²⁴

However, if we make the assertion that there is sacredness and transcendence in Chinese culture because some say otherwise and thus attack on

Chinese culture, this apparently assertive attitude is but the asserter's disguised insecurity about Chinese culture. This assertion is actually reactive rather than active, showing the lack of an autonomous self in the Chinese culture so rendered. This is like the situations with many New Confucians who, although bowing down to Western liberal democracy in their hearts, wish to argue and assert that Western democracy and science can all be derived from Confucianism. Contrary to Jiang's attempt, I believe that a unique feature of Confucianism is precisely its attempt to find a middle way between the sacred and the secular, or, as the pre-Qin Confucian philosopher Xunzi put it, a "cultured" way that is understood by exemplary people and is (mis)taken by the masses as something sacred or supernatural.[25]

Generally speaking, if we start from the belief of an exclusive either/or relation between the absolute and the sacred on the one hand and the relative and the secular on the other, the fact that, without oppression, pluralism is inevitable seems to mean that those in free societies are doomed to live a vulgar life clouded by relativism and nihilism. In other words, because we demand a too strong sense of sacredness, we are doomed to lead the most vulgar life. As a Chinese saying goes, "there won't be any fish left when the water is too clean." However, in the realm of political philosophy, Rawls in his later period gives up the demand of an a priori, comprehensive doctrine as *the* bedrock for liberal democracy, but, at the same time, he tries to preserve a "weak" kind of certainty and a "thin" universality in his political liberalism, thus avoiding bouncing between the two extremes (absolute sacredness and a state of all hell breaking loose). While acknowledging the fact that pluralism is inevitable and desirable, he tries to offer a universal political arrangement. In doing so, Rawls frees liberal democracy from its historical background (Christianity in some cases) and what is often believed to be its theoretical basis (such as Kantianism), making liberal democracy a political concept endorsable by people with different, reasonable comprehensive doctrines. If we understand liberal democracy this way, we cannot insist on the inseparability between liberal democracy and Christianity, and cannot reject liberal democracy because we reject Christianity, as Jiang and many others do. Moreover, Rawls's pluralism is not built upon a "strong" version of nihilism or relativism that denies the existence of truth. Repeatedly, Rawls emphasizes that it is necessary and desirable for each person to have a comprehensive doctrine for himself or herself. But he understands that, as long as we do not appeal to oppression, even wise and virtuous people will differ on fundamental questions of human life, and so he hopes to find a political arrangement that allows the differences and the continuous debates over the fundamental issues.[26] Rawls's attempt to find a middle way between dogmatism and nihilism, in my view, echoes well with the Confucian middle way between the sacred and the secular, as is seen from the pre-Qin Confucians' (especially Confucius's) attitude toward the political.

In spite of my criticisms of him, I share Jiang's concern with the erosion of Chinese culture and politics by Christianity.[27] However, in my view, the danger posed by Christianity does not come from its teachings of transcendence. Rather, my worry lies in the fact that Christianity has adapted itself to the industrialized and postindustrialized world. It has preserved and developed various organizations, making it easier to spread among the populace in modern times. In contrast, Confucian organizations (family and the extended kinship as well as the rituals and cultures associated with them) and their influence on daily lives have been severely weakened, if not totally annihilated, through the turmoil that China has experienced in the past one hundred or more years. This fact also sheds doubt on any political theory that tries to understand East Asia, especially China, through the lens of Confucianism. Moreover, especially in mainland China, Confucianism has yet to develop a new organizational structure that is adaptive to a highly mobile modern society. For example, the migration of a large number of farmers into the city is a huge blow to the regulative power of the clan structure and customs that were supported by and supportive to Confucian political structure. A lover of China's traditional cultures cannot help but feel a sense of crisis here. By the sense of crisis, I did not mean to suggest that we resist Christianity and not allow it to be spread in China. After all, the introduction of Buddhism to China not only did not destroy the Chinese traditional cultures, but enriched them. Buddhism (or Chinese Buddhism) has become a part of Chinese cultures. What worries me and other lovers of the Chinese traditions is that Christianity, with the advantages of being a modernized and "industrialized" religion, of the financial, political, and institutional supports from the West, and of having the halo of being "Western" (read as "advanced"), will further weaken and even destroy the already weakened Chinese traditions. One might hold onto the belief that the beauty of Chinese cultures, and some Chinese elite's appreciation of it will help the traditions to prevail in the end, but we have to remember that, after the commoners of the Roman Empire were converted to Christianity in large amount, the exquisite, refined, and sophisticated Roman culture of the upper class was soon to be destroyed (through the hands of authoritarian emperors). In a China that still faces so many potential uncertainties in the near future, a lover of this nation and its traditions must be concerned. However, what we need to do here is to develop Confucian institutions, rituals, codes of conduct that address the challenges of the industrialized and globalized world, and not to develop a transcendent and a priori system, as many New Confucians and Jiang have done.

The "Old State" of Confucianism as a Political Philosophy: The Middle Way

As is discussed above, Jiang wishes to make Confucianism a transcendent doctrine, and to do so he argues that the essence (the "old state") of Confucianism is the tenet that the sovereignty lies in heaven. This understanding came from the Han *Gongyang* school (perhaps the oldest religious version of Confucianism), particularly from the master of this school Dong Zhongshu. Jiang takes this school's rendering of Confucianism as the orthodoxy of Confucianism. But we have to ask, if we wish to go back to the root of Confucianism, why don't we go back to the pre-Qin Confucianism that was the earliest version of Confucianism? For example, Jiang challenges how claims such as "heaven hears as my people hear" are interpreted by some contemporary Confucian scholars. The first political philosophical interpretation of this claim and other related claims was offered by the pre-Qin Confucian Mencius. Clearly, it is a grave misunderstanding of Mencius when today's scholars take his interpretation as his being in favor of democracy. For, on the one hand, Mencius does identify heaven's will with people's will. But, on the other hand, what the people's will is and what we do with it are not fully determined by the people, and the (Confucian) elite have to play a significant role in this. Those who are too eager to make Confucianism compatible with democracy ignore the latter aspect, but Jiang is no less wrong than they by neglecting the former aspect of Mencius's understanding. As Liang Tao, a contemporary Confucian scholar, nicely put it (in a conversation), Mencius's political ideal is that "sovereignty lies in the people, but the right to rule lies in the wise and virtuous." To apply this ideal to today's world, the regime Mencius would support may have to be a hybrid regime that combines elements of popular will and the involvement of the elite. Jiang's political design is a hybrid as well, but, based upon his tenet of the sovereignty of heaven, he includes in the three houses a house representing heaven, and, in addition to the three houses, he adds the Academy and the symbolic monarch that represent heaven and earth, respectively. If we say that the sovereignty of heaven is a misunderstanding of Mencius, we can at least say that Jiang's institutional design is not supported by Mencius's ideas.[28]

Moreover, it is almost a consensus among Confucian scholars that a key feature of pre-Qin Confucianism is to disenchant heaven and to humanize it. They adopt an attitude of the middle way between the sacred and the secular, ridding heaven of the sanctity that can serve as the basis for a theocracy, but maintaining a reverence to it through "decorum" or culture, rites, and rituals. In political institutions, an important development pre-Qin Confucians made was to assert the power of the educated elite. As the famed historian and philosopher Qian Mu pointed out, this development made traditional Chinese political regimes never a pure absolutism, but ones with strong elements of the rule by the educated elite.[29] In my view, this humanism and the emphasis on rule by the elite (combined with the importance of the popular will) are the essence of Confucian political philosophy. It is true that some Han Confucians apparently try to enchant heaven, making it transcendent and sacred, which is why Jiang, who wishes to turn Confucianism into a Christian-like transcendent religion in order to counter the influence of Christianity, favors this interpretation of Confucianism. But, in my view, one reason Han Confucians did this was to vie for power from the emperor through the monopoly of Confucians over the interpretation of the will of heaven when the emperor was already firmly in power, could not be dismissed, and could be tamed only by the Confucian elite at best. This is in line with the Confucian ideal of the rule by the educated elite that is shared by almost all Confucians over generations, and to enchant heaven was merely a means in a special context.

In practice, since Jiang's way of heaven is independent of, and higher than, the way for human beings, it makes it possible for the way of heaven to be independent of the well-being of human beings, which may then lead to the form of totalitarianism that has appeared in the West. In contrast, even the most despotic governments in traditional China had to use the flag of serving the people, and the legitimacy of these governments can be thus challenged by looking into whether people are actually served or not. Those that fail the test may even be overturned (such as the overturnings of tyrants Jie and Zhou in the Tang and Wu revolutions that are celebrated by Confucians). This "for the people" feature of traditional Chinese culture and, in particular, Confucianism is dissolved in Jiang's reading of Confucianism, which is why he has to dilute the revolutionary side of Confucianism.[30]

Moreover, to deal with practical problems from such a transcendent perspective can be extreme and dogmatic, suffering from the same problems many Western doctrines do, and thus decreasing the degree of significance of a Confucian revival to the world. For example, Jiang wants to promote the environmental values to the level of the way of heaven,[31] and he has argued repeatedly that the heavenly elements of his political arrangements help to deal with environmental problems.[32] His theory gives environmental issues a sacred status independent of, and even higher than, human concerns. This is similar to the attitude of many radical environmentalists in the West. The radical attitude of the latter has made it hard for many to accept their ideas. For many, especially those in developing countries, the choices they are facing often constitute a dilemma: either they damage the environment to survive, or they save the environment while starving themselves to death.

Those with the aforementioned radical attitude (Jiang included) basically tell the people in poor countries or in desperate situations that "to starve to death is a small matter, compared to saving the environment."[33] I think that what is distinctive of a Confucian attitude toward the environment from the radical or overly ideal attitude is precisely the humanism that is the core of Confucianism. A Confucian should not damage the environment, not because it is part of sacred heaven, but because it is what we human beings have to rely upon for our long-term survival (in terms of satisfying both our physical and spiritual needs). This attitude may be more appealing to the many, and it will also be more sympathetic to, and pay more attention to, the needs of common people. It will thus try to address both the environmental issues (which are important for our long-term survival) and the basic, short-term needs of the poor and the disadvantaged, trying to find a solution of these apparently conflicting concerns.

Another example of the problems with the transcendent version of Jiang's Confucianism is his argument that the emphasis of China's Way of the Humane Authority on winning over people by virtue can change the Western hegemonic way that conquers others by force. But first, his understanding of the Western way is much too narrow. For example, Kant, the Western philosopher, and Woodrow Wilson, the Western politician (after whom Wilsonianism is named), among other Westerners, advocate an idea against hegemony and for something similar to the Way of the Humane Authority of winning over people by virtue. But a danger of this kind of idealism is that it tends to lead its advocates to neglect political reality. The once powerful American neocons take precisely an (aggressive) Wilsonian attitude in international affairs. With an idealism that carries with it an almost religious zeal, they supported the war on Iraq, believing that this would bring democracy and happiness to the world. What they did bring about, however, was the unnecessary suffering of many Iraqis and the cynicism of many in the world toward good-willed interventions. This in fact encourages moral relativism and indifference to others and is opposite to the original intention of some good-willed neocons. There are so many examples in history in which people with good intentions do horrible things. In contrast, in the *Analects*, Confucius has strong reservations of the *Realpolitik* the hegemon Duke Huan of Qi and his political advisor Guan Zhong practiced, and, at the same time, he praises them for de facto protecting civilization from being ruined by unnecessary wars and the attacks of barbarians (*Analects* 3.22, 14.9, and 14.15–17). This shows Confucius's middle way between idealism and realism in international politics. This middle way might offer a better hope for humans, compared to the swing between the two extremes (idealism and realism) in today's international politics. Another expression of this middle way is the ideal of loving all people in the world as family members and all things in the world as friends that is nevertheless based upon a gradation or hierarchy of love (i.e., the love one has for, say, one's family member should in general be greater than one's love of a stranger, and so on). This ideal does not restrict one's love to one's friends or compatriots on the one hand and does not pin hope on a hopeless ideal of loving everyone equally. This again is an attempt to find a middle way between *Realpolitik* (like the one emphasized by Carl Schmitt and expressed through the idea of nation-state) and the Christian kind of fraternity.

A NEW MISSION THAT DEALS WITH POLITICAL REALITY

Another general problem with Jiang's proposal, as Daniel Bell, another important figure in promoting a Confucian constitutionalism, points out, is that Jiang's Confucian constitutionalism is almost exclusively derived from the dogmas—"dogma" in its literal sense—of his own version of Confucianism (understood as a transcendent religion), and does not sufficiently take into account realistic political concerns.[34] Of course, as we have already seen, Jiang wants to show how his Confucian constitutionalism is superior to other alternatives in dealing with practical problems. But the core of his design is about how to derive a political system from the sacred dogmas of Confucianism. Due to this fact, his reflections on problems of Western political issues tend to be superficial, and he does not offer a thorough analysis of the legitimacy and justification of his political designs.

For example, in his view, Confucian constitutionalism is a choice we have to take in an imperfect age, when sagely politics is no longer available. But why are we doomed to live in an imperfect age, and why is the age of perfect harmony no longer available? Even in an imperfect age, why are sage rulers no longer available? Of the times we live in, Jiang only makes assertions. He offers no arguments. Moreover, if the age we live in is merely a coincidence, should we give up Confucian constitutionalism when the sage rulers (Jiang's Confucian counterpart to Jesus?) come back to this world? How do we know that they are back? Through some apocalyptic signs similar to those described in the *Book of Revelation*?

One thing common to both the political structure offered by Jiang's Confucian constitutionalism and what I offer in my own works is to add an elitist element to the democratic regime. The reason that this element needs to be added, in Jiang's view, is that when we are neither in the age of perfect harmony nor in the times of sage rulers during the imperfect age, heaven entrusts sovereignty to the educated elite. But why should we believe that Jiang, or the Confucians he approves of, actually represent the will of heaven? Whom should we listen to if there is a difference of opinion among them? If we follow the arguments for pluralism, it is not possible to attain even a common understanding of Confucianism among a large number of Confucians without resorting to oppression. Moreover, Jiang thinks that one reason for trusting the Confucian elite is that the popular will—due to the poor educational, moral, and political quality of the populace—cannot be trusted. But is it not a Confucian tenet that the government and the Confucian elite have the duty to educate the common people and that, if we follow Mencius and Xunzi, every human being is educable and can become a sage through education? We thus come back to the aforementioned question about why the age of perfect harmony, in which everyone becomes a sage, is not available anymore. Jiang fails to offer an argument about why we cannot improve people's wisdom and virtue to such a degree that the popular will becomes identical with the heavenly will. In fact, many Western democratic theorists also recognize the unsatisfactory quality of the voters and wish to improve it from within in order for the popular will to be trusted.[35]

Jiang adds to his institutions a House of the Nation and a House of *Ru* to the House of the People, and then adds the symbolic monarch and the Academy to the three houses. All these additional elements are elitist, and one cannot help but ask if these arrangements make the whole political institution overly elitist. Will these almost redundant elements thwart smooth political operations? If these additional institutions fail to achieve what Jiang wishes them to achieve, what can we do about them?

In Jiang's institution of the Academy that serves the guiding role in the state, I appreciate one particular design, that is, the modernized version of the institution of the imperial historians that offers unembellished and comprehensive records of the rulers and the modernized version of the honorary titles for the deceased rulers that, in Chinese history, offer a one-phrase summary of an emperor's lifelong performances in his job.[36] One reason Jiang offers for establishing these institutions is his "theological" argument based upon his reading of Confucianism as a religion. But he does offer another political consideration that can be accepted by me and many others. That is, these institutions can play a role of watching over the rulers, and, when the rulers have to think about the long-term consequences of their policies (because these policies will be faithfully recorded and their long-term results will be evaluated through these institutions), they may have an incentive to plan policies beyond mere short-term interests. Very interestingly, the economist Sheng Hong who is sympathetic to Confucianism, offers an argument similar to this one and supports the aforementioned institutions.[37] This fact shows the universality of arguments in political philosophy. Moreover, Jiang also points out that the problem with these institutions in history is that they were not really independent of the power of the emperor and thus were subject to interference from the emperor. Therefore, he argues that these institutions should be independent of, and even higher than, other branches of the government. I fully endorse his idea of these institutions being independent, although I do not see why they have to be higher than other branches of the government.

I share Jiang's underlying concern with the continuity and sacredness of national identity, which led him to suggest a symbolic monarch. A state needs a unifying force. Based upon some Western theories of nation-state, some contemporary Chinese scholars think that only by adopting the idea of a nation-state can China become a modern state. But "Chinese" (and its opposite, the "barbarians") has been a cultural rather than a racial or a Western-style national concept since the pre-Qin era. This cultural concept of national identity has many merits compared to the concept of nation-state. For example, it is not built on a friend-enemy divide deriving from a narrow sense of nation, and is more inclusive than the latter.[38] Thus, I am sympathetic to Jiang's attempt to use a cultural symbol to unite the Chinese people. But in Western nominal monarchy, the monarch either becomes an appendix to the political body from a bygone era or harms the image of the state through his or her own despicable conduct. There is a danger in having a concrete person as the unifying symbol of the state. If we wish to maintain the continuity of the identity of a state, why can we not simply appeal to patriotic education? We can use the abstract national spirit that shows itself through mountains and rivers and people and history to perform the role of a nominal monarch, maintaining the unity and continuity of a nation. Not only can this avoid the possible harm an individual monarch might cause, it can also channel patriotism into a concrete feeling for the land and the people of the state.

A problem with Jiang's institutional design is its failure to take pluralism into account. For example, the House of *Ru*, the symbolic monarch, and the Academy are all based upon Confucian dogmas interpreted by Jiang. But in a Chinese society that has different ethnicities, religions, and cultures, the legitimacy and inclusiveness of the institutions based upon (a special version of) Confucianism become dubious, let alone the legitimacy and inclusiveness of these institutions in other states (the lack of which would make Jiang's design culture-specific).

Of course, among the three houses in Jiang's design, the House of the Nation takes into account ethnical and religious pluralism. But, first of all, what is the basis for the pluralistic arrangements? Second of all, the pluralism in this house is a "neutered" pluralism. For in Jiang's design of this house, only Confucians are given the prestige of actually ruling, and those from other religions and cultures are not really offered a strong participatory role. A cynic may argue that pluralism in the West is also neutered (and he or she might be right to say this in many cases). For one thing, it is possible, justifiably so, for those holding a doctrine that is geared toward aggression and intolerance not to be accepted by a pluralistic society. But we can still claim that, in Jiang's arrangement, pluralism is more severely curtailed than in a pluralistic democracy. Third, there are many pluralistic arrangements in Western regimes and education, and Jiang fails to offer an argument for the distinctive merits of the institution of the House of the Nation.

One function of the House of the Nation is to preserve the nation's cultural and historical heritage.[39] But are the members of this house, in Jiang's design, able to maintain this heritage? One kind of member of this house is the descendant of former emperors and rulers, such as Liu Bei. Liu Bei was the de facto ruler of one of the three kingdoms—his kingdom arguably ruled over what is now the Three Gorges Dam area, among other areas— vying for dominance and unification of the Chinese state during the Three Kingdoms era, and was recognized by some as having legitimacy because he was of royal lineage (though merely a distant relative of the incapacitated and merely nominal emperor of the times). Jiang argues, because his descendants would not want their ancestral shrine to be submerged as a result of building the Three Gorges Dam, they would not support the building of this dam.[40] Clearly, Jiang believes that the building of the dam is a bad thing. But if it is a good thing, then its construction should not succeed owing to objections from Liu's descendants (if Jiang's logic holds). Generally, this is letting national interest be beholden to an individual's or a clan's interests. Moreover, who can guarantee that Liu's descendants would not support the building of this dam out of other concerns, such as the possibility of being promoted within the ranks? Jiang further points out that protecting the ancestral shrine of the Liu family is a reflection on the cultural legitimacy because Liu Bei was from the legitimate Han royal line. But this is highly debatable. The descendants of Cao Cao—the de facto ruler of another kingdom of the three kingdoms and someone who kidnapped the Han emperor to wield influence over other de facto rulers—may have been disqualified, if we follow Jiang's reasoning. But many would argue that Cao made a far greater contribution to Chinese culture. More generally, how should we deal with the rulers of the many small states during the dynastic changes and the rulers of a few foreign dynasties (i.e., dynasties that were not founded by those who were then considered culturally Chinese)? If fact, if the building of the Three Gorges Dam harms the long-term interests of the Chinese people and the Chinese cultural heritage and should thus be opposed, whether Liu's descendants are in the House of the Nation or not does not really matter. For we only need to make sure members of this house should not be beholden to short-term interests. In this sense, we do not really need a separate House of the Nation. We only need people who can be farsighted and virtuous to be members of the legislature. Generally, I believe that many of the functions (those I and perhaps many other reasonable people, Confucian or not, can approve of) of Jiang's House of the Nation and his House of *Ru* can be performed by the Upper House (the "senate" in its original sense, i.e., the house of the learned, experienced, and virtuous) in my own design.

On the detailed points he is making, Jiang is not very careful sometimes. For example, rather arbitrarily (without any concrete data, adequate empirical support, or theoretical argument), Jiang asserts that monarchy is a reason that environment was not damaged badly in the old days.[41] He claims at another place that sovereignty by the people is a result of Western linear thinking; more generally, the Western thinking pattern is dualistic, black and white.[42] But is it not also a result of black and white, linear, and prejudiced ways of thinking when it is claimed that the Chinese think this way, and the Westerners think the other way?

From his *Political Confucianism* to "Political Confucianism—A Sequel," Jiang has made great contributions to the Confucian revival, in particular by calling people's attention to the political philosophical dimension of Confucianism. Insisting upon a sincere and full embrace of Confucian principles, Jiang develops many ideas that preserve the traditions and are creative at the same time. But as I have argued in this chapter, to defend the contemporary legitimacy and relevance of Confucianism, we will need to go back to the spirit of Confucianism and not to a dogmatic system of a certain era. We will then need to face the political reality of today, showing how, following the Confucian spirit, we can answer questions from today's reality. This is to offer a new mission and mandate to an "old state" (meaning both China and its traditions), and our attempt is made to solve not only some fundamental political problems in China but also similar problems in the world. In so doing, we can make sure that a Confucian revival is not only for the well-being of the Chinese but also for the betterment of world politics.

CHAPTER 6

Transcendent Heaven?

A CRITIQUE OF JIANG QING'S GROUNDING OF THE RIGHT TO RULE

Chenyang Li

Among contemporary Confucians, Jiang stands out in several important ways.[1] Whereas most Confucian authors are interested in ethics, Jiang's focus is primarily on political philosophy, an area of study eschewed by most Confucian thinkers for at least half a century. In contrast with the liberal wing of New Confucianism, Jiang's conservative approach points unmistakably in the direction of restoration.[2] Unlike the majority of Confucian writers who are professors, focusing mostly on texts and scholarly publications, Jiang seeks to promote the reading of the classics in society in general. His position appears radical to many and even out of sync with the time. However, there is no question that his scholarship is serious, rigorous, and systematic. Those of us who take Confucianism seriously cannot ignore it.

This essay offers a critique of Jiang's conception of the Confucian "heaven" (*tian*), a concept that serves as the key to his philosophical system. My critique is internal to Confucianism, in as far as I accept most Confucian concepts. I argue that the Confucian notion of heaven, understood appropriately, should be the heaven of the "heaven-earth-humanity" triad, not the transcendent heaven Jiang promotes.[3] It is my claim that, whereas the concept of heaven is intrinsic to Confucianism, Jiang's move to add a transcendent heaven in today's Confucianism is misguided and counterproductive. The notion of heaven in his philosophy is vacuous and unnecessary. It cannot serve as a solid foundation for Confucian political philosophy as he purports.

THE TWO HEAVENS

In Jiang's philosophical system, there are two "heavens." One is "transcendent heaven;" the other is a "differentiated" and diversely manifested heaven. The latter is what I have called the heaven of the "heaven-earth-humanity" triad. In the triad, heaven is correlated with earth and humanity and interacts with them. However, Jiang's transcendent heaven not only occupies a higher position than the differentiated one but also generates it. It is the transcendent heaven that is the ultimate foundation for his theory of a modern Confucian political system.

"Sovereignty," or *zhu quan*, is Jiang's notion of governing rights. In his interpretation, the right to govern a society comes from the transcendent heaven. In this sense, there is no difference between "heaven" and "God" (*shang-di*). The two terms have the same reference. Jiang's heaven at this level is transcendent, absolute, and sacred. However, just as the Judeo-Christian God generates a Son in order to reach out to humanity, so too Jiang's transcendent heaven generates a differentiated heaven, that of the "heaven-earth-humanity." In doing so, the abstract heaven takes on an "embodied" form.

For some reason, this transcendent heaven needs to detranscend itself and to enter into the human world. According to Jiang, although sovereignty ultimately lies with the transcendent heaven as the ultimate metaphysical reality, as far as we human beings are concerned, as far as we are dealing with the world of politics, the unitary transcendent heaven cannot but separate into a differentiated heaven. For Jiang, that implies that politics must embody, exhibit, and realize the oneness of heaven at different levels. The transcendent heaven is just too lofty, after all; it has to become differentiated into one that relates directly to the human world. Before it becomes differentiated into the heaven-earth-humanity triad, the transcendental heaven at best possesses only symbolic significance. The very fact that Jiang's transcendent heaven needs to become differentiated into that of the "heaven-earth-humanity" triad indicates the hollowness of Jiang's transcendent heaven. Such a heaven is not related directly to the human world. Without differentiation, it is ineffectual.

Let me be clear that I endorse the Confucian notion of the "heaven-earth-humanity" triad, which includes Jiang's notion of the "differentiated" heaven. Such a notion is central to Confucian metaphysics and to Confucian moral philosophy. The question, however, is with Jiang's notion of the transcendent heaven, the heaven that is beyond the "heaven-earth-humanity" triad. In today's world, it may be asked if such a notion possesses any real significance. I think not. Given that in Jiang's scheme the heaven of the "heaven-earth-humanity" is already placed at a higher position than earth and humanity, there is simply no need to posit a transcendent heaven above and beyond it as Jiang does.

In the following, I discuss this issue in two steps. First, I show that, in pre-Qin thought, there is a transition from the notion of a transcendent heaven to one of a differentiated and therefore "embodied" heaven, that of the "heaven-earth-humanity." In mainstream classical Confucianism, the notion of heaven is already that of the "heaven-earth-humanity." Jiang's move to go back to the transcendent heaven is a regress, not a progress of thought. Second, through analyzing Jiang's philosophy, I argue that the transcendent heaven in Jiang's system is actually a vacuous notion and does not possess real significance. Such a notion cannot serve as a foundation for today's Confucian political philosophy.

FROM TRANSCENDENT HEAVEN TO IMMANENT HEAVEN

In the history of Chinese thought, the notion of heaven has acquired a variety of meanings. A major transformation of this notion took place prior to Confucius and continued through the early stages of Confucianism. In this process, the notion of "heaven" was transformed from one that is primarily a transcendent and personal deity to one of that is in the triad "heaven-earth-humanity." Jiang's move to bring back the transcendent heaven is a backward move.

Feng Youlan gave five different meanings for the ancient notion of "heaven" (*tian*):

> (1) A material or physical *Tian* or sky, that is the *Tian* often spoken of in opposition to Earth. . . . (2) A ruling or presiding *Tian* . . . in which anthropomorphic *Tian* and *Di* are signified. (3) A fatalistic *Tian*, equivalent to the concept of Fate (*ming*), a term applied to all those events in human life over which man himself has no control. This is the *Tian* Mencius refers to when he says: "As to the accomplishment of a great deed, that is with *Tian*" (*Mencius* 1B:14). (4) A naturalistic *Tian*, that is, one equivalent to the English word "Nature." This is the sort of *Tian* described in the "Discussion on *Tian*" in the *Xunzi* (Ch. 17). (5) An ethical *Tian*, that is, one having a moral principle and which is the highest primordial principle of the universe. This is the sort of *Tian* which *The Doctrine of the Mean* refers to in its opening sentence when it says: "What *Tian* confers (on man) is called his nature."[4]

Feng's account is comprehensive and largely accurate. However, when it comes to specific usages of *tian* in Chinese classics, different interpretations emerge. For instance, Feng Youlan held that in the *Analects*, "heaven, for Confucius, meant a purposeful Supreme Being or 'ruling heaven.'"[5] Meng Wentong, however, believes that *tian* in the *Analects* carries a natural meaning, connoting the natural course of things.[6] I think Feng Youlan probably overstated his claim regarding the *Analects*. The expression of *tianxia* (all under heaven) appears repeatedly in the *Analects* and clearly does not connote anything close to God.

Jiang's notion of transcendent heaven is related to the second and fifth meaning of *tian* in Feng's summary, namely the deity that controls the world and the ultimate moral principle of the universe. However, Jiang makes his *tian* a transcendent heaven, unlike the heaven of "heaven-earth-humanity" as advocated in early Confucianism. In early Confucianism, heaven is already a differentiated one—it is already in the triad of "heaven-earth-humanity."

During the early developmental period of Chinese thought the notion of *tian* underwent a metamorphosis from a transcendent and personified deity to a member of the triad of "heaven-earth-humanity." In his *Ancient Religions and Ethics*, Chen Lai writes about this transformation of *tian* during the Shang (ca. 1600–1046 BCE) and Zhou (ca. 1046–256 BCE) periods:

> An important difference between the worldview of the Yin/Shang dynasty and that of the Western Zhou did not lie in whether the Shang took *tian* to be the ultimate God. For if *tian* was merely the personified God who could display anger, then such a notion of *tian* was no different from that of *di* (God). As a matter of fact, the two terms were interchangeable. The crucial difference between the worldview of the Shang and that of the Zhou was this: whereas in the Shang's beliefs *di* and *tian* did not have moral import—their religion was not yet a moral religion—in the Zhou's understanding, *tian* and *tian ming* (heaven's mandate) acquired moral significance, with "revering virtues" and "protecting people" as primary characteristics. *The divine characteristics in the notion of "tian" were gradually weakened. In contrast, the status of people became elevated. This was the direction of Zhou thought.*[7]

On Chen's account, *tian* in the Yin/Shang period was a transcendent and personified God. During the Zhou period, the godly characteristics of *tian* were downplayed and the status of humanity became augmented. Moral significance became its primary characteristic. In other words, the "focus" of heaven was shifted from a transcendent realm to the human world.

Another scholar, Ouyang Zhenren, agrees that, during the Yin/Shang and Western Zhou periods, the divine characteristics of *tian* became gradually weakened, and humanity was further promoted. According to Ouyang, in the Yin/Shang period, the power of *tian* was so overwhelming that humanity appeared insignificant in contrast. This situation changed during the Zhou period:

The Zhou notion of *tian* was evidently enriched with rational content. The status of humanity was elevated. In such a notion of *tian* as a spiritual force, we see the dignity and spirit of humanity.[8]

To put it a different way, in Zhou thought, *tian* was no longer a transcendent being as was the case during the Shang. It has become correlated with humanity. Such a correlated notion paved the way to a notion of the heaven of "heaven-earth-humanity." It was against this background of "Renaissances" that Confucianism emerged. By that time, the notion of *tian* Confucianism had to work with was already no longer the transcendent notion, which at most had merely a residual significance. Continuing in the direction of Zhou thought, Confucianism developed its notion of an immanent heaven within the triad in such works as the *Book of Changes* and the *Doctrine of Mean*. The heaven of the "heaven-earth-humanity" is that of mainstream Confucianism.

As discussed above, in the *Analects*, *tian* seems to have been used to mean a controlling God, moral principle, as well as the natural course of things. Confucius said, "[I]f you have offended *tian*, you have nowhere to turn to in your prayers" (*Analects* 3.13). When his favorite disciple died, he lamented, "Heaven has bereft me! Heaven has bereft me!" (*Analects* 11.9). In these uses, *tian* most probably refers to a deity. When the word is used in such expressions as *tian ming* (will of heaven) (*Analects* 2.4) or *tian dao* (the way of heaven) (*Analects* 5.13), it clearly carries a strong sense of moral principle. Finally, in numerous occurrences of the expression of *tian xia* (all under heaven), and when Zigong said that "the Master cannot be equaled, just as the sky cannot be reached by climbing stairs" (*Analects* 19.25), *tian* refers to the sky. Perhaps for this reason, the prominent philosopher Zhang Dainian holds that, during Confucius's later years, his notion of *tian* transformed from that of a controlling God to the natural course of things.[9]

In the *Mencius*, heaven correlates directly to *xin* (human heart) and *xing* (human nature). Such a heaven is by no means transcendent. Similarly, in the *Doctrine of Mean*, the mandate of heaven is found in human nature (*xing*). In the *Book of Changes*, the rigor and strength of heaven correlate with the perseverance of human efforts. As the force of the *Qian* hexagram (*yang*) correlates with the force of the *Kun* hexagram (*yin*), heaven correlates with earth. Heaven is located indisputably within the framework of "heaven-earth-humanity." The *Book of Changes* states,

> There is the *way* (Way) of heaven, the *way* of Earth, and the *way* of humanity. The six components in the hexagrams are the duplicated representation of these three potent forces. These six components indicate nothing other than the *way* of these three forces.[10]

A hexagram is composed of two trigrams and therefore consists of six lines. Within each hexagram, each of these three forces is represented twice, to achieve a balanced scheme. Together, all three potent forces are integrated to generate a grand triadic structure of "heaven-earth-humanity."

In the *Xunzi*, *tian* as the totality of natural phenomena is not transcendent either. It participates in the triad of "heaven-earth-humanity." Xunzi describes *tian* this way:

> Not to act, yet bring to completion; not to seek, yet to obtain—thus indeed may be described as the work of Nature. In such a situation, the [Perfect] Man, however profound, does not apply any thought to the work of Nature; however great, does not apply his abilities to it; and however shrewd, does not apply his acumen for inquiry to it. This indeed may be described as "not competing with Nature in its work."

And,

> heaven has its seasons; Earth its resources; and Man his government. This, of course, is why it is said that they "can form a Triad." When man abandons what he should use to form the Triad yet longs for the [benefits that result from] the Triad, he suffers from delusion![11]

Tian is the natural course of things: "The course of Nature is constant; it does not survive because of the actions of a Yao; it does perish because of the actions of a Jie."[12] Heaven is not affected by good rulers (Yao) or bad rulers (Jie). Such a notion of *tian*, of course, cannot be a transcendent deity.

The Han Confucian, Dong Zhongshu (179–104 BCE), advocates the close connection between heaven and Humanity. Heaven does not exist without interacting with humanity. In Dong's writings, heaven manifests itself in the *way* of heaven. The *way* of heaven, the *way* of earth, and the *way* of humanity work together to promote world transformation. Dong says, "The *way* of heaven bestows things, the *way* of earth transforms the world, and the *way* of humanity promotes morality."[13] Clearly, for Dong, heaven is not apart from "heaven-earth-humanity."

The above brief visit with early thinkers of Confucian philosophy shows that from early on the mainstream Confucian notion of heaven was already one of the triadic "heaven-earth-humanity." This immanent notion of heaven is crucial to the very foundation of Confucian philosophy. Today, Confucian philosophy must take this triadic notion of heaven as its foundation, as its starting point, and as its end point. Going back to the Yin/Shang notion of heaven as a transcendent and personified deity is a step backward and can be only counterproductive to the mission of Confucianism.

Jiang's notion of transcendent heaven cannot serve as a solid foundation for today's Confucian political philosophy.

REDUNDANCY OF THE TRANSCENDENT HEAVEN

Jiang's primary concern is with Confucian constitutionalism. Laboring on the notion of transcendent heaven, Jiang purports to establish that sovereignty comes from heaven, not from the people. From such a perspective, Jiang develops a comprehensive theory of Confucian constitutionalism. Admittedly, Confucianism upholds the notion of heaven, particularly in a spiritual and moral sense. The view that the right to govern is ultimately rooted and justified in the mandate of heaven can be grounded in the Confucian tradition. However, the heaven that Jiang is considering is a transcendent heaven, one that is beyond earth and humanity. For him, only such a transcendent heaven possesses the capacity to confer the authority to rule over human society.

With the transcendent heaven as its source, Jiang maintains that Confucian constitutionalism is also transcendent and sacred, that is, religious in nature. Accordingly, a Confucian constitution is not a secular matter. It is also sacred and transcendent in character. In this regard, I find myself in fundamental opposition to Jiang. In my view, constitution, along with government establishment, is mundane in nature. It has a practical character and is neither sacred nor transcendent.[14]

Because Jiang's heaven here is transcendent, it does not directly reach the human world. Realizing this deficiency, Jiang has to make it generate a second form of heaven, one that is related with earth and humanity. We must ask, if the transcendent heaven itself cannot function, why does his system need such a transcendent heaven? Why is he not satisfied with the heaven amid earth and humanity as is the case in mainstream Confucianism?

Jiang's system is reminiscent of the doctrine of the Trinity in Christianity. According to this doctrine, God the Father is God, God the Son is God, and the Holy Spirit is God. Yet God the Father is not God the Son, God the Son is not the Holy Spirit, and the Holy Spirit is not God the Father. Logically, if the verb "is" connotes identity, then the two terms before and after "is" denote the same object. If A is B, and B is C, then A is C. While this doctrine may work in religion, from a purely logical, philosophical perspective, it is definitely problematic. It would appear to violate the simple logic of identity.

I am not claiming that Jiang's system is the same as the doctrine of the Christian Trinity. It is obviously not. But, his system surely contains a similar logical problem. One may ask, is the transcendent heaven the same as the heaven of "heaven-earth-humanity"? If so, why should we need a transcendent heaven in addition to the heaven of "heaven-earth-humanity"? If they are not the same, besides saying that one generates the other, what else can be said of them meaningfully? Is just saying that one heaven generates the other heaven expressive? It seems to me, Jiang's notion of the transcendent heaven does not have any substantive meaning.

A closer look into Jiang's system may reveal the real reason for having a transcendent heaven. Positing such a notion may serve a stylistic purpose in Jiang's construction of a religious-political system. His stylistic need may have propelled him to go so far as to violate basic logic. In designing his political system, Jiang includes an Academy alongside the parliament. The Academy is the national council of Confucianism. It is the embodiment of the national spirit, with a higher status than the parliament. The parliament consists of three houses that correspond perfectly with the "heaven-earth-humanity" scheme in his metaphysics. Here is how it looks:

TABLE 6.1.

Symmetry between Philosophical Concepts and Political Arrangements

Philosophical Concepts			Political Arrangement		
[?]			Academy		
Heaven	Earth	Humanity	House of Ru	House of the Nation	House of the People

Without a transcendent heaven, the Academy would have no grounding. Thus, the question mark in the above grid has to be filled with a transcendent heaven. One cannot but admit the elegance of Jiang's design here. It is perfect. But does an aesthetic need of the system justify the positing of such a heavy-handed notion? Of course, without knowing Jiang's mental map in developing his philosophy, no one can say with certainty how his notion of transcendent heaven first emerged. If it was called up to serve a stylistic need of his political system, then that is not a good justification.

Furthermore, does the transcendent heaven have real, practical efficacy, besides a rhetorical function? I think not. Jiang admits that the sovereignty of heaven does not imply that it can manage human affairs directly. It has to be brought down to earth, to human society. He maintains that the transcendent heaven acts through Confucian sages. Because only sages can fully represent heaven, authority to rule lies with sages, not with the people. In Jiang's view, the sage king is a sage because he is the mediator between heaven and the human. Therefore, in politics, only sage kings are able to represent and act on behalf of the transcendent heaven.

A problem arises here. If heaven has no other way to reach out and can be represented only by the sage kings, would the sage kings themselves not become de facto heaven? If heaven can be represented only by sage kings, and no one else, through whatever means, heaven has become a de facto empty notion. Thus is the fate of the transcendent heaven in Jiang's philosophy.

To make the situation worse, Jiang's process of the entrustment of governing rights from heaven does not stop with sage kings. For at that point, even sage kings are nowhere to be found. The sovereignty has to be further delegated the Confucian scholar-officials. If so, what use or value does the transcendent heaven possess, besides being an empty concept playing a nominal, aesthetic role of adornment? We have to conclude that Jiang's transcendent heaven does not have real, practical significance. Suppose someday Jiang's political system becomes a reality, would people not want to seize the power to interpret heaven from Confucian scholar-officials?

CONFUCIAN CONTENT WITH DEMOCRATIC FORM

Finally, I would like to take this opportunity to present my own view of the ideal relationship between Confucianism and democracy, as an alternative to Jiang's system. I see my own position as somewhere in the middle between today's conservative and liberal Confucian thinkers. It is to the left of Jiang's but to the right of liberal Confucian thinkers, who consist of the majority in the field.

In previous work, I proposed that Confucianism and democracy are two independent value systems and should be treated as such.[15] Instead of integrating them into one system—which would result in a significant loss of some core values in both systems—we should keep them in a relationship of checks and balances in the same society. This position, although I believe it is still relevant to the discussion of the relationship between Confucianism and democracy, has its limitations. Joseph Chan, for instance, has argued that the view of democracy implied in my proposal is "an inclusive view of democracy," too inclusive to make productive inferences in our discussion.[16] I now partially agree with him. Democracy is not one single, iron block; there are many forms of democracy. Taking this reason into consideration, I would propose a revised relationship between Confucianism and democracy. This new relationship may be labeled "Confucian content with democratic form."

"Democratic form" refers to a political arrangement that adopts a democratic electoral mechanism. Such a form is political in nature. It is an organizational procedure by which society generates political leaders. "Confucian content" refers to Confucian social and moral ideals. When these ideals are preserved in society, the lives of the majority of the people manifest Confucian philosophy. In such a society, the government takes people's well-being as its top priority, and people support their government. Family is highly valued, education is vigorously promoted, and people are mostly virtuous. In order to achieve this goal, Confucianism must acquire popular support at the grassroots level on the one hand and, on the other, Confucian values and convictions must be constitutionally guaranteed (e.g., integrity of the family and priority of citizen's livelihood in the agenda of the government).

This view endorses a limited degree of integration of Confucianism and democracy, an integration that is external rather than internal in character. It does not change Confucianism. It is just that Confucianism adopts the democratic political mechanism for governmental affairs, in some way similar to how Christianity adopts a democratic form in the West without changing its fundamental beliefs and ideals. To be sure, a democratic form does not guarantee the implementation of Confucian values. As a matter of fact, no social form can guarantee a particular value. Democratic elections can give us Winston Churchills or they can give us Adolf Hitlers. (This of course does not mean all political systems are the same.) It all depends on people's effort in promoting social ideals in real life. Confucians must keep that in mind.

In three ways my proposal differs from the model of "Chinese Substance with Western Function" (*zhong ti xi yong*). First, although the Chinese Substance with Western Function model can be applied to political arrangement, its primary consideration has been with Western science and technology. My proposal is thoroughly political in nature. Second, the Chinese Substance with Western Functions model takes science and technology as a good. My proposal adopts democratic form without making a value endorsement. In fact, Confucians maintain a critical stance regarding the inherent deficiencies of any democratic form. Finally, both "substance" and "function" (*ti* and *yong*) are ancient Chinese concepts, with exceedingly complicated meanings and overly broad applications. In comparison, "Confucian content" and "democratic form" are self-explanatory and less ambiguous.[17]

CHAPTER 7

Is the Way of the Humane Authority a Good Thing?

AN ASSESSMENT OF CONFUCIAN CONSTITUTIONALISM

Wang Shaoguang

JIANG QING'S CONCEPTION OF THE WAY
OF THE HUMANE AUTHORITY

Keping Yu's phrase "Democracy is a good thing" is already well known at home and abroad, though not everyone who reflects on China's future would necessarily agree.[1] In today's China, Jiang Qing is somebody who is not afraid to stand alone and refuse to follow the herd. Jiang Qing may not have actually used those words, but he would surely agree that the politics of Way of the Humane Authority is a good thing.

Over the past twenty years or so, Jiang has devoted himself to establishing the structure and theory of political Confucianism.[2] He started with a study of the *Gongyang* school,[3] and has now moved on to say that "the Way of the Humane Authority is the direction in which contemporary Chinese politics is heading."[4] Most recently he has been promoting Confucian constitutionalism with the Way of the Humane Authority at its center.[5] His untiring efforts and dedication to this one cause are said to be so as to resolve the question of legitimacy. He sees the fundamental problem of political power as one of legitimacy, or of "legitimizing the Way." He believes that this question has not been properly handled either in China or in the West, which some people take as the model. Furthermore, it could even lead to a serious crisis. The Way of the Humane Authority is his prescription for resolving this problem of legitimacy.

China's problem is said to be its lack of legitimacy. The reason for this, according to Jiang, is that over the past hundred years "China's own culture has collapsed and its leading role in the formation of culture has been completely taken over by foreign culture—liberal or socialist cultures. This has displaced Confucian culture from its orthodox status as a guide in politics and society and led to a falling away from the path of development of Chinese culture."[6]

In the West the problem is that legitimacy is unbalanced. Jiang thinks that "the politics in the West is colored by its cultural one-sided tendency. Thus, when dealing with the issue of legitimacy, the West has often gone from one extreme to another. While it exclusively focused on the divine source of legitimacy throughout the Middle Ages, now the excessive weight is given to the will of the people as the sole guarantor of legitimacy in the modern time." Due to its bias toward the will of the people, Western democracy has become "excessively secularized, vulgarized, flatten, and full of human desires."[7]

Jiang thinks that it is possible to resolve the problem of legitimacy both for China and the West and the solution is his idea of the Way of the Humane Authority. Of course, the Way of the Humane Authority is not the ideal Confucian solution since it would not be required once we have entered into the world of great harmony.[8] But in the imperfect world of today, the Way of the Humane Authority is the best possible choice. It should be accepted both in China and the West as the direction in which politics develops.[9]

The key term in the Way of the Humane Authority is "royal." Confucian classics explain the term according to either sound or form. The *Discussions in the White Tiger Hall* (*Baihu tongde lun*) explains "royal" (*wang*) as "coming towards (*wang*), that towards which all under heaven come." Confucius notes that the character *wang* (王) is composed of three horizontal lines united by one vertical line. Dong Zhongshu explains further, "[T]he three horizontal lines represent heaven, earth and the human realms and the one vertical line which unites them stands for the Way."[10]

On the basis of the Confucian classics, Jiang argues that legitimacy must be threefold. The popular legitimacy is the easiest to understand since Jiang defines it as based on the will of the people. The legitimacy of earth is that the political order of each state should be in conformity with its own culture. In China that means conforming to Confucian culture and the Confucian way. It is much more difficult to understand the legitimacy of the way of heaven. Feng Youlan noted that the term "heaven" had five meanings in ancient China: a material heaven, a ruling heaven, a fatalistic heaven, a naturalistic heaven, an ethical heaven.[11] In writing *Political Confucianism (Zhengzhi Ruxue)*, Jiang would appear to agree with Feng, but he draws attention only to the latter four meanings. Whether we read five or four meanings is not important though; in both cases the term "heaven" is unclear and can give rise to misunderstanding. It is perhaps to avoid such misinterpretations that in his most recent writings Jiang speaks of sacred legitimacy as "morality" or "applied morality."[12]

In his *Political Confucianism*, published in 2003, Jiang put the legitimacy of the human way in first place, calling it "the first principle of the Way of the Humane Authority."[13] In his more recent writings he has moved the legitimacy of the way of heaven into first place. His reason is that heaven is "'the first among the many things' and 'the great prince of the hundred spirits.' It is the sovereign and so the three forms are not equal or on the same plane."[14]

The Way of the Humane Authority at the level of legitimization must be realized at the level of the implementation. Otherwise, it will remain somewhat abstract. Jiang recommends a tricameral parliamentary system at this level; each of the houses represents one form of legitimacy.[15]

Jiang's theory is such as to create a school apart. He throws out a challenge to all those who discuss Chinese politics to reflect over many theoretical and practical issues as well as historical and contemporary issues. Given that Jiang's study of political Confucianism and his advocacy of the Way of the Humane Authority and Confucian constitutionalism are not on academic grounds alone, but to provide a remedy for enduring political ills and "a theoretic alternative for China's future political reform,"[16] and to resolve the political difficulties faced by all human societies, this critical essay focuses on his identification of those ills and the remedy he proposes with such single-minded dedication.

DIAGNOSIS: A CRISIS OF LEGITIMACY?

Jiang focuses on the issue of legitimacy because he believes that both China and the West are facing a crisis of legitimacy.

Putting to one side the question as to whether legitimacy is the root problem of politics, we first must note that any political setup will have to face the question of legitimacy because no political arrangement can win the minds and hearts of every single person. For instance, when the Republic of China replaced the monarchy in 1911 there were some Qing loyalists who doubted the legitimacy of the Republic. The People's Republic of China was founded sixty years ago, but there are still those who think it is illegitimate. But that some people question the legitimacy of a political arrangement does not mean that there is a crisis of legitimacy. We need to ask what exactly Jiang understands as the crisis of legitimacy faced both by China and the West.

Legitimacy can be explained in two ways: At the level of norms, legitimacy involves asking if the origins of political power are rightful or justifiable.[17] At the practical level, legitimacy is a matter of whether or not the political setup is able to make people believe that the current polity is the best feasible alternative for their country.[18] It is clear that the latter is a political matter. When people in general hold that the present political arrangement is not best suited to their country, then legitimacy faces a crisis. Legitimacy at the level of norms is a matter of moral philosophy. If the questioning of legitimacy of moral philosophers, or politicians under the guise of moral philosophers, has no influence on the thought or behavior of the people who live in the country, then it is of purely academic interest and does not constitute a problem of legitimacy. To sum up, then, whether or not a political system faces a crisis of legitimacy depends on whether the people who live there doubt the rightness of its power, and whether they consider it the appropriate system for their country. In Confucian terminology, the key to determining whether or not there is a crisis of legitimacy lies in whether or not "all under heaven" "turn toward" the system. By this criterion, does China face a crisis of legitimacy?

Jiang thinks that Chinese politics have lacked legitimacy for a long time. It so happens that mainstream Western theorists say much the same thing. Having been said time and again over the last few decades it would seem to have become an unshakeable truth. Many articles, newspapers reports, and speeches by politicians in the West, Hong Kong, and Taiwan all take China's supposed lack of legitimacy as the basis for their theories. In time some people in China have begun to share the same view.

If we first use normative legitimacy as our standard, Jiang is quite right to assert that China's lack of legitimacy is a very serious problem because the Way of the Humane Authority and three forms of legitimacy are quite absent in the present time. The problem is that Jiang himself acknowledges that the Way of the Humane Authority is an ideal model developed from the rule of the three sage kings as known in legends. Since the time of the three dynasties this ideal has never been able to be put into practice. In other words, China's problem of legitimacy in this sense has a long history, of at least over two thousand years. Likewise, if we use the Western standard of legitimacy at the normative level, then China certainly has a problem of legitimacy because, without competitive elections, China's political system does not match Schumpeterian criteria for electoral democracy.[19]

However, if we consider things from whether or not all under heaven turns toward the authorities, then the situation is very different. Since the 1990s Western scholars (or scholars born in China and working in the West) have carried out many large-scale surveys into the legitimacy of Chinese political power. Initially the high degree of acceptance of the regime was interpreted by the Western scholars as a result of the persons questioned being afraid to tell the truth. As a result, later surveys added various mechanisms to prevent the people being questioned from telling lies (such as providing the options "don't know" or "no response"). But the results

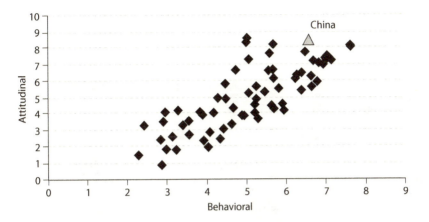

FIGURE 7.1. The Ranking of Legitimacy in Seventy-Two States

of each survey were always the same.[20] There was a time when articles with this conclusion had great difficulty in being published in Western academic journals because the anonymous assessors used their own subjective opinion to cruelly shoot down such results.[21] However, iron-fast facts are hard to denounce. By now scholars familiar with the field have virtually all arrived at a consensus: the degree of legitimacy of the Chinese political system is very high.[22]

At the turn of the century, Bruce Gilley made a chart of legitimacy ratings in seventy-two countries (Figure 7.1). The total population of the countries is 5.1 billion, or 83 percent of the world population. Gilley's chart has two axes: attitudinal and behavioral. The data for people's attitude to their government come from the World Value Survey. The data on how much people's behavior indicates support for their government are derived from three indicators: rate of participation in elections, frequency of violence in popular opposition to officials, and proportion of revenue from income tax, capital gains tax, and real estate tax in the total revenue of the central government. In terms of attitude, the chart shows clearly that China comes in second place at 8.5, a long way above the United States (7.12) and India (5.89). Gilley's axis on behavior is not quite fair to China since China has only recently brought in income tax, and it is shared equally between the central and local governments. Also, China has no real estate tax yet. Moreover, these systems of taxation have nothing to do with whether the ordinary people support the government or not. Nonetheless, Gilley's chart still places China in thirteenth place, well above many supposedly democratic countries.[23]

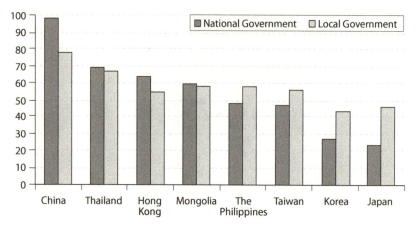

FIGURE 7.2. Trust in National and Local Governments

In 2008 Columbia University Press published a most interesting book: *How East Asians View Democracy*.[24] This book looks at eight countries or regions in East Asia. The case studies in the book are all based on comprehensive, strictly random sample surveys. Among the questions, two are relevant to the legitimacy of the state: people's level of trust in central and local government. Figure 7.2 is drawn up according to the data in the book and shows that of all the eight countries or regions studied, the Chinese state comes closest to the ideal of all under heaven turning toward it. From the above it would seem that China does not suffer from any lack of legitimacy.

Jiang's criticism of Western liberal democracy is that its legitimacy relies solely on the people's will. This criticism seems to imply that Jiang has accepted the mainstream Western view that Western liberal democracy does enjoy the legitimacy of the popular will. What he objects to is that this form of legitimacy is lopsided and unbalanced. But does Western liberal democracy really enjoy popular legitimacy?

Surveys in Europe and America often include the question, "Are you satisfied with the performance of democracy?" The surveys in such countries regularly report that over 70 percent of respondents are "satisfied" or "comparatively satisfied."[25] On the basis of this, many people conclude that American and European countries enjoy the legitimacy of the popular will. But the question itself is too vague. It could be understood as asking (1) if you satisfied with the present government, or (2) satisfied with the present political system, or (3) satisfied with democracy as an ideal form of political arrangement. It could also be understood as any possible combination of the above. In other words, it is a bit like a rubbish bin and is a pretty meaningless question and should not be taken too seriously.[26]

If instead we ask "What degree of confidence do you have in the government?" the situation is very different. Among ninety countries for which data are available, Vietnam and China come in at the top, with the people having great confidence in the government while most European and American countries are in the bottom half, with the United States at fifty-eight, the United Kingdom at sixty-eight, France at seventy-seven, and Germany at eighty-seven.[27] If a large proportion of the citizens have no confidence in the government, how much popular legitimacy does such a political system have?

In Western liberal democracy, the so-called representatives of the people, the national assembly members or parliamentarians, are chosen by election. However, as Fareed Zakaria, the editor of Newsweek, so ironically pointed out that, in many polls, when Americans are asked which public institutions they most trust, there are always three in the lead: the Supreme Court, the army, and the Federal Reserve Bank.[28] What all three have in common is that their directors are not chosen by election, and these organizations are not ones that supposedly represent the people. But it is precisely the elected institutions such as the U.S. Congress that most opinion polls show to be placed in the lower ranks. Zakaria said that in 2003. On April 18, 2010, the Pew Research Center published its latest survey, "The People and Their Government: Distrust, Discontent, Anger," which again proved the same point. Only 24 percent of those polled indicated support for what the U.S. Congress did, and a massive 65 percent indicated disagreement. The reputation of the Congress is only slightly better when compared to the badly discredited banks and financial institutions at the height of the financial crisis.[29]

Not only do institutions that are supposed to represent the people have very little popular legitimacy in the United States, even in Europe the situation is much the same. The results of the 2005 European Social Survey (ESS) are shown in Figure 7.3.[30] Apart from two tiny countries—Luxembourg with a population of 0.5 million and Cyprus with a population of 1 million—people have more confidence in the police, who are a symbol of violence, than in the members of parliaments who are the supposed representatives of the people. The average rate of trust in the people's representatives of the twenty-nine countries taken together is 37 percent. While this is better than that in the United States, it is still very low. The gap between trust in the police and in the people's representatives is 25.9 percent, while in the United Kingdom, France, and Germany it is between 40 percent and 50 percent.

If the people's representatives chosen by election are held by most people as not representative of the will of the people and do not enjoy the trust

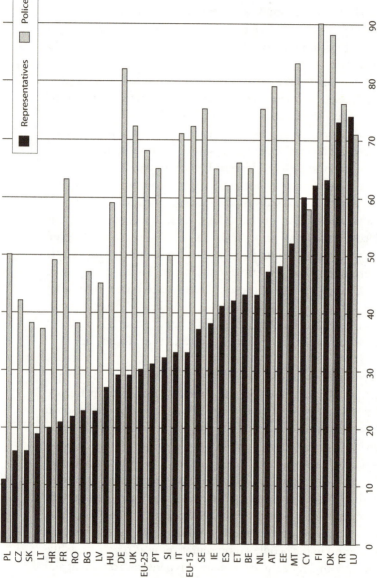

Figure 7.3. Trust in Representatives and Polices, 2005

Source: http://www.eurofound.europa.eu/areas/qualityoflife/eurlife/checkform.php?idDomain=0&Submit1=List.

Note: AT = Austria; BE = Belgium; BG = Bulgaria; CY = Cyprus; CZ = Czech Republic; DE = Germany; DK = Denmark; EE = Estonia; EL = Greece; ES = Spain; EU-15 = 15 EU member states (before May 2004); EU-25 = 25 EU member states (after May 2004); FI = Finland; FR = France; HR = Croatia; HU = Hungary; IE = Ireland; IT = Italy; LT = Lithuania; LU = Luxembourg; LV = Latvia; MT = Malta; NL = Netherlands; PL = Poland; PT = Portugal; RO = Romania; SE = Sweden; SI = Slovenia; SK = Slovakia; TR = Turkey; UK = United Kingdom.

of the majority, then Western liberal democracy based on competitive elections would appear to not have much popular legitimacy; still less can it be said that popular legitimacy is monopolized as the only form of legitimacy.

While Jiang thinks that Western liberal democracy is too democratic, I think that its problem is that it is not democratic enough. In recent years the term "democracy" has been preceded by such adjectives as "liberal," "constitutional," "representative," "electoral," "pluralist." The aim of all those modifications is to restrict democracy. "Liberal" democracy and "constitutional" democracy bar many important things that involve people's everyday life (e.g., property ownership, work, family life) from democratic decision making. "Representative" democracy makes democracy a ritual of power endorsement that happens only every few years, between which people hardly play any role in decision making. "Electoral" democracy in practice deprives most people of the right to be elected such that elections result in what Aristotle referred to as oligarchy,[31] or Francesco Guicciardini (1483–1540) called aristocracy.[32] "Pluralist" democracy papers over the serious inequalities in the distribution of economic, social, and political resources among social classes and the effects of this. In each case the addition of the adjective leads to a defective form of democracy, a powerless democracy, a democracy less dangerous to the ruling class, a democracy that represents the interests of powerful social groups rather than the will of the people.[33]

Clearly, it is a misjudgment to say that China lacks legitimacy or that the legitimacy of the Western democracy relies solely on the will of the people.

PRESCRIPTION: THE WAY OF THE HUMANE AUTHORITY?

When you see the doctor, he needs to make a correct diagnosis in order to provide the right prescription. If the diagnosis is mistaken, then it is hard to prevent the prescribed medicine from having little effect. What is at stake here is a matter both of reasoning and of practicability.

In terms of reasoning, if China's problem is not a lack of legitimacy and the West does not suffer from the supremacy of popular will, do we need the Way of the Humane Authority as the option for improving China's politics in the future? Could it also serve as the political ideal for the whole world?

An ideal is worth pursuing only if it is possible to realize it in practice. This is what Rawls calls a practical utopia. If the ideal is altogether unrealizable, then it is merely a pipe dream. We have already mentioned that the Way of the Humane Authority vaunted by the ancient Confucian worthies is an ideal model based on the governance of the sage kings of the three dynasties. The term "three dynasties" was coined in the Eastern Zhou era to refer to an ancient golden age. Archaeological evidence cannot yet confirm the existence of the Xia dynasty. Up to now, it is purely the stuff of legends.[34] Jiang himself admits that after the three dynasties this ideal was no longer practiced. However good it was as an ideal, if it has not been put into practice for over several thousand years, one has good reason to wonder if it is not a mere pipe dream. There is even more reason to wonder if something that could not be achieved when society was under hierarchical leadership could possibly be implemented in China today after a socialist revolution and the acceptance of the idea of equality.

Even through Jiang's reinterpretation, his idea of the Way of the Humane Authority or Confucian constitutionalism based on threefold legitimacy is not necessarily a practical utopia worth pursuing. In a nutshell, Jiang's Confucian constitutionalism is an elitist blueprint, not an ordinary kind of elitism but a Confucian elitism or an elitism in which Confucian scholars are the elite.[35] Propagation of this kind of elitism is based on two presuppositions: (1) the political structures of both China and the West are insufficiently elitist and (2) only elitism by Confucian scholars is able to understand the way of legitimizing politics and also comprehend its implementation, representing the way both of heaven and of earth. The vast mass of the people cannot understand either legitimization or implementation, nor can they represent heaven or earth.

But neither of these presuppositions can stand.

Let us consider the first of them. Under Mao Zedong there was probably not much elitism in China because from the late fifties onward, he began to search for a way to wipe out "bourgeois rights," that is to change the unequal relationships between people. This search was called "combat and prevent revisionism."[36] In 1957 Mao noted that though the socialist transformation of the means of production had been largely complete, the transformation of human mind-sets was not yet complete.[37] The next year, in his criticism of Stalin's *The Economic Problem of Soviet Socialism*, Mao went on to say,

> Following the changes wrought by the socialist transformation, we have basically resolved all the problems with regards to the ownership of the means of production. However, equal relationship between people in the process of production would not emerge automatically. The existence of bourgeois rights will certainly prevent in all ways it can the formation and development of this equality. It is essential to do away with bourgeois rights which still exist between people. Such bourgeois rights manifest themselves in the pyramid of power, condescending attitudes, withdrawing from the masses, not treating people as equals, not relying on work or physical strength to eat but relying on one's post or power, division between cadres and the masses, hierarchical relations like those

of cat and mouse or father and son. These must all be destroyed, utterly destroyed. Once destroyed, they will return so they must be destroyed again.[38]

At the time the methods Mao used to destroy bourgeois rights involved rectification, encouragement of grassroots experimentations, criticism of hierarchy, sending cadres to work in the countryside, and "two participations and one reform" (the participation of cadres in manual work and the participation of workers in management, and the reform of unreasonable regulations). Later on, the Socialist Education Movement (1963–66) in both town and countryside was also designed to solve this problem. But he still felt that these measures were insufficient to destroy bourgeois rights and prevent the danger of a restoration of capitalism.

On the eve of the Cultural Revolution (1966–76), Mao published the ideal of his later days in the May 7th Directive. From this we can see that Mao wanted to gradually abolish division of labor in society and abolish commodities and that he was looking for a completely equal society in which the three great inequalities of workers and peasants, town and country, physical labor and mental labor would be destroyed. He wanted complete equality in work, culture, education, politics, and material conditions of life.[39]

The first part of the Cultural Revolution (1966–68) focused on criticism of so-called "capitalist roaders," while the later part of the Revolution (1969–76) shifted to nurture so-called "socialist new things" (e.g., May 7th cadre schools; educated youth going up to mountains and down to the countryside; revolutionary model operas; workers, peasants, and soldiers going to university and running universities; workers' propaganda team; poor peasants' propaganda team; barefoot doctors; cooperative medicine; three-way union of the elderly, middle aged, and youth; and three-way union of workers, cadres, and intellectuals). All these things can be seen as Mao's ways of realizing his ideal.

However, after eight years of the Cultural Revolution, Mao realized that one revolution alone could not achieve his goals. In a speech on theory in 1974, he revealed his true feeling:

China is a socialist country. It resembled capitalism in many ways before Liberation (1949). Even now we still have eight grades of pay, distribution of resources according to work, currency exchanges, all of which are not very different from the old society. The main difference is that the ownership of the means of production has changed. China is now implementing a commodity system, the wage system is unequal, there are eight grade wage scales, and so on.[40]

This became the basis for his theory of continuous revolution. Between October 1975 and January 1976, before he died, Mao spoke many times of the problem of bourgeois rights. His conclusion was that in a hundred years a revolution would still be needed and again in a thousand years.[41]

In brief, throughout his last years Mao was fully engaged in combating against bourgeois rights and using all means to bring about equality of all (excluding class enemies) in the economy, in society, in politics and culture. Consequently, China did not develop serious class divisions. The pre-Liberation old elite and the post-Liberation new elite all were held down.

The policy of reform and opening up began in opposition to the ideology of leveling everyone to the lowest common denominator. In the thirty years since then, the lives of hundreds of millions of ordinary workers and peasants have been improved, but their political status has plummeted substantially. Meanwhile, with the support of the political elite, the capitalist class and intellectuals, who were at the bottom of politics in Mao's era, have returned to the upper echelons of society. They have also used the resources and knowledge they have in hand to throw themselves into politics. By now the political elite, economic elite, and intellectual elite have formed a kind of triangular alliance, which is tending to harden.[42]

Changes in the political standing of each class are reflected in the composition of the National People's Congress (see Figure 7.4). In the period when Mao sought to eradicate bourgeois rights in the later part of the Cultural Revolution, workers, soldiers, and peasants were the mainstay of the Congress, with over two-thirds of the seats, of which workers and peasants accounted for more than one-half. This proportion fell after the Cultural Revolution from 51.1 percent in the Fourth Congress in 1975 to 18.46 percent in the Tenth Congress in 2003. In the Eleventh Congress convened in 2008, it was said that "numbers of frontline workers and peasants have greatly increased," but the exact figure is unknown. We do know, however, that currently the mainstay of the Congress is cadres of all levels and intellectuals, who together compose two-thirds of the total.[43] Meanwhile the National Political Consultative Conference is a veritable elite club, whose 2,237 members represent thirty-four fields of work. While this body also contains representatives from the All-China Federation of Trade Unions and the agricultural field, who are mostly union officials or agronomists, there are practically no ordinary workers or peasants.[44]

Western liberal (capitalist) democracy was elitist from the start. When, in the late nineteenth and early twentieth centuries, the theory of majority rule was beginning to be widely accepted, Gaetano Mosca advanced the theory of the ruling class, while Vilfredo Pareto advocated an elitist theory.[45] They thought that universal suffrage would give rise to the illusion that the

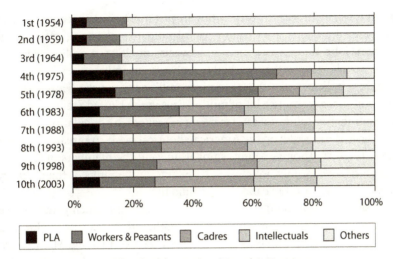

FIGURE 7.4. The Composition of the National People's Congress

Source: http://www.people.com.cn/GB/14576/15117/2350775.html and http://www
.people.com.cn/GB/shizheng/1026/2369476.html.

people had become the ruling class but in fact society would still be run by elite, and these elite would be composed almost entirely of members of the bourgeoisie.[46] Whatever motive they had for advancing elitism, the development of European and American states in the last century or so has proved their prediction to be correct.

In a liberal democracy, the main form of participation by the mass of people is in elections. The degree to which people with varying social resources participate in elections shows a huge discrepancy. Data gathered in various countries throughout the years confirm that the more resources one has, the more one is likely to vote, and the less resources one has, the less one will go to the polls. In other words, social elites have a higher turnout than people lower down the social ladder.[47]

Not only are social elites more ready to vote, they also make up by far the largest proportion of persons elected. Research into the background of political elites in European and American countries was relatively large in number in the 1950s and 1960s, because at the time the influence of Marxist analysis was more marked. After the sixties this type of studies gradually disappeared, and by now they are exceedingly rare. But the presence of social elites in state apparatus is beyond any doubt. In the U.S. Congress, the House of Representatives has 435 members, of whom at least 123 are millionaires, which amounts to one-third. In the Senate, among its 100 members, at least 50 are millionaires, which is one-half of the total.[48] In fact, it is not quite true to say that they are just millionaires because some of them are billionaires. For instance, one candidate in the 2004 presidential election, John Kerry, had a household wealth of US$340 million. Perhaps some people will say that the high proportion of millionaires in the U.S. Congress indicates that there are more millionaires in the United States. In truth, there are quite a lot of millionaires in the United States, but their total number certainly does not exceed 1 percent of the population. Clearly, they have a large stake on the American political scene. A researcher of the U.S. Congress, Thomas Mann, sums it up well: the members of the U.S. Congress are certainly not chosen from among the ranks of the ordinary people. They are an elite band through and through.[49]

Besides actively taking part in elections and influencing the choice of policy makers or themselves taking public office, the social elite will unsparingly lobby to influence the process of decision making. Mainstream Western pluralism would seem to have won most people to believe that any-one can form their own group to present their own demands. According this theory, the existence of innumerable groups means not only that they can keep an effective check on government but also that they can keep a check on each other and ensure that no one group becomes dominant, and so together they make up the pluralist playing board. But the actual situation is very different. The power of groups that represent the particular interests of elite circles is vastly superior to that of groups that represent ordinary people.[50]

Unequal participation in politics results in serious inequality in political influence: the influence of elites on the government far surpasses that of the masses. In the heat of the 2008 American presidential election, Professor Larry M. Bartels of Princeton University published a book with the title *Unequal Democracy*.[51] It was reported at the time that Obama read the book.[52] This book analyzed the response of the Senate's responsiveness to the demands of groups with different incomes in the period of the 101st to 103rd Congresses. He found that the response of the Senate to groups with high income was the strongest, to those in the middle income bracket it was less, while to those with the lowest income it was the weakest, to the point of even being negative and contrary to their interests. This rate of responsiveness was roughly the same throughout the whole period of the three Congresses. There are those who will say that the United States has two main parties and that if one party neglects the poor and favors the rich, the other will bring things back into balance. Facts prove that this way of thinking is illusory. Is there a difference between the Republicans and the Democrats? Yes. The Republicans tend to favor the rich more, but the Democrats are also unfair to the poor. Both parties react negatively to the poor. Clearly there is a difference between the parties, but it is negligible since both are dedicated to representing the interests of the elite.[53]

Western liberal (capitalist) democracy is excessively elitist. This is perhaps why its popular legitimacy is not high at all.

If the political systems of China and the West already have a highly elitist tendency, one might well ask, is Jiang's championing of elitism an asset in establishing a balanced political system, or will it lead to the very lack of balance he so fears?

Let us turn to Jiang's second hypothesis now. Could the elite or great Confucian scholars represent what he calls "transcendent, sacred legitimacy"? The answer of course depends on the meaning of the "transcendent, sacred legitimacy." If it means "practical morality," is such "practical morality" a universal value? Yet Jiang would seem not to recognize any universal morality or global ethics, so it can only be a native Chinese ethics.[54] The problem is that if we use Jiang's argument in denial of a global ethics, people could also argue in the same way that Confucian ethics is merely one strand of China's native ethics and that it should not monopolize the entire field of ethics, especially in China today, or else it will commit the same error as the Western-centered theory in proposing a Confucian-centered theory. If Confucianism cannot monopolize ethics in China, then to form a House of *Ru* to represent transcendent, sacred legitimacy would seem to be lacking in legitimacy itself.

Even if it is not from a fear of equating Confucian ethics with Chinese ethics, people will still question whether great Confucian scholars can represent this transcendental legitimacy on the basis of the history of Confucianism in China. Jiang himself separates political Confucianism, moral Confucianism (New Confucianism), and politicized Confucianism. In his view, New Confucianism that fails to develop a new theory of political authority presents nothing more than an "eye-catching but meaningless scene" with many serious negative consequences.[55] He is even more critical of politicized Confucianism, saying that

> it has completely given up any ultimate concern for an ideal of higher values or hope for future harmony in society. It has lost its ability to criticize the present system and engage in self-criticism. It has integrated itself wholly to the existing political order and has become transformed into a pure ideology, descending to the level of a political tool to defend the interests of the present system and the rulers.[56]

In the history of Confucianism, Han Confucians turned Confucianism into a theology lost in the smoke of corruption and ghost stories. In the Wei-Jin period, the scholar-officials pursued abstruse studies and made

Confucianism into abstruse metaphysics. Under the Sui the system of state examinations was established. In the following thirteen centuries, Confucianism essentially became a stepping stone for one generation after another of clueless scholars to pursue a career in officialdom. Popular sayings in Chinese—"A mouth full of virtue and morality; a stomach full of burglary and concubinage," "hypocritical Confucian scholars"—are the result of observations that the words and deeds of Confucians did not match. Were the corrupt officials in Chinese history not also Confucians who had applied themselves wholeheartedly to reading the books of sages and worthies? A book like the *Anecdotal History of the Scholars* lets us see how many Confucians were lazy loiterers, yes-men, in search of petty gains.[57] In fact even great Confucians were not necessarily better. The colorful tittle-tattle about the great Zhu Xi's private life in unofficial historic records is not entirely unfounded.[58]

During the Japanese invasion of China, a great master of Confucianism, Wang Jitang (1877–1948), became one of three most notorious traitors serving the puppet North China Political Council (1940–43). A leading academician thoroughly acquainted with the classics, he cooperated with the Japanese in north China in the Strengthening Security Movement, which led to the slaughter and harassment of Chinese people opposed to Japanese rule. He also opened an Academy of Confucianism and ran training in Confucian studies for youngsters, using these as a means of turning the people into slaves. He was executed for treason in 1948. The former director of the Chinese Philosophy Research Centre of the Chinese Academy of Social Sciences, Zheng Jiadong, was famed for his study of Confucius and could probably be counted as a great Confucian of the present time, but in 2005 he was arrested for smuggling six women into the United States.[59] Some would argue that Zheng's crime had nothing to do with Confucianism. Perhaps, but the problem is how people can distinguish genuine Confucians from insincere Confucians.

If Jiang's criticism of moral Confucianism and politicized Confucianism is correct, if Confucianism has gone off the rails for a very long time, if many contemporary Confucians are hypocrites, then what reason do we have for believing that simply be reading the *Four Books* and *Five Classics* Confucians will be able to represent transcendent, sacred legitimacy? Will we have to sort our Confucians into true and false ones, as previously we had to distinguish true and false Marxists? Who is qualified to make this kind of assessment?

If undifferentiated Confucians are incapable of representing sacred legitimacy, can they represent historical, cultural legitimacy along with other elite persons? To answer this question, it is necessary to spell out the meaning of "historical culture." "Culture" is very difficult to define. Back in 1952 two researchers gathered 164 different definitions of culture.[60] Jiang's "historical-cultural" must refer to the historical-cultural tradition, that is, the total sum of the system of social values that are transmitted over time. If this is indeed his understanding, then this tradition must include the great tradition of what is recorded in the classics and transmitted by the social elite, and the little tradition formed by the daily life and oral tradition of the masses.[61] Here we do not need to worry about whether the great tradition determines the little one or vice versa. Yet we must acknowledge that both are alive and both change and evolve with the times. They are mutually interrelated. But Jiang would seem to tend to essentialize historical-cultural tradition, as if it were some "heavenly book" written a long time ago by the sages, whose code can be read only by Confucians and the cultural elite. If the historical-cultural tradition is a living synthesis of the great and little traditions, then ordinary people ought to have a say in interpreting it. It should not become the exclusive preserve of Confucians and the cultural elite.

In the above, I have addressed the desirability of what Jiang calls the Way of the Humane Authority; let us now turn to the practical aspects and ask if it is feasible.

Jiang states very clearly that if the Way of the Humane Authority or Confucian constitutionalism is to be realized in China, "at least three conditions must be met . . . : Firstly, there must be a complete revival in society of a Confucian-centered Chinese culture. Secondly, within the country there should be the spontaneous formation of a substantial body of scholars in China who keep to Confucian beliefs and practices. Thirdly, the way of Yao, Shun, Confucius, and Mencius must be added to the constitution." He also optimistically concludes, "It is not impossible that one day they should all be realized." Here it might be better to speak in terms of probability rather than possibility. Of course, no one can completely rule out the possibility that the three conditions will be met, but it would appear that the chances of Confucianism returning to its status as China's orthodoxy and becoming the Palace School again are fairly low. Daniel A. Bell observes that in China there is "hardly anybody really believes that Marxism should provide guidelines for thinking about China's political future."[62] If Bell is right, then the chances of Confucianism being the guiding principle of the country are even slimmer.

I have used the Baidu Index (http://index.baidu.com) to gather support for my view and show that it is not just my own personal opinion. The Baidu Index is a statistical tool for measuring the volumes of keyword searches, based on Baidu's web search statistics. It can show how much interest people have in certain keywords.[63] Figure 7.5a looks at to what extent Internet users are interested in three key terms: Confucian thought, liberalism, and Mao Zedong thought. It informs us that since 2006 Internet users are much more interested in Confucian thought than in liberalism. However, they are more interested in Mao Zedong thought than in Confucianism. This is reflected in the three curves that respectively indicate the number of searches on each keyword; the three lines are not in the same order of magnitude. Figure 7.5b is based on the names of three persons: Confucius, Hu Shi, and Mao Zedong. Clearly, there is no great difference between 7.5a and 7.5b. Hu Shi, the standard bearer of Chinese liberalism, is always in last place (if the name Li Shenzhi, another representative of Chinese liberalism, were used in place of that of Hu Shi, the line on the graph would be invisible). The venerable founder of Confucianism, Confucius is in second place, and Mao Zedong is in first place. Only at the beginning of 2010 did the search volume of "Confucius" abruptly soar; this was because a movie titled *Confucius* was released at that time and not because there was any fundamental change in direction. If Google Trends (http://www.google.cn/trends?hl=en), another tool for displaying search trends, were used to carry out the same kind of search, the results would be more or less the same. This shows that Confucianism has indeed enjoyed a restoration, but this does not mean that it will become the sole form of ideology. Hence, implementing the Way of the Humane Authority or Confucian constitutionalism is not a "realistic utopia," at least not yet.

CONCLUSION: CHINESE SOCIALIST DEMOCRACY

Jiang advocates elitism in politics, rule by sages, because he remains fundamentally opposed to equality for all. He thinks that "in practical morality the difference between people is very great. There are distinctions between sages and commoners, between gentlemen and small-minded person. Moreover these moral distinctions have significance in politics and government."[64] This implies that he has wholly accepted that "[o]nly the superior savants and inferior fools cannot be changed" (*Analects* 17.3), "[w]hile the people may be made to obey they cannot be made to understand" (*Analects* 8.9), and "[t]hose who work by their minds govern others; those who work by their strength are governed by others" (*Mencius* 3A:6). Probably no reasoning will be able to shake him from his obstinate belief in this matter.

Other supporters of Confucian politics have not necessarily gone as far as Jiang in their views. As an advocate of elite rule, Bai Tongdong, for instance, does not deny the equal capacity of sages and commoners to participate in politics. What he stresses is that most ordinary people (including

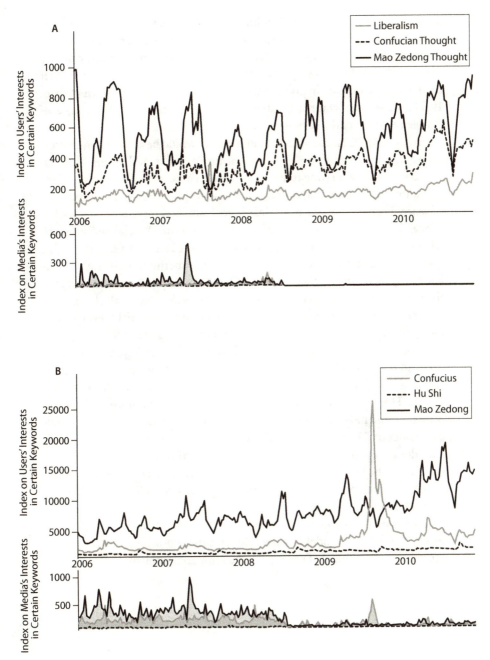

FIGURE 7.5. Popular Interest in Certain Keywords

most "petty bourgeoisie" or "middle class" such as white-collar workers, technicians, engineers, doctors, financial workers, teachers, and the like) simply lack the time, energy, interest, or ability to participate in running the state.[65] But if ordinary people do not have the chance to exercise their capacity to participate in politics, then there is no need to press for elitism. It is far more important to create the conditions under which the mass of people can in fact take part in politics.

In my view, "Chinese socialist democracy" would be a much better alternative than the Way of the Humane Authority, as it would lay institutional foundations for everyone to become equal to Yaos and Shuns (even Mencius admits, "All men may be Yaos and Shuns" [*Mencius* 6B:2]).[66] For want of space, I cannot elaborate my ideas here. I simply want to emphasize what I mean by the three terms of this expression. For me, "socialism" refers to what China has painstakingly developed over the last sixty years through a history of taking a step sometimes to the left, sometimes to the right.[67] It is a form of socialism that has been sought by global progressive forces over the past century or so.[68] "Democracy" is not merely what I call electocracy. Rather, it should be a new form of democracy that tries to enable everyone to take part in politics through sortition, deliberation, and modern electronic forms of communication and that extends popular participation from the political realm to other areas, including that of the economy.[69] More inclusive than Confucianism, "Chinese" refers to the Chinese civilization (not just the Han civilization) that is culturally rooted in a tradition of "unity in diversity" and never-ending self-revitalization. The goal of "Chinese socialist democracy" is to eventually achieve the great harmony instead of merely a moderately prosperous society. In fact, according to Jiang's own theory, the Way of the Humane Authority is not suitable for a harmonious world.

If we were to borrow Jiang's terminology, then "socialism" would be the way of heaven (sacred legitimacy), "democracy" the way of humanity (popular legitimacy), "Chinese" the way of earth (cultural and historical legitimacy). Would this model of threefold legitimacy not be a "more realistic utopia" than his model of the Way of the Humane Authority?

PART III

Response to the

Commentators

CHAPTER 8

Debating with My Critics

Jiang Qing

I n my book *Political Confucianism (Zhengzhi Ruxue)* I outlined the idea of the politics of the Way of the Humane Authority. Seven years later I have developed the plan of Confucian constitutionalism on the basis of the Way of the Humane Authority. The Way of the Humane Authority touches on the political ideas of the state, while constitutionalism deals with the setup of the state. My ideas have drawn interest and criticism at home and abroad, largely from the perspective of liberalism and the new Left.

From May 3 to May 5, 2010, Professors Fan Ruiping and Daniel A. Bell arranged a conference at the City University of Hong Kong on Confucian constitutionalism and the future of China. This was an opportunity for me to present my ideas and receive feedback. The criticisms of the liberals and new Left were serious, systematic, and well grounded. At the conference I replied orally. I later gathered the papers I have written over the years on this topic into a book called *Political Confucianism—A Sequel: The Way of the Humane Authority and Confucian Constitutionalism: Confucian Thought for China's Future Political Development (Zhengzhi ruxue: xupian: wangdao zhengzhi yu rujiao xianzheng: weilai Zhongguo zhengzhi fazhande ruxue sixiang)*. Professors Fan and Bell hope that this book can be published in English for an international audience, so that the world, especially observers of Chinese political Confucianism, will fully appreciate Confucianism. The editorial committee of the book has asked me to reply in writing to the criticisms made of my ideas. Here I address the criticisms presented in the essays by Joseph Chan, Bai Tongdong, Li Chenyang, and Wang Shaoguang. Since their thought largely reflects the position of liberalism, I have also replied in a systematic way to the whole system of values of liberal democracy. Moreover, given that liberalism and the new Left are the dominant trends in scholarship in China today, it is also an opportunity for me to present the response of China's Confucianism to these trends. The reader will be the judge of the reasonableness of my replies. Alas! What is today called "response" was termed "debate" in the old times. I can do nothing else but debate! Mencius had no choice but to debate; Xunzi said that the gentleman must debate. Coming after these two masters, I also have no choice but to debate. Below are my replies to the criticism of the Way of the Humane Authority and Confucian constitutionalism advanced by liberalism and the new Left.

REPLY TO JOSEPH CHAN'S CRITICISM OF CONFUCIAN CONSTITUTIONALISM: A WHOLESALE PROMOTION OF CONFUCIANISM IS NOT HARMFUL TO CIVILITY

In his essay "On the Legitimacy of Confucian Constitutionalism," Professor Joseph Chan has made a systematic criticism of Confucian constitutionalism. Professor Chan allies himself with perfectionism rather than liberalism, but the foundations of his thought are still those of liberalism, especially the political liberalism of Rawls. In my reply to him, I therefore initially address the issue of political liberalism.

The Alleged Pluralist Society of Political Liberalism

Along with other liberals, including even recent New Confucians, Professor Chan thinks that Confucianism need not be restricted to a purely critical role in society. It should, rather, take part by playing a political role, "point to a direction of change, or better still, an alternative to the object being criticized, be it a value, a policy, or an institution." This participation will be, in Chan's words, as follows: "to positively shape political institutions, legislation, and policy making. In a sense, this can be regarded as a version of 'Confucian constitution.'" From this statement we can see that Professor Chan does indeed view Confucianism as a positive force for politics. In this he differs greatly from the modern roaming spirits, who view it as merely serving a critical role. He acknowledges that Confucianism has a certain positive value in positively influencing politics in contemporary society. Given that he is someone who has been heavily steeped in political liberalism, it is particularly remarkable that he has such a positive assessment of Confucianism. This is what makes me appreciate him.

Professor Chan identifies two ways or two kinds of constitutionalism, in which Confucianism can contribute to legislation and policy making: the promotion of Confucian values in an extreme and a moderate form of perfectionism. The former is characterized as "the state should adopt a comprehensive doctrine of the good life as the basis of state constitution, legislation, and policy" and "rank those goods into a certain hierarchy." The characteristic of the latter is, "the state may appeal only to specific judgments about the good life, not comprehensive doctrines." According to Chan's standard, Confucian constitutionalism is a form of extreme perfectionism, while his own preference is for a moderate version. Chan makes the distinction between these two forms, not for its own sake but in order to reject the extreme version.

He lists five features of extreme political perfectionism:

1. A comprehensive doctrine of "the good life that involves systematic theorization about human life" and "explains why certain things are good to human life";
2. It "ranks those goods into a certain hierarchy";
3. It "[specifies] concrete ways to realize those goods";
4. It "promotes Confucianism as a comprehensive doctrine of the good"; and
5. "The state takes the comprehensive doctrine of Confucianism as the basis for legislation and policy-making."

Chan rejects this version of Confucianism, since it would harm civility. He argues that in a pluralist society, ways of living, ideas about life, and religious views are not uniform, and so society is obliged to seek those values, about which there is consensus, so as to reduce differences of opinion over morality. When consensus is impossible, then each side must withdraw or else there will be conflict and civility will be upset.

Yet it is worth asking if wholesale Confucian values would really lead to social conflict and harm civility. In my view, they would not do so. Below I prove the point from both theory and history.

Leaving aside Chan's support for Rawls's political liberalism for a moment, we can say that any society must have a comprehensive, systematic, leading orthodoxy to direct its values for the betterment of human life and social order. On the basis of this set of values society can arrive at a basic consensus and maintain social stability and harmony.

We know that by nature human beings tend to want to be autonomous, their own masters, respecting themselves alone, having laws unto themselves, and even holding themselves to be holy. Thus, in the matter of human and social betterment, in moral beliefs and philosophical thought, people also exhibit these same tendencies. This is the self-centeredness of humanity. It is reflected in society, as can be seen in the anarchism reflected in the ancient Chinese sayings: each person has his or her own reason, ten persons ten reasons, even a hundred persons a hundred reasons. This form of anarchism in which social values are divided pluralistically will inevitably lead to society as a whole becoming one of moral relativism in which each person is a law unto himself or herself. When this moral relativism develops to an extreme, it inevitably leads to a negation of all values: social anarchy results in moral anarchy. Thus, moral relativism can lead only to unending conflict of values. In a morally anarchic society, the interests and evil desires of people will lack any restraint from orthodox, guiding values and society will lapse into the most primitive eternal conflict of interests.

To prevent this degradation into moral anarchy, any human society must establish one comprehensive, systematic, leading, orthodox set of values for human and social betterment and by means of these values bring society to basic consensus and overcome moral relativism and moral anarchy, and the eternal social conflict they entail. Only in this way can the most basic stability of society be maintained. Its complete collapse is not impossible. Hence, such a set of comprehensive values will not harm civility, it will lead to the exact opposite. A society grounded on these comprehensive values can overcome conflict and lay the basis for the long-term stability of civic harmony.

However, having said that, there is a basic practical condition for a given comprehensive set of values to ensure civility, namely that it is internally harmonious, before it can overcome external conflict. Comprehensive values such as those of social Darwinism (nationalist values), class struggle (Soviet values), or maximization of profit (capitalism) can lead only to social conflict. On the contrary, Confucianism is a comprehensive system of values that is harmonious and can protect, rather than destroy, civility.

Professor Chan thinks that it is not possible to promote Confucian values as a comprehensive doctrine. The fundamental reason for this view of his is that of Rawls's political liberalism. But Rawls's political liberalism is hypocritical. Although Rawls believes that his theory of justice is founded on the overlapping consensus of Western liberal-democratic society, in matters of religious belief, values, and political thought, Western liberal-democratic society is not a completely level playing field of pluralist equality but one in which, in these areas, there is one dominant thread that rules over a plurality.

In Rawls's own America there is freedom of religious belief, values, and political thought, but only at the level of the individual person. At the level of the state and in the public domain, it is not so. We know that since modern times it has been the state that has ruled over society, and to do this the state must establish a comprehensive, systematic, leading orthodoxy to govern the values for human and social betterment and guarantee stability. In the United States it is specified that there is to be no national religion. Nonetheless, the orthodox belief remains Protestantism. The leading values in society come from a Protestant value system, and the directing thought in politics is based on constitutional democracy, which comes from the natural theism of Protestant Christianity. This appears mainly in the Constitution. These Protestant religious beliefs, values, and political thought form the comprehensive system of values that regulates American society. Robert N. Bellah held that in the United States there was a common national state religion, which he called its "civil religion."[1] As I see it, in America this civil religion is Protestantism. While it is true that there are many religions in America, including Judaism, Catholicism, and innumerable Protestant denominations and even some non-Western religions, the mainstream political concepts are the values of Protestant Christianity. Values of other Christian denominations and non-Western religions may be freely believed in but only at the individual level. They are not the leading belief of the state. Still less are they established in the Constitution as its political principles.

So in the United States individuals enjoy freedom of belief, values, and political thought, but the rule of the state over society can be comprehensively based only on the values of human and social betterment of Protestant Christianity. In this matter there is no freedom to speak of because the Protestant values are already written into the Constitution as its founding principles and supreme political norms. In terms of values and of the setup of the state there is only one comprehensive system with power to direct and enforce itself. The United States could not choose Islamic, Hindu, or Confucian religions, values, or political ideas as its civil religion, that is, for its mainstream values or constitutional principles. It is precisely for this reason that we can say the one rule that dominates the American social scene is that of Protestantism. It is the official doctrine. Other religions or religious denominations or political ideas are the pluralism of American society, where there is freedom and the hundred schools, or better the individual schools, contend. In other words American society in terms of religion, values, and politics is not one in which there is a perfectly level playing field of equal pluralism, but one in which one form of religion, values, and political ideas rules over the plurality in a hierarchical way.

Here we must again stress the point that in a democratic, pluralist society Professor Chan thinks that we should promote moderate perfectionism. Yet if we look at the history and state of democracy in America, or even in the whole of the West, we find that democracy is based on what Professor Chan calls a "comprehensive doctrine" because the democratic idea of sovereignty lying with the people is itself a system of political legitimacy and a comprehensive metaphysical system. It is also the systematic and comprehensive orthodox political basis for Western democratic political power and authority to rule.

Furthermore, in democratic pluralist societies, freedom, rights, and equality are not adopted in a specific or piecemeal fashion, as Professor

Chan contends, but are treated like sovereignty of the people as a systematic and comprehensive system of thought. Western democratic countries do not adopt metaphysical ideas such as freedom, rights, and equality in a specific or piecemeal fashion but use them as a comprehensive foundation for political legitimacy. Rawls's political liberalism may believe that Western democratic societies should exercise value impartiality in the way they rule, but in reality they have a comprehensive value system that plays a leading role in enforcing the official doctrine of the constitution. Democratic values in a Western society are not on an equal footing with other values, hence Rawls's theory of a pluralism does not match the reality of the pluralism in Western countries. It is in this sense that his theory is hypocritical. Not that he is morally hypocritical, but the theory and practice do not match. What is surprising is that Professor Chan is hampered by Rawls's theory of political liberal democracy and so fails to see that the promotion and realization of free democratic values in Western democratic pluralist society is comprehensive and systematic. Still less is he able to see that those values play the leading, orthodox, guiding, dominant constitutional role of the one rule and the official doctrine. Instead, he thinks that it is not necessary to promote Confucian values in China comprehensively. This surely cannot but leave one amazed.

Complete Confucianization and Civility

The central point of Professor Chan's essay is to differentiate between complete and moderate versions of Confucianism and to reject the former. He bases his arguments on the existence in a pluralist society of many rational values that are equal in nature and different and so cannot be subsumed under one umbrella. An attempt to enforce such a complete synthesis of values would lead to serious conflict between them.

Above, we have already noted that Western pluralist society, both historically and in practice, works under the umbrella of liberal-democratic values, which are not accepted in a specific or piecemeal fashion. In Confucian terms, Western society is one of one rule with many elements under it. The one rule is that of the official liberal-democratic values. Other values that are not those of liberal democracy are allowed to add their own voices under this one rule, but this does no harm to civility. Hence, the complete propagation of any integral set of values does not necessarily harm civility, so there is no reason to object to the complete propagation of Confucianism in China as detrimental to civility.

In the United States or in the West the subordinate values are in harmony under certain conditions. They must accept liberal democracy and not undermine its predominant status, that is, they cannot attain constitutional status as the ruling, orthodox, guiding, dominant, official political doctrine. For instance, in the United States and in the West, Islamic values or other religious values may not change the values of liberal democracy and become the official values of the state. If they were to do so, there would be no pluralism to speak of and no harmony since Islamic values or other religious values would strictly prohibit the propagation of liberal-democratic values. If the West is thus allowed to take liberal democracy as its ruling set of values, why should China not be allowed to do the same with Confucianism? Why should liberal-democratic values be allowed full development and not those of the Way of the Humane Authority? Or could it be that the widespread propagation of Western democratic values is being used as a cover for increasing domination by Western values? Could it be just another sign of the hypocrisy of the West? The West perhaps judges it inopportune to freely admit that it seeks to spread its liberal democracy over China as well. Could it be that it wishes for specific and piecemeal adoption of Confucian values in order to allow it to spread its own liberal democracy as the comprehensive umbrella over all? We cannot say more about this, except to ask Professor Chan to think harder over the matter.

Since the Reformation, many Protestant denominations have emerged, and each has its own way of interpreting the Bible and its own ceremonies. Yet these divisions in the church cannot change the historical fact that, in the broad context of civilization and religion, there is but one Christian society and one Christian politics. In the face of the development of different denominations and the conflict or war between them, today's Western philosophers have proposed the idea of religious tolerance and freedom of conscience and, on this basis, have established a constitutional freedom of belief, namely, the constitutional separation of church and state, thus resolving political chaos in society brought about by the many denominations. The separation implied here is simply said with regard to certain particular Christian denominations.

There is no separation between politics and Christianity as such, since it is still Christian values that are the accepted religion in politics (especially Protestantism). It is just that, in politics, the West rationalizes Protestant values into a universal philosophical principle—this is especially true of Locke's philosophical principles. On the basis of this universal philosophical principle, a universal political-legal framework has been established to guarantee the concrete implementation and organizational realization of Protestant values such as liberty, democracy, and equality. In other words, the way the West resolves the diversification of denominations is by the integral transformation of substantive religious values into an integral formal, public rational system, on the basis of which a comprehensive constitutional legal framework is erected. By virtue of this transformation, the one rule over the many is achieved in the West. In other words, there is tolerance for the many under the governance of the liberal-democratic values of Protestant philosophy and their constitutional status.

However, this one rule over many is not, unlike what Western liberals believe, an ideal society or the highest model of politics. In my view a serious problem exists. The rational form in which liberal-democratic values are promoted has led to an erosion of religious, moral values and to a valuing of relativism, even nihilism. This is the reason why American scholars have criticized liberal democracy for bringing about an absence of values, an empty civic space.[2] We know that in the matter of values there must necessarily be distinctions between the dominant and subordinate, high and low, specific and comprehensive, great and small, strong and weak. This factual background to our discussion of values cannot be avoided. Moreover, these distinctions are significant not only for individuals in a society; they are also significant publicly in politics. Political power and the political setup must support and realize the high, strong values as the leading, orthodox, comprehensive, and guiding values of the state. If public rationality in democracy and in the constitution undoes these distinctions, then this amounts to undoing values themselves, since the hierarchy is a necessary part of what values are, and an unraveling of that hierarchy can result only in value relativism and value nihilism.

Although in the West liberal-democratic theory and the constitutional framework ensure a basic minimum level of tolerance in society, they do so by paying the price of a devaluation in the political sphere, such that politics becomes a valueless blank screen. This is the fundamental reason why MacIntyre and Strauss criticize liberalism.[3] The curious thing is that while the West promotes a thorough spread of liberal-democratic values, this leads to a politics with no values at all. The cause lies not in the method of propagation, whether it be complete or moderate, but in that essentially liberal-democratic values are a formal form of Protestant values, that is, a value of no values, based on reason, autonomy, enlightenment, equality, and pluralism. It itself is the source of value nihilism, and so it leads to the wholesale promotion of the value of having no values in the realm of politics, leading, inevitably, to a political absence of values or a politics with no values. For this reason we cannot entirely stand in the place of liberalism if we want to criticize Confucian constitutionalism because liberalism itself is problematic. While Professor Chan is sympathetic to Confucianism, his basic political standpoint is still that of liberalism.

The comprehensive one rule of the formal public rationality used in the

West to deal with social conflicts at the level of plurality is a historical fact in recent Western history. Its classic example is also, therefore, suited to the West. It is a specific product of Western history and culture and lacks any universality. It is thus inappropriate in China. There is a big difference between the one rule and plural diversity in Chinese and Western society. The Chinese model accomplishes tolerance for plurality and harmony among the masses in a different way. I describe the Chinese model as one of "practical leading values." This model does not need to seek formal universality or public rationality. It has one substantive leading value but does not reject the existence of other substantive values provided they are not the leading ones. It tolerates, and coexists with, the latter such that there will be no serious conflict between the leading and nonleading values. In this way, stability and harmony are upheld in society.

However, there must be clear lines drawn between leading and nonleading values. The former are the official teaching and have public significance in politics; the latter are confined to the private thoughts of individuals in society. The lot apportioned to each is different, and so there can be no confusion. If the nonleading values are elevated to the status of the official leading values, then this implies the distinction is not respected and confusion will result, and there will no longer be a plurality existing under the one rule. The erosion of the distinction will result in the plurality in society leading to very serious conflict affecting the stability and harmony of society.

In Chinese history, the promotion of Confucianism is the one rule of a substantial leading value under which the plurality can exist. We know that the promotion of Confucianism means to elevate it to become the substantial leading value, the official doctrine of public significance, but the "rejection of the hundred schools" does not mean a prohibition on their existence or transmission but a prohibition on their becoming of equal status with the official substantive leading values, that is on becoming the official doctrine. The hundred schools may exist only within their own remit as the values of individuals in society and not as the public political doctrine. However, they can freely exist, be believed in, and be transmitted in society.

Throughout Chinese history Confucianism has held the leading position, but over the past two thousand years Confucianism, Buddhism, and Daoism have been able to coexist in Chinese society. True, there may have been a few isolated political conflicts, yet it has never come about, as Professor Chan fears, that the promotion of Confucian values as a comprehensive doctrine has led to society necessarily becoming disharmonious. The reason is that Buddhism and Daoism have never sought to go beyond their limits and challenge the leading role of Confucianism. They have been happy to remain as private values with their own subordinate status. Hence, the public, leading values and the private, nonleading values have never been engaged in a struggle for survival of one against the other. Still less could there be any religious wars because the various kinds of values can happily coexist for a very long time. There could never be upheavals and divisions in society as a result of religious conflicts as in traditional Western society.

We may take the example of the erection of statues of Confucius in state universities in China today. Many campuses of state universities have erected such statues recently. Since these universities are government universities, the erection of these statues is an act of public conduct and of public political significance. But we find that Chinese Buddhists, Daoists, and Christians are not opposed to these acts, unlike in Singapore, where the foundation of Confucian classes was stopped following opposition from other religions. The reason is because in China the non-Confucians are very clear in their minds that Confucianism is a public value with political significance, while their own beliefs are purely the private values of individuals in society. It is only natural that Confucian values should enter into the public political domain and be of educational significance for all citizens while the private values of one's own belief do not enjoy this status. Hence, non-Confucian believers can accept the erection of these statues.

It is possible to erect a statue of Confucius in a public university in China without provoking any contention, but we can imagine that if a public university attempted to erect a statue of Jesus or the Buddha this would give rise to contention because the values of Christianity and Buddhism are only private and not official in China. In other countries Christianity and Buddhism could be the official doctrine, as is the case for Christianity in the United Kingdom, Finland, and Greece and for Buddhism in Thailand. Since Christian values and Buddhist values have no public, political significance in China, they cannot enter into the public political domain and be of educational significance for all the citizens. But this does not prevent them from being taught in theologates and Buddhist centers in China. It is perfectly possible to erect a statue of Jesus in a theologate or one of the Buddha in a Buddhist college because these places are ones of educational significance for private beliefs. This shows that in any society it is simply required that each set of values finds its own place as a private doctrine that does not play a leading role and that respects the official doctrine formed over history and does not challenge it. Not only can the leading and nonleading values find their place in society in harmony, but many other kinds of nonleading values can also realize their specific value. The result will be a society with an orthodox ruling set of values and a tolerance of many private values.

Professor Chan is concerned that the realization of my Confucian constitutional order will have dire consequences. He writes, "constitutional order be grounded on the worldview of Confucianism" would imply "a total rejection of liberalism, socialism, Buddhism, or Christianity as possible grounds for the constitutional order." In fact he need not be so afraid. If my Confucian constitutionalism were really realized, I think that liberalism, socialism, Buddhism, and Christianity would all find their place as private doctrines among Chinese citizens who could freely believe and transmit their values. It is just that they could not challenge the official doctrine of Confucianism.

In China Confucianism has been the official doctrine and must remain to be so today. This is not the mere opinion of a few individuals. It is the requirement for the essential particularity and historical continuity of Chinese culture or Chinese civilization. Over the past hundred years, liberal democracy has sought to overthrow Confucianism and make itself China's official doctrine. Even though Professor Chan would appear to be sympathetic to Confucianism, he is guilty of using a new version of pluralist theory to overthrow the role of Confucianism as the official doctrine. In this he is in fact no different from the old liberals who wanted to replace Confucianism by liberal democracy. It is just that their aim was clearly stated as such, while the new liberals influenced by Rawls use complicated and hidden tactics to seek the same goal.

Joseph Chan's Confucian Constitutionalism

Professor Chan describes my Confucian constitutionalism as promoting Confucianism as a comprehensive doctrine. He dislikes its comprehensiveness and proposes his own version instead, which he describes as being moderately perfectionist. He favors a specific and piecemeal approach, by which Confucian values could be chosen in legislation and policy making. This is what he calls Confucian constitution.

In my opinion the selective adoption of certain Confucian features in legislation and policy making cannot be called Confucian constitution. We know that a constitution is not only a matter of limiting power. It is, more importantly, an affirmation of values and concepts, which is systematic and legitimizing. A piecemeal selective approach could only mean a utilitarian choice of Confucian values, as circumstances require. It would lack a systematic exposition of values or concepts. Hence, a piecemeal approach can never justify the name Confucian constitution. Only a systematic adoption of Confucian values and concepts can justify the name Confucian constitution.

The reason why Western liberal democracy is called "constitution" is because there is a complete and comprehensive set of values and concepts, which systematically serves as the basis to guarantee legitimacy. This complete set of values and concepts is "sovereignty lies with the people," "social contract theory," "natural human rights," "representative government," "parliamentary sovereignty," "civil society," "civic participation theory," and the like. If there were only a piecemeal selection of aspects of liberal democracy for use in legislation and policy making, as Professor Chan suggests, rather than the systematic adoption of these notions, then there would be no democratic constitution. We can see that there are countries, castigated by the West as nondemocratic, that do indeed have elections, parliaments, constitutions, and to a certain extent democracy and human rights.

To count as Confucian, a constitution must adopt a thorough system of Confucian values, and that is what the Way of the Humane Authority is. The selective adoption of certain features does not affect the overall constitution, as when the United States passed a House resolution in honor of Confucius's birthday and paid selective respect to some Confucian values, or when an authoritarian regime selectively adopts some Confucian features as Chiang Kai-shek did in China and Taiwan. But can this selective use on occasions and the refusal to adopt a full-blooded system really be termed Confucian constitution? Does Professor Chan not see that China's current socialism with Chinese characteristics selectively adopts the values of a moderate Confucianism? Does it not also selectively adopt certain Confucian values such as "harmony" as the basis for government policy? According to Professor Chan's criteria, China is already a Confucian constitutionalist state! I do not know if the Chinese socialist Confucian constitution is the liberal Confucian constitutionalist state Chan envisions. I also wonder what the difference between the socialist and the liberal versions is.

From the above it is clear that any political body can selectively adopt certain Confucian values to help in its formulation of policy, but this fact does not alter the basic nature of the body politic as such. If, as Chan proposes, a democracy adopts benevolence, practical wisdom, and courage—which Chan describes as the three necessary virtues for human living—to help in its formulation of policy, this does not alter its still being a democratic polity. Likewise, if an authoritarian polity adopted these same values, it would still be an authoritarian polity. The nature of the polity is decided by its comprehensive system of values and concepts and not by its selective adoption of some other values. A democratic regime is defined by its democratic system, an authoritarian one by its authoritarian system and a Confucian one by the Way of the Humane Authority.

The definition of a system as Confucian is not defined by its piecemeal selection of Confucian values but by its systematic, wholesale adoption of those values. This is a fundamental requirement of Confucian constitution. Hence Professor Chan's Confucian constitution is not what its name claims to be. It is democratic constitution with a Confucian nameplate. The basic system defines it as democratic and not the selective adoption of Confucian values.

Promotion of Confucianism and Ideology as a Comprehensive Doctrine

Professor Chan holds that comprehensive doctrines are often tied "to a tradition of thought" and that "Confucianism began life more than twenty-five hundred years ago." Hence he concludes that Confucian thought is both comprehensive and traditional in nature. He also holds that "promoting Confucianism as a comprehensive doctrine is a kind of ideological politics that has to be rejected if we regard civility as an important virtue." The problem here is to determine if Confucianism is an ideology or not and then to ask if its wholesale propagation will harm civility.

I agree that Confucianism is a comprehensive traditional system of thought, in which there is a transcendent, sacred metaphysics of the way of heaven, but comprehensive theory or systematic metaphysics should not be equated with an ideology. We know that being comprehensive and being systematic are features of all traditional thought, but this does not make something an ideology. Whatever meaning is given to "ideology," the basic idea comes from political modernity and refers to the systematic body of concepts posited by modern Western rationalist philosophers. Hence, the basic nature of an ideological politics is not as Shils says "obsessed with totality" but a rational thing that is closed and exclusive. Being comprehensive is not the hallmark of an ideology. Rather, it is its being a closed and exclusive rationalism that is its defining feature.

Before the modern era there were many systems of traditional thought, but these were not ideologies. Ideologies arise with the modern Western "-isms": racism, liberalism, democracy, socialism, capitalism, nationalism, and totalitarianism of either Left or Right. These -isms went on to influence the whole world. Thus, we cannot say that traditional Chinese Confucianism was an ideology, just as we cannot say the same of traditional theology in the West or traditional Islamic legal studies in Muslim countries. It is true, however, that these traditional ways of thinking do have a certain strong tendency to being comprehensive.

Furthermore, for the most part traditional thought is based on a religious sacred or transcendent foundation, which is experienced or grasped by the human soul. Traditional thought is the appearance in human history of an ultimate origin of sacred transcendence and eternal truth, even though different traditions have different ways of understanding this. Ideology, on the other hand, is the conceptual creation by the special talent of the individualistic extreme secularism of modern Western philosophers and bears no relationship whatsoever to sacred transcendence or eternal truth. It is simply an empty distinction—to use Buddhist terminology—created by these individual philosophers.

Finally, traditional thought is always tolerant and open. Confucian thought tolerated Daoist thought and Buddhist thought. Christian thought tolerated Judaic thought and Greek thought. Islamic thought also tolerated Judaic thought and Greek thought. Traditional thought is thus tolerant of other thoughts and open to absorbing their thought, unlike ideological -isms, which are firmly based on a rational spirit of being closed and exclusive, because the nature of reason lies in the principle of noncontradiction and either x or y.

Hence, Confucianism shares with other traditional systems of thought a comprehensive nature, but that does not prevent it being tolerant and open. It lacks the closed exclusiveness of rational ideologies. This is because Confucianism is not grounded in political modernity, which is ideology based on rational philosophy. It is grounded, rather, on the way of heaven. Promoting Confucianism as a comprehensive doctrine is, then, not like the spread of an ideology and will cause no harm to civility. Instead, Confucianism is a tolerant political tradition that respects social harmony. It is a politics of royal transformation and not of an ideology. For instance, my own Confucian constitutionalism includes a tricameral parliament and an Academy that supervises the state and that thereby absorbs some elements of parliamentary democracy and constitutional balance. My system is not, as Chan alleges, in outright opposition to Western democracy. The difference between the Way of the Humane Authority and ideological politics is that between political traditionalism and political modernity, or between Confucian politics and ideological politics. I hope Professor Chan will be able to understand this correctly.

The Way Is among Human Beings and the People Who Grasp the Way

Professor Chan holds that it is a principle of Confucian thought that "the human embodies the Way," that is, that it exists among the masses as the will of the people. As a result, he is opposed to my Confucian constitution placing the people outside the way of heaven. He thinks that it is contrary to Confucianism to select one group of persons as those who grasp the Way, as in my scheme.

It is correct to say that in Confucianism the Way is among human beings, but Confucianism draws a clear distinction between the way in which the Way exists and the state of human existence. The Way, in Confucianism, is the way of heaven, and is the source of the way of humanity. As the way of heaven, the Way is ultimate existence and does not exist among human beings. The Way, in this sense, is not in the will of the people. This is because, in Confucianism, the Way is absolute, external, transcendent, sacred, ultimate existence. This is what the Confucian classics, the *Book of Odes*, the *Book of Historical Documents*, the *Record of Rites*, and the *Spring and Autumn Annals*, refer to as August heaven and God or the way of heaven—the two names refer to the same thing. Precisely because this Way exists outside the will of the people, the *Book of Historical Documents* says, "The way of Heaven is to bless the good and publish the bad."[4] Or the *Book of Odes* says, "Great Heaven, unkind, Is sending down this great miseries";[5] or again, "How vast is God, The ruler of men below."[6] And the *Spring and Autumn Annals* uses the theory of disasters and portents to refer to how heaven can judge human affairs by rewarding the good and punishing the evil. This all goes to show that the Way of Confucianism is not among the people as Professor Chan believes.

Confucianism also holds that there are people in whom the Way becomes present, resulting in distinctions between wise and foolish, worthy and unworthy, that is, between sages and commoners, gentlemen and small men. The life of the wise sages and worthies derives purely from the principle of heaven. They are heaven's wooden bell mallet (*Analects* 3.24). Heaven does not speak, but they can speak on heaven's behalf and can experience and grasp and speak about the way of heaven. The life of the foolish people is full of human desires, and they cannot grasp the way of heaven. It may be that at times their senses, speech, and action happen to accord with the way of heaven, but this is only accidental, for their own hearts are normally veiled in obscurity, and so if their conduct is in accord with the way of heaven they themselves do not realize it, and so in politics they can but yield to the guidance of others.

It is for this reason that Confucius thought that the positions of wise and foolish could not be exchanged, and so he proposed the politics of the sage kings of the three dynasties. Mencius thought that only those who labor with their minds can know heaven and hence be qualified to rule, while those who labor by the strength of their hands cannot know heaven. Or again, Dong Zhongshu bluntly says that the people are ignorant, that they do not know the way of heaven. So for Confucianism only the sages, worthies, and gentlemen can experience and grasp the way of heaven and become people who grasp the way, to use Professor Chan's expression.

Commoners and small people cannot become people who grasp the way.

Moreover, Confucianism has a political dimension. Even Moral Confucianism recognizes that Confucians can discuss politics. Here Confucianism believes that the Way of the Humane Authority is hierarchical in nature. It is a rule by sage kings or by sages or by scholar-officials and not an egalitarian politics of the masses or democracy or politics of the common people. The political aspect of this grasp of the way of heaven can be embodied only by the sage kings, sages, or scholar-officials directly ruling in person.[7] It is also embodied in the basic nature of the state in the royal rule of the sage kings, the rule by rites of the sages, and the appointment and examination system for scholar-officials—these being the three ways in which the ideal has been put into practice at different stages of history.

The priority given to those who grasp the way is expressed in my Confucian constitutionalism by the priority assigned to the House of *Ru* and to the Academy. The result is the traditional political privilege by which people who know heaven and work with their minds rule others.

I am quite well aware that this privileged Confucian hierarchy is something that democratic liberals are most opposed to because it smacks of a substantive religious and ethical politics. As a democratic liberal, Chan is forcefully opposed to this political attitude. I quite appreciate that, but my idea of the relationship between the Way and the people is not a departure from Confucianism, as he suggests. Indeed, it is the exact opposite. It is what truly embodies the one thread running through the rule of the sage kings, of the sages, and of the scholar-officials.

Ranking Confucian Values

One reason that Professor Chan has for opposing the extreme perfectionism involved in the promotion of Confucian values is that this will lead to "explain why certain things are good to human life, rank those goods into a certain hierarchy, specify concrete ways to realize those goods." Therefore, he suggests, "as a normative basis of political action [Confucianism] should present a noncomprehensive conception of the good life that contains only specific judgments about virtues and desirable goods, without trying to rank them into a hierarchy." Professor Chan's own thought is in practice based on the political leveling of values of liberalism, which is itself a denial of Confucian politics.

We know that Confucian learning is the learning of the sages and the way of Confucianism is the way of the sages. Confucianism, then, makes a distinction between high and low values in its plan for human improvement. It categorizes people according to their type in the hierarchy described by

Zhou Dunru as "scholar-officials are below worthies, who are below sages, who are below heaven." Below the scholar-officials are the people (commoners and foolish people). Confucianism recognizes the four classes of sages, worthies, scholar-officials, and the people because the experience and grasp of each rank is different. The difference is not one of equality but of hierarchy. Higher ranks experience and grasp higher level values. This ranking is not only a practical reality in society. It also reflects the ranking of values. If all values were equal and there were no hierarchy of values, then there would be no values to speak of because without it we would not know how to choose when faced with pursuing different values or when values themselves conflict.

Confucianism believes that the difference in rank of values is not only of religious or moral significance, it is also of political significance in matters of direction and setup. This is what Professor Chan refers to as "specify concrete ways to realize those goods." In accordance with the distribution of power in the Way of the Humane Authority by which those with the Way receive more and those with the Way have all under heaven—the Way is what we today call "values"—greater ruling power is granted to those who have a grasp of higher values than to those who have a grasp of lesser values. Sages should receive more power than worthies, who receive more than scholar-officials. The same tendency should also be protected in the structure of the state so as to ensure that those with a grasp of higher values inevitably enjoy more power. In ancient China this protection was given by royal rule, in the later period by rule by the rites and by examination and appointment, and in the present time by my Confucian constitutionalism.

My opinion is the exact opposite of Professor Chan's. The spread of Confucian values must promote the values of human betterment, and so the values must be ranked and a method of realizing this ranking must be established. In today's China that means this hierarchy of values must be implemented in Confucian constitutionalism.

Possible Flaws in Confucianism

Professor Chan has one further cause to criticize promoting Confucianism as a comprehensive doctrine. He says, "[T]here is no reason to consider Confucianism as completely correct." This is because "given all the great minds in history around the world, there has never been anyone whose thoughts have not been questioned and criticized. No matter how brilliant Confucian scholars in the past might have been, their thoughts could not have been flawless." On account of these possible flaws, Chan thinks that one cannot promote Confucianism as a comprehensive doctrine lest these flaws harm civility. He gives the example of filial piety as one of the flaws.

Here Chan fails to see that there is a distinction in level to be made between the orthodox, systematic, comprehensive, guiding leading social thought and theory and partial, particular, piecemeal flaws. As Chan notes, there is indeed no flawless orthodoxy without partial flaws that lies beyond criticism. This holds for Confucianism. The same applies to any society. In fact over the past two thousand years Confucian thought and theory have had certain partial flaws and so have been criticized by Confucians and non-Confucians alike, with the result that Confucianism has been forced to correct its mistakes and improve. But these partial flaws do not affect the orthodox status of Confucianism in Chinese society, or else it would not be Confucianism. The flaws of Western liberal democracy do not prevent its remaining the leading thought. Indeed, the presence of these partial flaws leads the orthodoxy to improve itself and strengthen its hold on society.

In the course of history Confucian and non-Confucian criticism has not altered the fundamental nature of Confucianism as such, and so these partial flaws are no obstacle to its wholesale promotion. Therefore, we can clearly state that today there may be partial flaws in Confucianism, but these do not influence our wholesale propagation of Confucianism today. Our propagation today is of the essence of Confucianism and its basic spirit and not of some partial flaws, which do not represent this essence or basic spirit.

Furthermore, here we come up against the question as to how to understand the flaws of Confucianism. Different schools of thought will point out different flaws. Professor Chan is a liberal and relies on enlightenment thought and so judges the obedience of children to their parents in filial piety as a manifest flaw. Obedience of children to parents runs counter to the basic principle of liberalism and enlightenment thought: personal autonomy and rational obedience. Today we cannot accept filial piety, still less accept promoting Confucianism as a comprehensive doctrine that includes filial piety. But from a Confucian perspective, the filial piety of children's obedience to their parents is not only not a flaw, it is a basic principle of Confucianism.

Since Chan misunderstands filial piety, it is necessary to give a simple explanation of it here. There are five aspects of filial piety in Confucianism: serving parents with piety, running the state with piety, respecting spirits with piety, sacrificing to sages with piety, and treating things with piety. These five aspects touch on piety in the family, in society and politics, in religion, in the culture of the sages, and in ecology.[8] The five have an organic relationship that together, or rather comprehensively, embodies the basic nature and spirit of Confucianism. To deny these ways of piety, or any one of them, is to deny the basic nature and spirit of Confucianism, which amounts to denying Confucianism itself. Yet Chan's filial piety refers only to the obedience of children at the level of the family. Chan is well aware that children's obedience to their parents is conditional in Confucianism, but he deliberately takes the part for the whole and stresses that filial piety is a matter of children's obedience to their parents.[9] This sort of understanding runs contrary to the real meaning of Confucian filial piety.

As a result, at this time of a Confucian revival it is necessary to engage in promoting Confucianism as a comprehensive doctrine, which will include promotion of filial piety. This is a matter of life or death for Confucianism and is something on which no ground may be ceded. We must destroy the demonization of Confucianism of May Fourth. The complete overturning of tradition of May Fourth started with an attack on filial piety, an attack that was fiercer than any other in Confucian history, except that of the so-called authoritarianism.

Even if Confucianism today still has some partial, particular, and piecemeal flaws, this does not prevent it from being promoted as a comprehensive doctrine. However, what those flaws are is for Confucianism itself to point out. One may not use liberal-democratic thought to judge because it will only use its own logic to judge the basic principles and positive values of Confucianism as flaws.

CONCLUSION

I have thus replied to Professor Chan's criticism in the above seven points. As a result, my conclusion is the exact opposite of his. At a time when Confucianism is reviving, it is not right to adopt a moderate or piecemeal approach. What we must do is to promote Confucianism as a comprehensive doctrine. In summing up the above seven points, there are a further three that call for special emphasis.

Firstly, Confucian values are not like other values, such as those that stress individual freedom, rights, or class struggle. The central values of Confucianism are the practical values of overcoming the self, acting morally, and keeping to the mean. Moreover, these practical values were established by the sages in preference to all other values as the high values. They embody the way of the sages and the values of the sages. When everyone in society universally accepts these values of the sages, social harmony—Chan's civility—will be realized. This social harmony requires, therefore, that from the top downward there be a promotion of Confucian values as a comprehensive doctrine.

Secondly, Confucian values are practical moral values and universal values. All people should accept them, and the more people accept them the greater the welfare of society will be. In other words, there is a proportional relationship between the rate of acceptance and social welfare. If all of humanity accepts them, then all of humanity will benefit. These universal values are the many values of Confucianism such as benevolence, justice, humility, yielding, filial piety, mercy, loyalty, altruism, moderation, shame, sincerity, fidelity, the mean, and harmony. These universal values of Confucianism are not like the values promoted by salvation religions, which are special values and that not everyone can be expected to accept, such as believing in some particular god, religious doctrine, or rite. Therefore, promoting Confucianism as a comprehensive doctrine implies the spread of universal values, which are practical and moral, and this not only will not lead to social conflict but also is the necessary means to bring about civility. The wholesale promotion of the special values of salvation religions, however, does not bring about civility but social or civic conflict. The conflict of values in Western, supposedly pluralist, society is mainly the result of the special values of salvation religions and not from the universal values that everyone should adopt. This is because the way of resolving value conflict in the West, the use of formal public rationality to dissipate practical moral values, cannot be the right one for all. This form of resolution is suitable only for Western societies that have a unique historical and cultural tradition and is not universally adaptable to the whole of humanity.

Finally, only promoting Confucianism as a comprehensive doctrine can overcome the sad fate of the past hundred years in which it has been thoroughly beaten down and deconstructed. Only then can the contemporary revival of Confucianism be fully, systematically, authentically, and completely realized, and only then can Chen Yinke's words be fulfilled to refound Chinese culture on the basis of Chinese culture while absorbing foreign civilization. A specific and piecemeal adoption of Confucianism cannot perform this mission because the remnants of Confucianism that have survived the battering of the past hundred years cannot be revived or reestablished in a piecemeal fashion, only in a comprehensive holistic way. It is for this reason that, on the basis of the Way of the Humane Authority, I have proposed Confucian constitutionalism, which is an attempt to comprehensively revive Confucian values in China's society and politics today. Naturally, I am well aware that China's liberal democrats will not accept Confucian constitutionalism with its promotion of Confucian values as a comprehensive doctrine. This does not matter. No conflict of basic values has ever been resolved in a wholly satisfactory manner by rational, equal debate. Rational, equal debate is important, of course, but ultimately we look to changes of fate and the way of the world, fluctuations in the human heart and in strength as well as in cultural power and political power to see which side will win. There is no end to correct debating. Let us each make our own effort and wait in patient expectation.

REPLY TO BAI TONGDONG'S CRITICISM OF CONFUCIAN CONSTITUTIONALISM: THE ORIGIN OF LEGITIMACY FOR THE HIGHEST POLITICAL POWER IS THAT SOVEREIGNTY LIES WITH HEAVEN AND NOT WITH THE PEOPLE

Bai Tongdong describes his own version of Confucianism as a middle way, which is opposed both to the neo-Confucian wholesale acceptance of democratic values and my own so-called Confucian fundamentalist version of Confucian constitutionalism.[10] His basic thread of thought is the pluralism of the later Rawls, which seeks a middle way between dogmatism and nihilism. On the premise that liberal democracy itself need not be changed, Professor Bai suggests that we can "improve [democracy] from within in order for the popular will to be trusted." As a result, Professor Bai thinks that my Confucian constitutionalism does not take into account the metaphysical system of pluralism by which "Confucian constitutionalism ... cannot even be a constitutionalism for all Chinese." In response to the present time, Bai wants to "strip off the particular and contextual expressions" of Confucianism and "generalize the ideas beneath," that is, to understand Confucianism as an "a priori system," even as a "transcendent, sacred, religious, and metaphysical system." In short, Bai thinks that Confucian constitutionalism means a "contextual expression of Confucianism (the Han *Gongyang* interpretation of Confucianism) as the fundamental teaching of Confucianism, making it a dogma and a sacred teaching and imposing it on today's world." Thus, Bai rejects Han Confucianism because Han Confucians, especially Dong Zhongshu, "enchant heaven, making it transcendent and sacred." They produce "the oldest religious version of Confucianism," while the pre-Qin Confucians sought a "middle way between the sacred and the secular." Hence, Professor Bai calls for a return to pre-Qin Confucianism and even holds that this form of Confucianism "echoes well" with Rawls's search for a "middle way between dogmatism and nihilism."

Here I will not discuss Rawls's thought but look rather at the supposed distinction between Han and pre-Qin Confucianism. Is there really, as Bai suggests, a difference in their attitude to the transcendent, a priori, sacred, absolute, and supreme nature of heaven. Is disenchantment of heaven a feature of pre-Qin Confucianism? I do indeed acknowledge that there is a difference between Han and pre-Qin Confucianism, but this difference is merely one of a few aspects of Confucianism itself that differ. Inasmuch as Confucianism is Confucianism, there can be no basic disagreement about fundamental ideas, or else it would not be Confucianism. Let us consider Mencius, whom Bai proposes as the representative of pre-Qin Confucianism. Even if heaven for Mencius has a degree of *xin-xing* Confucianism (moral metaphysics), when we take into account the Confucian and the complex nature of Mencius's thought—namely that Mencius speaks both of the inner moral significance of heaven as a form of innate moral knowledge and of the external, objective transcendent heaven that grants supreme political power—in the matter of legitimacy, that is the transcendent, sacred legitimacy by which sovereignty lies with heaven, Mencius's heaven is not fundamentally different from that of the Han Confucians. While Mencius's thought may indeed not have a specific elaboration of the three forms of legitimacy, it does in fact already contain a three-dimensional pattern of three forms of legitimacy.

Let us look at a passage where Mencius is commenting on the classics about succession after abdication and hereditary succession:

> Wan Zhang said,
> "Is it true that Yao gave the Empire to Shun?"
> "No," said Mencius. "The Empire cannot give the Empire to another."
> "In that case who gave the Empire to Shun?"
> "Heaven gave it him." (*Mencius* 5A:5)

From this passage we can see that Mencius thinks that the ultimate holder of the highest political power is heaven and not a human person, that is, sovereignty lies with heaven. Heaven grants political power to men and to Shun. It is not a man (Yao) who grants it to Shun or anyone else. For Mencius, sovereignty lies with heaven and not with human persons or with the people. This is in conformity with what Han Confucians held about sovereignty. For instance Dong Zhongshu says, "The great origin of the way is in heaven," and the way of politics is founded on the transcendent, sacred sovereignty of heaven, which grants political legitimacy.[11] This sovereignty, or royal power, and political legitimacy, legitimization, has its origin in heaven, not in human beings or the people. Hence, in politics to say that the great origin of the Way is in heaven means that the great origin of royal power and legitimacy is in heaven. In the political discourse of today, we can rephrase this as the great origin of sovereignty and political legitimacy lies with heaven. Hence, in the traditional language of politics we may say that, in Mencius's political thought, sovereignty and legitimacy are what heaven grants, and not that sovereignty and legitimacy are what man grants. Given

Mencius's beliefs about sovereignty lying with heaven, it is natural that the transcendent, sacred legitimacy of heaven is higher in terms of legitimacy than legitimacy based on the people. Professor Bai's interpretation of Mencius's political thought as one in which sovereignty lies with the people cannot but be said to be in error.

Furthermore, when Wan Zhang asked once more, "You say Heaven gave it him. Does this mean that Heaven gave him detailed and minute instructions?"

"No. Heaven does not speak but reveals itself through its acts and deeds. . . . The Emperor can recommend a man to Heaven but he cannot make Heaven give this man the Empire. . . . In antiquity, Yao recommended Shun to Heaven and Heaven accepted him; he presented him to the people and the people accepted him. Hence I said, 'Heaven does not speak but reveals itself by its acts and deeds.'"

Wan Zhang asked again, "May I ask how he was accepted by Heaven when recommended to it and how he was accepted by the people when presented to them?"

Mencius replied once more, saying, "When he was put in charge of sacrifices, the hundred gods enjoyed them. This showed that Heaven accepted him. When he was put in charge of affairs, they were kept in order and the people were content, this showed that the people accepted him. Heaven gave it to him, and the people gave it to him. Hence I said, 'The Emperor cannot give the Empire to another.'" (*Mencius* 5A:5)

Here Mencius would seem to say that the Son of Heaven can only propose a candidate to heaven and the final verdict in handing over supreme political power is not made by a human being. Supreme political power is given by heaven and not by a man, by the Son of Heaven, because sovereignty lies with heaven. In doing things, heaven does not speak but relies on the way things are done to express its sovereignty.[12] There are two kinds of ways in which heaven exercises its sovereignty. One is in performing rituals, whereby acceptance by the spirits proves that political power and its legitimacy ultimately come from heaven and not from men. The second is by the security the people experience when the person manages political affairs, which shows that political power and its legitimacy also need to win the recognition of the people. But, for Mencius, political power and its legitimacy originates with, or is primarily rooted in, heaven while its recognition by the people is a secondary or derived origin. If it were not so, Mencius would not have rejected Wan Zhang's suggestion that Yao gave all under heaven to Shun by saying that heaven granted it. He would have had to reply simply that Yao, or a person, or the people gave it. Hence, Mencius and Dong Zhongshu both agree that heaven is the ultimate source of political power and its legitimacy.

Mencius goes on to say,

> Shun assisted Yao for twenty-eight years. This is something which could not be brought about by man, but by heaven alone. Yao died, and after the mourning period of three years, Shun withdrew to the south of Nan Ho, leaving Yao's son in possession of the field, yet the feudal lords of the Empire who came to pay homage as well as those who were engaged in litigation went to Shun, not to Yao's son, and ballad singers sang the praises of Shun, not of Yao's son. Hence I said, "it was brought about by Heaven." Only then did Shun go to the Central Kingdoms and ascend the Imperial throne. . . . The T'ai shih says, "Heaven sees as my people see; heaven hears as my people hear." (*Mencius* 5A:5)[13]

From this passage we can see that Shun received his position from heaven and not from human beings, and when Yao died the people's hearts gravitated toward Shun and not toward Yao's son. Heaven showed the justification of its giving power to Shun through the people's hearts. It was not the case that political power was made the property of the people so that they could give it to Shun directly. Only the owner has the right to give something to someone. Heaven owns sovereignty, and so heaven alone can give heaven's property, sovereignty, to Shun. Mencius's citation of the *Book of History*'s "Heaven sees as my people see; heaven hears as my people hear" simply explains that heaven does not speak. In its rightful exercise of sovereignty, heaven must be shown in one form of action, the gravitation of the people's hearts, which is a sign of the decision taken by heaven to transfer sovereignty, supreme political power, to another. It does not mean that sovereignty is owned by the people, still less that the will of the people is the will of heaven. Rather, the will of the people is but one form of sign of the will of heaven. Even if the will of the people were absent, the will of heaven would still be present. There would merely be the lack of an exercise by which the will of heaven was revealed.

In other words, the people do not hold ultimate political sovereignty. Hence, the will of the people itself lacks the justification of ultimate, supreme, self-sufficient political power. If one wants to say that sovereignty can be parceled out, then the sovereignty granted to the people is derived from that of heaven, and hence the justification of the will of the people is also derived from that of the will of heaven. It is not the case that the popular will simply is the will of heaven. Therefore, when Professor Bai maintains that "Mencius' political ideal is 'sovereignty lies with the people, but the right to rule lies in the wise and virtuous'" and that in terms of legitimacy the will of the people is that of heaven, this is clearly a serious misunderstanding of Mencius's thought. Because this way of speaking puts the power of the people, their sovereignty, above that of heaven; it makes the power of the people the ultimate, supreme, and self-sufficient form of sovereignty. This is clearly at variance with Mencius's theory of sovereignty lying with heaven and heaven granting power. It is, on the other hand, in accordance with the Western idea of sovereignty of the people, especially with the thought of Locke, because in part 1 of his *Treatise on Government*, Locke is opposed to the derivation of political power and of legitimacy from divine grant.

Professor Bai's way of thinking is by no means his alone. We know that, in recent times, many intellectuals, who are sympathetic to Chinese culture, have sought traditional resources in support of democracy to make it palatable.[14] But our analysis presented above shows that Confucianism acknowledges a higher and more important form of legitimacy, namely, that of the way of heaven. Hence, "Heaven sees as my people see; heaven hears as my people hear" can refer only to particular cases of the popular will and when that will is a sign of the universal will of heaven. It cannot be used to produce a theory of legitimacy as Professor Bai does. Still less can it be used to reduce Confucian thought on legitimacy to a statement such as the will of heaven is the popular will, or the popular will is the will of heaven. This is because the will of heaven can be made manifest in several different ways, and the popular will is only one of them. Other possible means are giving life to all that is, revealing auspicious omens, and sending down disasters, or in the heart of the king and the will of the sages. Moreover, these latter ways are the most important and most authoritative forms of manifestation of the will of heaven.

Precisely because Mencius held that sovereignty lay with heaven, when Wan Zhang went on to ask about Yu, who transferred power to his son and not to a worthy person who was not his relative, Mencius noted,

> No. It is not. If heaven wishes to give the Empire to a good and wise man then it should be given to a good and wise man. But if heaven wishes to give it to the son, then it should be given to the son. (*Mencius* 5A:6)

In other words, Mencius holds that sovereignty does not lie with Yu but with heaven. Hence when Yao transmitted it to a worthy person this was the will of heaven and it was in fact heaven that gave it. When Yu transmitted it to his son, this also was the will of heaven, and likewise it was heaven that gave it to him. A human being, such as Yu, does not have political sovereignty. A person, such as Yao, Shun, or Yu, can but recommend names to heaven.

Heaven tested the candidate by a particular process to ensure that he was up to the will of heaven before giving him the highest political power. Yao, Shun, and Yu were sage kings. If ultimate sovereignty is not even with the sage kings, how could Confucianism ever propose that the ultimate significance of sovereignty as lying with the people? If the sage kings, who held to the way of heaven, transmitted history, and understood the popular will, could not be the origin of sovereignty, then how could the people, who are very unclear about the way of heaven, know only their current reality and care about only the interests before their own eyes, be the source of sovereignty?

From the above it is clear that Professor Bai's version of sovereignty lying with the people is at odds with Mencius's authentic thought. Rather, his idea is in conformity with one tradition by which intellectuals have explained Confucianism, namely a misreading of Mencius and of the entire Confucian tradition so as to find resources in the Chinese tradition to support democracy. This is what I have referred to as the tradition whereby, under the powerful influence of Western culture, Chinese intellectuals use the West to explain China. This tradition takes Western thought as its guiding line and its comprehensive framework of thought so as to explain Confucianism. It goes from a misreading of Confucianism to a heretical form of Confucianism and leads to a structuring of Confucianism in which the West explains China.[15]

Furthermore, what is mind-boggling is that in this tradition of misreading Confucianism by using the West to explain China, the Confucian political notion that sovereignty lies with heaven is explained and deconstructed so that it becomes the Western idea of sovereignty lying with the people. As a result, Mencius is explained by many Chinese scholars as a great proponent of Lockean democracy in ancient China, or as the Chinese precursor of Western liberalism! The strange thing is that in part 1 of his *Treatise on Government*, Locke is opposed to rule by divine right. Yet in the *Wan Zhang* chapter, Mencius advocates that political power is given by heaven. I do not know if there is any difference between Locke's and Mencius's ideas of political power coming from heaven or God, but it is clear that Mencius's advocacy of sovereignty lying with heaven means that it is not democracy. Therefore, Mencius is not an ancient Chinese Locke.

Mencius also holds that heaven can freely decide to withdraw the highest political power from the person to whom it was granted. It can take it away from despots for instance. Mencius says, "[H]e who inherits the Empire is only put aside by Heaven if he is like Chieh or Tchou" (*Mencius* 5A:6).[16]

In short, Mencius acknowledges that heaven can demonstrate the power of ruling and supervision, of demoting or promoting by its acting without action in the human realm.[17] Mencius's action without action is heaven's independent and autonomous exercise of sovereignty and its rule, supervision, and decision over everything in the world.

Professor Bai believes that Mencius and Dong Zhongshu hold opposing views of heaven, which leads to two different political philosophies in pre-Qin and Han Confucianism. This sharp division in the common understanding of Confucianism is indeed contrary to the real situation of Confucianism and reflects the view of liberalism rather than that of Confucianism. Mencius talks a lot about the Way of the Humane Authority, and this is the common law of Confucianism. There is no difference in kind between the sovereignty of heaven and the three-dimensional three forms of legitimacy of Mencius and the Han Confucians because both are founded on the basic political idea of Confucianism: the Way of the Humane Authority, in which the way of heaven has the upper place.

Furthermore, Bai Tongdong writes, "[A] key feature of pre-Qin Confucianism is to disenchant heaven and to humanize it." This view is manifestly that of the post-enlightenment Western tendency that was accepted in China in the May Fourth movement. This movement cut off the origin of the most important, transcendent, and sacred value of Confucianism, the supreme pole of its thought, heaven. It interpreted Confucianism as a form of humanism as in Western culture, a form of enlightenment thought, even a form of liberalism and democracy. Confucianism became a humanist Confucianism, an enlightenment Confucianism, a liberal and democratic Confucianism, a fashionable modern Confucianism and a Westernized Confucianism. This Westernized humanistic Confucianism is contrary not only to the Han Confucianism Professor Bai belittles but also to the pre-Qin Confucianism that he so much admires. Both pre-Qin and Han Confucianism are grounded on the ancient classics that Confucius edited, and in these classics heaven, god, or the way of heaven and the decree of heaven are sovereign, transcendent, sacred, absolute, and supreme. It is not a matter of humanism or even less of the enlightenment or liberalism or democracy. Professor Bai notes that my Confucian constitutionalism is a "transcendent, sacred, religious, and metaphysical system." His observation is correct. My system is indeed rooted in the classics of ancient Confucianism. I am turning against the deviation of Confucianism that has been the orthodoxy of Chinese scholars since May Fourth and correcting it. I have established a Chinese form of politics with Chinese historical and cultural characteristics outside the province of democracy. Professor Bai may be sympathetic to some values in Confucianism, but we differ greatly in our basic political principles, so I can understand his criticism of Confucian constitutionalism, but I still hope to see more criticism emanating from his pen.

REPLY TO LI CHENYANG'S CRITICISM OF CONFUCIAN CONSTITUTIONALISM: THE TRANSCENDENT CONFUCIAN HEAVEN IS THE FOUNDATION OF POLITICAL POWER: THE FORM OF DEMOCRACY AND CONFUCIAN CONTENT ARE INCOMPATIBLE IN THEIR BASIC POLITICAL VALUES

Professor Li Chenyang's criticism of Confucian constitutionalism is largely focused on my understanding of heaven as the transcendent foundation of Confucian constitutionalism. Professor Li believes that the transcendent heaven is redundant. The question raised by Li is a very important metaphysical and religious metaphysical issue. Confucianism is not just any kind of rational metaphysics. It is a religious metaphysics with a faith belief. For this reason, its understanding of the transcendent, sacred, ultimate origin, heaven is a matter of prime importance.

We know that any form of metaphysics, Chinese or Western, ancient or modern, philosophical or religious, must have only one supreme essence or ultimate origin. The ultimate reality of all the myriad things can but be one, not many. This one is the final point of dependence or the supreme being by which the myriad things in the universe can rationally exist. The being of Parmenides is only one. Plato's idea is one. The Stoics' *Logos* is one. The God of Christian theology is one. In China, the Confucian heaven is one; Laozi's Way is one; the supreme ultimate of the Song dynastic Confucian cosmology was one. The mind of the dharma world in Chinese Buddhism's *Awakening of Faith in the Mahayana* is one. The tathatā of the Theory of the Origin of tathatā is one. The ālaya of the Consciousness-only School is one.

The reason for this is that any metaphysical thought must be founded on one transcendent, absolute, supreme, eternal, and universal being so that it can explain, demonstrate, or settle the real world. If the world lacks this transcendent being, then it will fall into chaos, becoming accidental, irrational, meaningless, aimless, disordered such that it can be neither understood nor relied on. Human life would descend into absurdity. Hence, metaphysics is what people need if we are to enjoy a life in conformity with reason. Metaphysicians may disagree on their understanding and interpretation of the one, but not on there being a one. If metaphysics dispenses with an ultimate one, then it is no longer metaphysics.

Though all metaphysics must have an ultimate one, this should be related to the real world and to human history if it is to be meaningful. When the ultimate one meets the world and history, it necessarily gives rise to many. But the many cannot dispense with the one. For the many to lack the one would imply that the one can no longer play its role in the world. In general there are two ways in which the one and the many are related:

as the ultimate, the one is the universal unifier of the many, or the concrete arrangement of one to many in the physical world, which is a reflection of the relationship of the one and the many in the metaphysical world. The first relationship is necessary to guarantee the universality of rationality, while the second is necessary for a statement of the rationality of the world.

All forms of metaphysics have these two relationships of one and many. In Mahayana Buddhism there is one mind that opens two gates. The mind of the dharma world is the one, and the two gates of the real world are the gate of tathatā and the gate of generation and destruction are the many. But the gate of tathatā is the mind of the dharma world as it appears in the world. In the Diagram of the Supreme Ultimate of Song Confucianism, the supreme ultimate is one and *yin* and *yang* are many, with *yang* being the visible presence of the supreme ultimate in the real world. *Yang* is the *Qian* hexagram, heaven, which is the supreme ultimate. Likewise, in Song Confucian metaphysics, one principle separates into many subprinciples. There is one supreme ultimate that gathers together the myriad things of the world and is the one principle such that there is one supreme ultimate for the myriad things. At the level of the subprinciples each thing has its own supreme ultimate, which is what accounts for the many within the one. Or in Aquinas's theology, God is one; form and matter are many, and "form" is the embodiment of God in the real world, so it is also one.

From this we can see that, in addition to the relationship of the one and the many in the physical world, there is also a metaphysical, ultimate, universal, coordinating, synthesizing one and that this is by no means redundant. Without this metaphysical one there could be no unity operative in the physical, subprincipled, limited, chaotic real world. The physical world of the many subprinciples would not then be a rational or meaningful world.

For this reason, in Confucian metaphysics, there must be a heaven, which is the one principle above the subprinciples of the triad of heaven-earth-humanity. This heaven is not, as Professor Li says, redundant or unnecessary. On the contrary it is something that Confucian metaphysics cannot do without because it would lack what Confucians call the essence of great origin. The lack of this implies that the world and history are doomed to eternal meaninglessness and absurdity. Confucianism would not be Confucianism because Confucianism is a heavenly study that places heaven in the multifarious world.

To help in our understanding, we could argue from the opposite point of view. If there were not a heaven as the one principle and there was only the heaven of the triad itself, then this would imply that there were no subprinciples in the world because the heaven of the triad would directly and completely include earth and humanity and so there would be a world where all that existed was only one principle. That is clearly impossible. Zhu Xi noted that there can only be a world in which there are myriad things and one supreme ultimate and not one in which there is one supreme ultimate for each thing because in the latter world each thing would lose its unique identity, purpose, and meaning. Not only could people not distinguish one thing from another, each thing would lose its identity and cease to exist.

Therefore, the heaven which is the one principle of the triad heaven-earth-humanity is the ultimate coordinator and synthesizer of the myriad things in the universe and gives them a universal purpose and meaning. The heaven of the triad itself is what gives each thing its particular purpose and meaning. For instance, in the triad the heaven of man and the heaven of things are different. In the physical world this difference ensures that humanity and things are different, but there must be another controlling, synthesizing universal heaven that overrides this difference. In other words, above one supreme ultimate for each thing there must be one supreme ultimate for the myriad things. This is the metaphysics of the *Book of Changes* whereby "everything obtains it correct nature as appointed (by the mind of Heaven)" under the premise of "great harmony are preserved in union."[18] The meaning is profound, and it is hard to put it into words. It can be grasped only by mystical comprehension.[19]

Professor Li also adds another criticism of my understanding of heaven. He says that the addition of a transcendent heaven is to take a step backward. His reasoning is that the heaven of the Shang and Zhou dynasties was a transcendent, metaphysical, sacred personified heaven, but by the pre-Qin thought had progressed to the differentiated heaven of the triad of heaven-earth-humanity. To understand heaven as a transcendent metaphysical, sacred, personified heaven is to take a step back from the pre-Qin into the Shang and Zhou dynasties, whereas the pre-Qin Confucian understanding of heaven is the more mature understanding.

This question is related to the criticisms of Bai Tongdong, but whereas Professor Bai accuses Confucian constitutionalism of employing a Han Confucian reading of heaven, Professor Li says it uses a reading of heaven that was even earlier than the pre-Qin period. Both agree in calling for a return to the pre-Qin understanding of heaven. They think that this understanding is more mature—it eliminates the transcendent, personified features of heaven—and orthodox—it accords with the spirit of Confucian humanism. Yet as I see it the Confucian understanding of heaven is not dependent on historical periods, or on a particular school of thought, but must refer back to the *Five Classics* edited by Confucius.

The understanding of heaven in the *Five Classics* as well as in pre-Qin Confucianism and Song-Ming Confucianism is the same. In the *Five*

Classics, heaven is clearly a sovereign. It is not a humanist, subjective psychological sense of heaven. Zhu Xi described the *Four Books* as a ladder to the *Five Classics*. Therefore, in understanding the Confucian heaven, the *Five Classics* are the highest source of authority. One may not rely on any one period of Confucian discourse as evidence for what heaven is, still less may one depart from the Confucian classics and judge any period of Confucianism as mature or orthodox. If pre-Qin Confucianism understands heaven differently from the *Five Classics*, then the *Classics* must be taken as the norm.

However, in fact Han Confucianism, especially that of Dong Zhongshu, understands heaven just as the *Five Classics* do, and so we have reason to believe that Dong's school of Han Confucianism embodies the understanding of heaven in the *Five Classics*. Hence, in our understanding of the Confucian heaven, Dong's school has been the key standard of reference. Likewise, any other form of Confucianism that shares the same understanding of heaven is an acceptable standard too, no matter of what period or founded by what person. In fact, my plan of Confucian constitutionalism was formed in reference to Dong's school's understanding of heaven as transcendent and sacred and also with reference to the understating of heaven as one principle with many subprinciples in the school of principle of Cheng Yi and Zhu Xi. I also absorbed what Mencius said about sovereignty, inasmuch as this conformed to the understanding of heaven in the *Five Classics*. This understanding of heaven can indeed be the foundation of political sovereignty, and not as Professor Li says, "cannot serve as a solid foundation for today's Confucian political philosophy."

It has already been noted above that Confucian metaphysics is a religious metaphysics. The highest essence and ultimate reality of a religious metaphysics is not something that reason can understand, but only something that can be grasped in faith. Therefore, the Confucian heaven is indeed much more abstruse than the being, or reality, of rational Western metaphysics. It is beyond the scope of understanding of human reason.

Professor Li says that the transcendent heaven above the triad "is not the postulate of a rigorous logic."[20] That is very true because this transcendent heaven is not something to which reason can attain. In Buddhist terminology we say "language is cut short; the road of the mind is severed." In terms of Christian theology, we can say "credo quia absurdum." Yet Professor Li thinks that the transcendent heaven is merely a postulate. This is quite wrong. The transcendent heaven of Confucianism is faith in the transcendent, sacred, august heaven, or God. This faith must rely on a mystical intuition that transcends reason and a dark-seeing and mystical understanding in the depths of the heart before it can be known or grasped. Hence, in Confucian religious faith, this transcendent heaven is really and truly alive. It is not just a postulate, as Professor Li says. Still less is it a "vacuous notion."

Li's difficulties with the heaven, which transcends the triad, have led him to think of the Christian doctrine of the Trinity. Li's is certainly an original view. The doctrine of the Trinity is above the myriad things of the world and certainly transcends reason, or is a-rational. It can be grasped only in sincere faith and intuitive comprehension and cannot be known by postulating from reason or by analyzing concepts, that is, it cannot be known by what Professor Li calls the "logic of identity." I think that the a-rational or supra-rational relationship between the transcendent heaven of Confucian religious belief and the heaven of the triad must also be viewed in a similar way.

The Form of Democracy with a Confucian Content

Although Professor Li does not accept Confucian constitutionalism as such, he does acknowledge certain Confucian values and also admits that democracy has some defects. In order to harmonize Confucian values and democratic politics, Li proposes his own plan, which is that of "Confucian content with democratic form."[21] By "democratic form" he means "a political arrangement that adopts a democratic electoral mechanism," that is "an organizational procedure by which society generates political leaders." By "Confucian content" he means that in a society with "democratic form," "when [Confucian social and moral] ideals are preserved in society, the lives of the majority of the people manifest Confucian philosophy." Professor Li hopes to use this "Confucian content with democratic form" to counter the idea that heaven granted sovereignty to the sages and then to the scholar-officials." He maintains, "Today Confucianism can fully and boldly accept democracy and use it to attain the Confucian goal of ruling the state and bringing peace to all under heaven."[22]

Here there is a matter that must first of all be clarified. At the level of basic political principles, are democracy and Confucianism compatible? If they are, then Li's proposal will succeed; if not, then it has no ground to stand on. In my view it must fail, the reason being that democracy and Confucianism are incompatible at the level of principle. We know that some Confucian values, especially values of personal cultivation and family morality, can exist in a democratic society with a form of democracy. Such values are those mentioned by Li: "Family is highly valued, education is vigorously promoted, and people are mostly virtuous."

However, Confucian political values, especially the basic ones, cannot exist in civil society in a form of democracy. The reasons are, firstly, that form and content are not on a level ground; still less are they mutually supportive or mutually restraining. Form plays a guiding, directing, and decisive role with respect to content because form is the structure, the norms, the framework and has an objective, unchangeable nature. It acts as a normative restraint on content, upholding some values and rejecting others. Form, especially political form, is not, as liberalism contends, neutral or impartial because any political form is established according to particular political values. For instance, the political form of liberalism is established according to the values of liberal democracy, while the political form of Confucian constitutionalism is established according to the values of the Way of the Humane Authority. Hence, the neutrality and impartiality of any established political form are only on the surface. In reality what is embodied or upheld are particular values, especially particular political values. In this way, it is determined that these particular values have permanence, which is supported by a supposedly public reason or objective framework. In this way, form guides content, directs content, and determines content. Once form has been established, then this determines the leading, guiding, and compelling role assigned to content. Content relies on form, obeys form, and serves form. In the matter of basic values, content that is not in accord with form will be excluded from the form and will not be allowed to realize its value under that form. The two not only influence each other, they are even produced in relationship one with the other.

The basic values of Professor Li's form of democracy are established according to democratic values. Therefore, the form of democracy protects democratic content. As a result, in the matter of basic values, any content that is not in accord with democratic values will be excluded from the form of democracy. In this sense, I think that the form of democracy and Confucian content are incompatible in their basic political values and principles. The form of democracy determines that the content of basic Confucian political values cannot enter into the form of democracy, nor can the form of democracy be used to realize basic Confucian political principles.

We know that the basic political values of Confucianism and those of democracy are not the same. The political attitude of the Way of the Humane Authority is rule by sages and worthies (in a broad sense) since it determines that sovereignty lies with heaven and sages. In concrete political terms, this requires a complicated, hierarchical system of recommendation and examination. It believes that a system whereby power is granted to worthy scholar-officials is just and maintains that genuine great sages and worthies do not need to be elected by the masses and ought to have the power to rule. It puts morality at the head of politics. In contrast, the political attitude of democratic values is rule by ordinary people (what the

American scholar Carl J. Friedrich defines as "the politics of the common man"[23]) as it determines that sovereignty lies with the people. This requires a simple, flat system with general elections. It holds that an equal distribution of power is what conforms to justice and political power can be won only through general elections. It puts interests in first place.

There are many other similar differences that all boil down to saying that the two forms of rule are different at the level of basic political values and these differences are the differences in the basic political values of the Way of the Humane Authority and of democracy. For this reason, the content of Way of the Humane Authority values and the content of rule by sages and worthies (including both value content and organizational content) will necessarily be excluded and be unrealizable in the form of democracy.

We do not think it is possible in a form of democracy to elect sages and worthies to rule. This is because rule by ordinary people can use only general elections to choose ordinary people who will represent the interests and desires of the masses. Some people have compared democracy to an objective, neutral, level stage on which everyone can dance their own dance. Everyone can win the power to rule and engage in politics through this framework. This is what Professor Li refers to as the form of democracy. But the democratic stage is far from being objective, or neutral, still less fair. It is tilted in favor of ordinary people (even small-minded men such as Chen Shui-bian and the like).[24] It is not for worthies and gentlemen, still less for sages. If sages, worthies, and gentlemen wish to mount the stage they must keep to the objective framework of the stage, that is, the form of democracy, and first make themselves into ordinary persons or small-minded persons, or else they cannot ascend the stage and hold the power to rule.

So Professor Li's desire to match the form of democracy and Confucian content is a hard task indeed. Still less is it possible that "Confucianism can fully and boldly accept democracy and use it to attain the Confucian goal of ruling the state and bringing peace to all under heaven."[25]

Moreover, there is something else that is scarcely credible, namely that some ten years ago the New Confucians were saying democracy has provided a structural protection in which Confucian values can be fully realized, and therefore China must take the road of democracy. In fact Professor Li's form of democracy and Confucian content is very similar to what the New Confucians were saying then. His form of democracy is their theory that democracy is the general consensus of humanity. Yet if we look at things from the point of view of the basic political values of Confucianism, from the moral cause of the subprime mortgage crisis in American democracy and the chaotic phenomenon of Taiwan's realization of democracy, they all show that democracy has not provided a structural protection in which Confucian values can be fully realized. On the contrary, we see that the interests of particular groups and particular democratic values are given structural protection by democracy.

Of course, I do not deny that in areas of general, nonpolitical values, in personal morality, political standing, and family ethics, the form of democracy and Confucian content are compatible. For instance, in 2009, the U.S. House of Representatives passed House Resolution 784 in honor of Confucius's 2,560th birthday, which honored Confucius in the following words: "Whereas Confucius counseled introspection, self-cultivation, sincerity, and the observance of respect within social relationships . . . loyalty, respect for elders, and recognition of the importance of family . . . 'what one does not wish for oneself, one ought not to do to anyone else' . . . politicians must be models of truthfulness and morality."[26] These are all matters of personal morality, political standing, and family ethics. However, at the level of basic political values, the form of democracy and Confucian content are incompatible. The acceptance of the U.S. House of Representatives of some general Confucian values cannot alter this. To hope to unite the form of democracy with Confucian content and seek to use the form of democracy to realize basic Confucian values has been the unrealistic, ill-conceived, naïve dream of Chinese intellectuals over the past century or so.

In Professor Li's essay, the form of democracy is largely a matter of universal suffrage. If, in the future, a sage should arise, he certainly would not take part in all that the form of democracy gives rise to: its secularism, pursuit of interests, agitation, demagogy, self-projection, performance, fawning, hypocrisy, pretence, pandering to the populace, including even absurdities, farce, and a great waste of money, which are part of mass elections. A sage would not seek to flatter or welcome unreasonable secular popular will, but would "experience disapproval without trouble of mind" and maintain his own moral ideal.[27] But a sage knows that by insisting on his own moral ideal, he could not possibly be elected. Hence, we can confidently assert that the form of democracy cannot elect sages, and so sages would not take part in elections.

Let us return to the form of democracy with a Confucian content. My own view is that a Confucian content requires a Confucian form, which will in turn uphold the Confucian content. In terms of basic political principles, Confucian content is the values of the Way of the Humane Authority and Confucian constitutionalism is the Confucian form.

The reason why I have gone into this link between democracy and Confucianism at such length is because many prominent scholars in China have been involved. The New Confucians have proposed a theory of "the expression of rational structure."[28] Fok Tou-hui suggested "elite democracy."[29]

Dr. Fan Yafeng and his colleagues have proposed "Chinese Liberalism."[30] Professor Tu Weiming has suggested the theory of Confucianism as Adjectival.[31] Twenty years ago Gan Yang proposed a theory of Western politics and Chinese morality.[32] What all these scholars have in common is that they accept the form of democracy as the common law for all humanity or think that Confucian values can be fully implemented within democracy. For instance, Mou Zongsan thought that the role of the mind of Confucianism could be fully expressed in the rational structure of democracy. Others have thought that Confucian values can improve democracy. For example, Fok Tou-hui thinks that the leveling of values produced by democracy can be remedied by the Confucian values of benevolence, justice, wisdom, and trust being used to improve the electorate and the personal virtue of politicians, so as to achieve a better level of democracy. Others think that Confucian values can remedy the defect of democracy in China, in that China lacks a religious or moral foundation for democracy. For instance, Yao Zhongqiu thinks that democracy works successfully in the West because there is a widespread basis of Christian religion and morals to act as a foundation for democratic society, but, since China can never be wholly Christianized, Confucian values are the only thing that can provide this foundation. Once that is done, democracy will work in China. Others think that Confucian values can provide an added supplement to democracy. For instance, Tu Weiming thinks that without altering the basic political structure of the West and its constitutional setup, Confucian values can act as an adjective in supplementing democracy. Others think that Confucian values can enable individuals to develop their own personal morality within a democratic frame. For instance, Gan Yang thought that the political modernization of China could be founded only on a democratic framework and each individual's personal values could be those of Confucian morality.

From the above we can see that Chinese scholars sympathetic to, or in support of, Confucian values all accept the form of democracy as the common law of politics, that is, as the universal structure of politics, and Confucian values are simply a supplement or something that elevates or completes the democratic framework. Here the form of democracy is the objective structure, which is universal, leading, guiding, normative, and decisive, and Confucian values are the subjective content, which is particular, led, guided, subject to norms and decisions that are not of its own making. In Aristotelian terminology, Western democracy is the form, which is the substance and mould for each thing, while Confucian content is matter. Matter is what makes up the material and basic nature of a thing. Form takes first priority and matter is secondary. Form is the end cause and efficient cause, and so form is dynamic and apparent, while matter is passive and hidden. Matter can be realized and come into existence only through form. Hence form determines the nature and realization of matter. Matter is governed by form and at the service of form. Once form is established it is the master, and matter can be only its servant. Hence, when there is the form of democracy and Confucian content, the form of democracy is the master and Confucian content the servant.

This state of affairs is clearly contrary to the basic principles of Chinese culture. We ought, instead, to propose the opposite thesis, of a Confucian form with a democratic content. This would imply making a Confucian form on the basis of basic Confucian political values to forcefully uphold the Way of the Humane Authority. At the same time we should accept some values from democracy that supplement, elevate, and complete Confucian politics.

Hence, when Chinese scholars, utterly without principle, engage in a leveling harmony of the form of democracy and Confucian content, from the perspective of China's own culture and that of a political order with Chinese historical and cultural characteristics, they cannot succeed. In fact, this kind of harmonization is a version of "the West as substance and China as the means" in which the form of democracy is the substance and the democratic content is the means.[33] But as Chen Yinke said, the history of Confucian learning in the Song dynasty tells us that any theory or political arrangement that departs from the substance of Chinese culture will not be successful in the long run.[34] When we in China today wish to establish a Chinese-style politics with the characteristics of Chinese history and culture, we must use the form of Confucian constitutionalism and selectively pick and choose elements of democratic content or of constitutional content, and not the other way around.

Professor Li's formulation of the relationship of democracy and Confucianism is based on a consideration of the current times. He notes that although "democracy has many deficiencies" and is "not perfect," "given the trend of the modern world, no other form of political arrangement, apart from selection by the people, can be considered reasonably possible. Confucianism must face reality and accord with the tide of history and accept a system of choice by the people." The reason is that "nowadays there is no better system. Even though the democratic system is not perfect, at least it provides an acceptable model to work with."[35] We may describe this idea as a mitigated form of Fukuyama's thesis. In practice, modern Chinese intellectuals sympathetic to, or accepting of, Confucian values have all accepted this mitigated form of Fukuyama's thesis. Its heart is that despite deficiencies, democracy is the only available form of governance in today's world, and therefore Confucianism must simply accept it. Admittedly, this thesis is true in part, and democracy may be the least bad form of politics in the world today, but knowing its imperfections and deficiencies and that there is currently no better alternative, do we not then have the task of creating a better, more perfect, less defective form of politics? The invasiveness of Western culture in the minds of Chinese intellectuals has been such that they have already lost their creative awareness and, in time, will also lose their creative ability, until finally they can do nothing else except accept Western democracy.

Faced with this situation, the first task of Confucianism in politics today is to arouse creative awareness and respond to the times and foster a creative ability based on basic Confucian political values, so as to create a better and more perfect political setup than democracy. This setup will be based on the values of the Way of the Humane Authority and be a Chinese style of politics with the characteristics of Chinese history and culture. This is what I have been doing over the past few years in promoting Confucian constitutionalism. I realize that this is simply my own idea, but it is not based on my own subjective musings. It is required and structured by the inherent principles of China's Confucian civilization on the basis of Chinese political values. It is my hope, then, that Chinese intellectuals sympathetic to, or accepting of, Confucian values reject a mitigated version of Fukuyama's thesis in politics and create a Chinese form of politics responsive to the opportunities presented by history and imbued with the mission of the times. Because this Confucian creation will be great and also require hard work, it will need the collective participation and efforts of many generations of Chinese intellectuals for it to come to fruition.[36]

REPLY TO WANG SHAOGUANG'S CRITICISM OF THE WAY OF HUMANE AUTHORITY AND CONFUCIAN CONSTITUTIONALISM: RECOGNITION OF POLITICAL LEGITIMACY, RULE BY SAGES, AND THE JUSTICE OF SEPARATION OF POWERS

Professor Wang Shaoguang's criticism of the Way of the Humane Authority and Confucian constitutionalism raises many questions. In this response I limit myself to the five most important and elaborate my own views further.

The Question of a Lack of Legitimacy

First of all, Professor Wang does not believe that China suffers from a problem of lack of legitimacy. He uses opinion polls based on empirical studies to prove that the Chinese people are very satisfied with the government and hence, in terms of popular legitimacy, argues that it is false to describe China as lacking in legitimacy. On this question, I want to stress that my lack of legitimacy refers to a lack of the three forms of legitimacy, that is, whether or not a political order lacks sacred, historical, and popular legitimacy. Sacred legitimacy is based on religious belief and transcendent values. The past century has seen the destruction in China of her national religion, Confucianism, that was at least five thousand years old. The result of this is that Chinese politics can no longer be grounded on religious belief or transcendental values, the sacred legitimacy of Confucianism. The role of Confucianism in Chinese politics is that of providing religious belief and transcendent values and of bestowing sacred legitimacy. It is in this sense that China can be said to be lacking in legitimacy.[37]

Furthermore, in respect to historical legitimacy and despite a recent renewal of domestic interest in China's traditional culture, the constant wave of antitraditionalism over the last century, especially in the sphere of politics such as the May Fourth movement and the Cultural Revolution, has led to severe restrictions on the space available for China's traditional culture. The Chinese political framework has basically been a translation of the model of the former Soviet Union. It still lacks ideas and a form of organization that is rooted in China's own historical and cultural tradition. As a result, China faces the problem of the lack of historical and cultural legitimacy.

In terms of popular legitimacy, China's economy has made great progress, and the standard of living has been greatly increased as a result of the policy of reform and opening up. This has, indeed, led to a rise in popular satisfaction and brought about a legitimacy of political achievement. Yet popular legitimacy is broader than this. Besides the satisfaction of material life, it also includes the protection of some basic rights such as freedom of speech, of religion, of media and the press, freedom to form associations, and the like. It also includes the sense of security of the people, their happiness, their sense of fairness, and assessment of social and political morality. In this sense, the Chinese masses are clearly discontented. Hence, the degree of satisfaction in terms of popular legitimacy comes at a considerably reduced discount, and so even in terms of popular legitimacy there is a lack. It is clear, then, that to different degrees China suffers from a lack of legitimacy and that Professor Wang's contention cannot stand.

Normative Legitimacy and Legitimacy of Recognition

To disprove my contention of the monopoly of popular legitimacy, Professor Wang uses empirical opinion polls to show that, in the West, people's confidence in democracy is very low, and so, in the West, there is no monopoly of popular legitimacy. On the contrary, there is a lack of popular legitimacy. They are not too democratic but rather not democratic enough. Here Professor Wang draws a distinction between "normative legitimacy" and "the practical level of legitimacy" and uses the latter to replace the former.[38]

We know that, in Western democracy, sovereignty lies with the people. This is a form of normative legitimacy based on a universal metaphysical principle. It is a rational standard by which political order and political power may be assessed and belongs to the realm of normative, metaphysical truth. However great or small the subjective endorsement of the actual political situation by the masses is, this does not alter the fact that the sovereignty of the people is the normative form of legitimacy in a democracy. Even if the people did not accept the political order or power in a democracy, or even if they were completely dissatisfied with the government, this would not alter the fact that, in a democracy, the sovereignty of the people is still the norm of legitimacy. This is because this norm plays a rational, objective, universal, determining role in a democracy, while the people's endorsement of the government is empirical, subjective, psychological, and subsidiary. It is the normative legitimacy that determines the legitimacy of a democracy and that determines if a democracy is legitimate or not. Subjective recognition does not play this role.

It is precisely for this reason that the thesis that popular legitimacy holds a monopoly of legitimacy in a democracy means that there is only one form of normative legitimacy. The other two forms, sacred and historical, are lacking. It is thus not held in check by any other form of legitimacy. As a result, democracy suffers from a serious flaw in the matter of legitimacy. Professor Wang writes from the point of view of the great democracy of the new Left and uses subjective legitimacy of endorsement at the practical level to replace objective normative legitimacy, holding that the problems of Western politics do not come from democracy but from a lack of democracy and so denies my assessment of the monopoly of popular legitimacy. In so doing, he confuses the two kinds of political legitimacy and contradicts the establishment of Western democracy on the sole normative legitimacy of sovereignty of the people.

Maoist-Style Great Equality Compared to Confucian Rule by Sages

The reason why Professor Wang has been described as belonging to the new Left is that he has a boundless longing and admiration for the Maoist great equality. He thinks that China's ideal politics is that outlined in Mao's May 7th Directive (of 1966): the elimination of distribution of work, of commerce, and of the distinction between manual and intellectual labor and the creation of a totally equal society.[39] Hence, Professor Wang is particularly opposed to rule by worthy scholar-officials and to the arrangements for the House of *Ru*. In his view, the House of *Ru* is an oppressive and unequal form of elite politics.

It is indeed true that rule by worthy scholar-officials in Confucian constitutionalism is an arrangement of inequality, but this inequality is not based on a capitalist monopoly, as Professor Wang holds, on what he calls the power of the capitalist class, but on natural differences in moral worth and ability, on the natural though unequal grades of worthiness and ability. This is what Mencius refers to as "the inequality of things is part of the nature of things" (*Mencius* 3A:4), or as Zhu Xi says, "the grades and distinctions of the principle of heaven." According to the Confucian principle of choosing the worthy and appointing the capable, worthy and capable persons should be in high positions. While their rule may be unequal, it is not unfair.

We know that political power is a very limited resource. Worthy and capable scholars hold an unequal position in society, and because of this it is fair to assign them to positions with access to greater political resources. In other words, to distribute political power to worthy and capable scholar-officials rather than to the ordinary masses is fairer to the scholars than the reverse situation would be. This is because worthy and capable scholar-officials have a heart of benevolence, moral conduct, breeding, ideas, learning, wisdom, and ability such that they must receive more political power so that they can use it to serve the people. The ordinary masses lack the virtues necessary for the exercise of politics, and so it would clearly be unfair to the worthy scholars to give more power to the masses than to them. It would also not benefit the use of power in the service of the people. The fairness discussed here is a form of natural fairness, the fairness of the order of the way of heaven, as Zhu Xi described it. It is also the rectification of names that Confucius spoke about or Plato's apportioning each person his office, or Aristotle's unequal treatment of what is unequal, or Burke's natural aristocracy. In short, it is a form of substantive rather than distributive fairness or justice.

In fact, Confucianism and the new Left do hold some things in common. Confucianism is also opposed to what Professor Wang terms the capitalist monopoly of power, that is, the capitalist alliance of a political and financial elite who oppress the masses. But Confucianism is not extremist and would not use this as a reason for doing away with all inequality, singing slogans such as "Everywhere a Hero" or "Six Hundred Million Shuns and Yaos." It would seek to replace the capitalist hold on power by a hierarchy, in which worthy and capable persons ruled. This is why, for Confucianism, only the worthy and capable scholar-officials are able to truly represent the interests of the masses thanks to their moral virtue and political ability, and hence once in power they can forcefully oppose the monopoly of power of capitalism and the oppression that this brings to the masses. Professor Wang should not fear the rule of worthy officials or be anxious about the arrangements for the House of *Ru* because the history of China tells us that the people who truly represented the interests of the masses and worked for them were Confucian worthies, that is, the Confucian officials. The learning, ideas, upbringing, and status of the Confucian officials determine that they are not the oppressors of the people but rather the natural representatives of their basic interests.[40]

Furthermore, in the time when there was no sage king, the Confucian scholars represented the Way of the Humane Authority. The Way of the Humane Authority has popular legitimacy as one of its form of legitimacy, and so what makes the Confucian scholars the proper representatives of the most basic and most long-lasting interests of the masses is precisely the sacred role assigned by heaven to the scholars. The Maoist great equality championed by Professor Wang is, to use his terminology, an unrealistic utopia, whereas the rule by Confucian scholars is a realizable utopia that has already been realized in history. This is because rule by worthy Confucian officials has been realized in history, and so the spirit of that rule can be continued today in response to the changing conditions of the times and recreated again. Mao's great equality with its elimination of the three great differences can never be realized in any society at any time and can be only a form of empty utopia, even if we are deeply moved by the sad nostalgia for that empty utopia.[41] Professor Wang's ideal of great equality is an unrealistic utopia, while the rule by worthy scholar-officials of Confucian constitutionalism is not an unrealistic utopia but one that can be realized by reflection and effort, to use the description of Professor Wang.

Justice in the Distribution of Power

It is clear from the above that the new Left and liberalism have much in common: Both are forms of political egalitarianism. On the basis of this egalitarianism they arrive at an equal distribution of political power. They differ only in that the new Left thinks that liberalism's one person one vote is insufficiently egalitarian, insufficiently democratic. Instead, it advocates that the masses should take part fully in politics as much as possible and should hold the greatest power. This is their great equality and great democracy.

In response, the Confucian Way of the Humane Authority has four questions to ask regarding the justice of this distribution of power: (1) Are there distinctions between commoners and sages, in a political sense, among real human beings? (2) If there are such distinctions, do they have a political significance in the distribution of power? (3) If they do play such a role, then are these distinctions in conformity with justice or not? (4) If a preference in granting political power to sages is in conformity with justice, then what kind of reasonable arrangement can effectively protect the justice of this preference?

The response to these questions by both the new Left and liberalism is essentially the same. (1) Since the Enlightenment, people have used their own reason to decide things in the public arena. In terms of reason, each person completely and autonomously realizes political endorsement, that is, a regime of complete equality. Hence, there are no politically relevant distinctions between commoners and sages. (2) The lack of political distinctions implies a lack of politically significant distribution of power. (3) This in turn means that there is no preference in favor of sages, and hence the question of the justice of such a preference does not arise. (4) The lack of such a preference means that there is no need for a system to ensure its existence.

The reply to these four basic questions by Confucianism is the exact opposite. The enlightenment of humanity is only on the surface and has nothing to do with morality. The Enlightenment has not brought about any substantive increase or progress in morality, or the universal good. Everyone seeks to use their own reason to fulfill their own autonomy, which simply means that people are proud and know nothing about transcendent, sacred values or common respect for morality. The representative democracy by which all people are equal is merely a selfish and self-sanctifying way of competing for power with God, or with the sages, a politics of everyone is a god or a sage. As a result, Confucianism is vehemently opposed to the proud politics of universal equality.

The Confucian response to the four questions is as follows. (1) There will always be a politically significant difference between commoners and sages in real human society. (2) This difference implies there is a distribution of power in a political sense. (3) The distribution of power is to be made according to the principles of treating unequal things unequally and of giving to people what properly belongs to them, by which a preference is shown in favor of the sages. (4) The justice of this distribution in favor of the sages implies that a reasonable arrangement be made, that is, a constitutional arrangement, so that the distinction in favor of the sages will enjoy effective protection. This kind of arrangement is a just arrangement.

It is precisely because of these four reasons that I thought of the Way of the Humane Authority and Confucian constitutionalism. Confucianism is in support of elite politics of rule by worthy scholar-officials. Confucianism's elitism is not that of modern society, which is a narrow, specialized, technical elitism, a specialized knowledge divorced from the ordinary world. It is, rather, an elitism of an understanding of the way of heaven, of attaining heavenly virtue, of believing in transcendent, sacred values, of being acquainted with specialized administrative knowledge, of morality and ability combined with excellence in carrying out politics as expressed in Zhang Zai's Four Sentence Doctrine. Since the new Left is even more egalitarian and more democratic than liberalism, a member of the new Left, such as Professor Wang, is even more fiercely, more actively, and more thoroughly opposed to my preference for granting power to the sages than liberalism is.

Chinese Socialist Democracy

Professor Wang criticizes my Confucian constitutionalism as "not a good thing." At the end of his essay he provides an alternative, which he believes is a good thing for China: Chinese socialist democracy. He articulates his vision in terms of the threefold legitimacy of the Way of the Humane Authority: "'socialism' would be the way of heaven (sacred legitimacy), 'democracy' the way of humanity (popular legitimacy), 'Chinese' the way of earth (cultural and historical legitimacy)."[42]

Here Wang fundamentally misunderstands the way of heaven. In Confucianism, this is a religious matter that can be grasped by faith and not by reason. The basis of the socialism embraced by the new Left is atheism and historical materialism. It is a theory of historical progress and scientism based on a post-Enlightenment rationality. Socialist theory denies faith in a transcendent, sacred, august heaven and God and faith in a metaphysical way and decree of heaven. It holds that reason (dialectical reason) can create a rational (i.e., one that is in accordance with the objective laws of history), materialist new world. It also holds that scientific technology is the revolutionary factor—the first element—that pushes the development of history forward. Obviously, this secular, rational, enlightenment, scientific, technical, atheist, materialist socialism is not on a par with the legitimacy of the way of heaven, which is one of the three forms of legitimacy of Confucianism. Socialism has no transcendent, sacred, religious nature, and so it cannot have any sacred legitimacy.

On popular legitimacy, Professor Wang is right to note that democracy is the way of the human, but the participation of the masses cannot be the only form of normative legitimacy for China. It cannot be the only standard by which one can judge the justice of politics. Since democracy does belong to the way of humanity, Confucian constitutionalism does not exclude it. The participation of all is granted a place in popular legitimacy and in the House of the People, which ensures it a place in the political setup and constitutional protection. But this form of mass participation is through representatives and not the Maoist form of great democracy, which Wang proposes.

Having said that, Confucian constitutionalism nonetheless remains elitist in nature because worthy and capable scholar-officials hold a greater share of power. It is, in Western terminology, elitist politics. The existence of the House of the People does not prejudice this elitism of the scholars. Here Wang has indeed correctly identified the heart of Confucian politics. However, in Wang's essay, the kind of elitism at stake is that by which, in the West today, capitalists hold power in the parliaments. This is clearly very different from Confucian constitutionalism, which is an elitism of knowledge and ability, not of money or wealth.[43] In terms of Confucian elitism, the dominance in the parliament of capitalists that Wang outlines is simply not elitism. Indeed, the people he portrays are part of the common masses; they are even small-minded people who rejoice in getting their desires. Confucian elitism is a matter of worthy scholar and gentleman. The *Record of Rites* says, "Superior men rejoice in attaining to the course (which they wish to pursue); and small men in obtaining the things which they desire."[44]

In summary, moved by the universal conscience of humanity and the benevolent heart of concern for people of Confucianism, I greatly admire the new Left's concern for the marginalized great masses. But on the basis of Confucian culture, I cannot accept the great equality and great democracy of the new Left. In my opinion, sympathetic concern for the marginalized great masses is not a matter of political justice but of religious love. This love is quite different from the justice of the preference for distributing political power to the worthy scholars and gentlemen. This Confucian love is what impels the Confucian scholar—when he is able to attain greater political power under the constitution—in implementing a government of benevolence. The attainment of power will enable him to decide laws and policies that show concern for the marginalized great masses.

Furthermore, when today we reflect on the history and state of democracy, we find that what capitalist liberal democracy calls political modernity has already run into a lot of problems in the matter of equality and democracy. It would seem that the new Left intends to continue the road set out by political modernity and use even greater political modernity to resolve the crises brought about by political modernity. It will do this by pushing the basic values of political modernity such as reason, the Enlightenment, autonomy, equality, democratic participation to an extreme with a view to opposing political modernity. I can see no hope in this use of the principles of political modernity to resolve the problems brought about by the same modernity.

The problems of political modernity can be dealt with only by political traditionalism because when we can see no hope ahead, the only hope lies in going back to tradition. In the case of China, a return to tradition is a return to Confucian civilization. Confucian constitutionalism is precisely such a return to the demands of Confucian civilization in the political sphere. This way is different from that of Chinese liberal democracy and from China's new Left. It is of course also different from the New Confucianism of Hong Kong and Taiwan. It is a Chinese form of political organization that bears the characteristics of Chinese history and culture.

This is my reply to the five questions raised by Professor Wang's essay.

CONCLUSION: POLITICAL TRADITIONALISM OPPOSED TO POLITICAL MODERNITY

In the above I have replied to five criticisms brought by liberalism and the new Left. It is a matter of political traditionalism replying to political modernity. The Confucian Way of the Humane Authority embodies the values of political tradition, even though it also absorbs, in part and where useful, some positive values of political modernity. Likewise, liberalism and the new Left embody the values of political modernity, even though they also absorb, in part and where useful, some general values of political tradition. In its basic political values, political Confucianism is traditional just as those of liberalism and the new Left are those of modernity. The partial use of some values from the other does not alter their basic difference of nature.

From the standpoint of Confucianism, reason, enlightenment, progress, humanism, autonomy, freedom, democracy, equality, inherent rights, separation of church and state, and political participation all amount to political modernity, and in these respects there is no difference between liberalism and the new Left. It is just that the new Left goes further than liberalism along the road of political modernity and takes it to an extreme.

Liberalism liberates man by talking about the enlightenment of man in the abstract; the new Left is not satisfied with this and talks about a thorough enlightenment and liberation of the great masses. Liberalism talks about universal humanism; the new Left goes further and talks about the humanism of the lowest classes. Liberalism talks about freedom under the law; the new Left wants an even freer economic society. Liberalism has limited representative democracy; the new Left talks about the great democracy of the masses. Liberalism proclaims equality under the law; the new Left wants the greater equality of Mao's thorough destruction of the three great differences. Liberalism discusses the abstract power of the law; the new Left wants a more thorough economic power. Liberalism seeks an abstract equality of opportunity; the new Left wants actual equality in practice for all. Liberalism reserves a place for God to oversee the world; the new Left does not want God. In all these instances, the new Left goes further in the way of political modernity than liberalism. The differences between the two are internal matters for political modernity and for Western thought.

However, in their opposition to tradition, the two have much in common. Both liberalism and the new Left deny the following: a personal transcendent sacred heaven, which can be the foundation of political legitimacy, the constitutional significance of the political legitimacy of heaven, the rule by scholar-officials in lieu of worthies in lieu of sages in lieu of heaven, the sovereignty lying with heaven, the moral difference between worthy and unworthy having any political connotations for the distribution of political power, the institutional union of "religion" (values) and "politics" (power) and that the historicity and continuity of the state need to be embodied and protected by a constitutional arrangement. The many things that both hold in common show that both stand with political modernity in opposition to political tradition.

In the terminology current in China today, this is primarily a struggle between old and new. My response to my critics is an important part of that struggle. Of course, the struggle is also one of China against the West, but this is only secondary. Modernity has brought along many problems and difficulties for human life, and many questions of China and the West ultimately boil down to ones of old and new. Today people must first of all face the difficulties of modernity, and only then can they go on to the problem of China and the West in the clash of civilizations.

Political Confucianism proposes the Way of the Humane Authority as a response to the difficulties of modernity that affect not only China but also the whole of humanity. Political Confucianism is not only intended for China. It is also of significance for all humanity. I hope that the reader will understand it and think seriously about the struggle between old and new because only in that way can my thought be understood, namely to understand that Confucianism is the representative of Chinese thought in China today.

Finally, there is one more point which must be emphasized. Tradition (old) is mystery, the sacred. Political modernity uses an extreme form of Western Enlightenment reason to disenchant and remove the sacred from politics, so that politics is freed from the transcendent values and completely secularized and humanized, leading to many difficulties and problems for politics. Hence, the struggle is also one of the sacred against the secular, or, in Confucian language, the principle of heaven against human desires. In my language it is one of disenchantment opposed to reenchantment. It is precisely here that we come up against an ultimate and basic value of all humanity in the struggle of the times. Confucian constitutionalism seeks to reenchant politics so as to overcome the extreme secularism of the enlightenment. Under the restraint of sacred values, it seeks to realize a political order in which human desires have a justifiable place, where they are harmonized and humanity is elevated. That order is Confucian constitutionalism.

INTRODUCTION

1. Gan Chunsong, "Qingmo minchu kongjiao hui shijian yu Rujia xiandai zhuandai de kunjing [The Establishment of Confucian Religious Associations in the Late Qing and Early Republican Period and the Difficulty of Transforming Confucianism Today]," *Qilu Xuekan* 3.186 (2005): 24–25. Gan shows that the debates were both substantial and open, and one cannot fail to note the contrast with the veiled decision-making process regarding the Confucius statue that was put up in Tiananmen Square in January 2011 and removed three months later.

2. As things stand (May 2012), Jiang cannot officially publish his institutional proposals in mainland China, but they have circulated samizdat-style among friends and supporters, and parts have been published in Taiwan and circulated on the Internet.

3. See, e.g., Fan Ruiping, ed., *Rujia shehui yu daotong fuxing [Confucian Society and the Revival of Dao]* (Shanghai: Huadong shifan daxue chubanshe, 2008), and Chen Lai and Gan Yang, eds., *Kongzi yu dangdai Zhongguo [Confucius and Contemporary China]* (Beijing: Xinzhi sanlian shudian, 2008).

4. Scholars and reformers have also debated experiments with subnational democratic deliberation and "democracy within the party," but these tend to be viewed as eventually paving the way for "full" democracy in the form of competitive elections for top leaders.

5. This section draws on Wang Ruichang, "The Rise of Political Confucianism in Contemporary China," in *The Renaissance of Confucianism in Contemporary China*, ed. Fan Ruiping (Dordrecht: Springer, 2011), 33–45; and Erika Yu and Meng Fan, "A Confucian Coming of Age," in Fan, *Renaissance of Confucianism*, 241–57.

6. Several of Jiang's cohorts went on to become prominent legal scholars, including Liang Zhiping (a distinguished legal historian of the Qing dynasty) and He Weifang (perhaps the most prominent liberal legal scholar in China).

7. This is not to deny that neo-Confucians also wrote on politics: Zhu Xi's idea of the community compact is a famous example. But political constraints meant that they could not be too explicitly focused on state-level politics (in some ways, the constraints were greater than they are today: for example, neo-Confucians did not have the option of publishing their works overseas in a different language).

8. See, e.g., Stephen Angle, "Rethinking Confucian Authority and Rejecting Confucian Authoritarianism," in *Zhongguo zhexue yu wenhua (di ba ji): Tang Junyi yu Zhongguo zhexue yanjiu [Chinese Philosophy and Culture (v.8): Tang Junyi and the Studies of Chinese philosophy]*, ed. Liu Xiaogan (Guilin: Guangxi shifan daxue chubanshe, 2010), 27–55.

9. See Guy S. Alitto's excellent intellectual biography of Liang Shuming that was somewhat prematurely titled *The Last Confucian*, 2nd ed. (Berkeley: University of California Press, 1986).

10. To be more precise, Jiang began to shift his focus from self-cultivation Confucianism to political Confucianism before the bloody repression of the student movement on June 4, 1989. In May 1989, Jiang participated in a conference held at Hong Kong Baptist University on the theme of ultimate concern for the postmodern world. Jiang presented a paper titled "The Meaning and Problem of Revitalizing Confucianism in Mainland China," in which he argued that the priority for Chinese scholars should be exploring how Confucianism can tackle problems faced by contemporary China rather than responding to challenges posed by the postmodern West.

11. Jiang's earlier works on political Confucianism include three books: *Gongyangxue yinlun* [*Introduction to the Gongyang Commentary on the Spring and Autumn Annals*] (Shenyang: Liaoning jiaoyu chubanshe, 1995); *Zhengzhi ruxue: dangdai ruxue de zhuanxiang, tezhi yu fazhan* [*Political Confucianism: The Transformation, Special Characteristics, and Development of Contemporary Confucianism*] (Beijing: Sanlian Shudian, 2003); and *Shengming xinyang yu wangdao zhengzhi: rujia wenhua de xiandai jiazhi* [*Faith in Spiritual Life and Politics of the Way of the Humane Authority: The Modern Value of Confucian Culture*] (Taiwan: Yang Zheng Tang Chuban, 2004). These books have yet to be translated into English.

12. For an account of my visit to the Academy, see "A Visit to a Confucian Academy," *http://www.dissentmagazine.org/online.php?id=146*, September 22, 2008 (accessed June 19, 2011).

13. Wangdao is more commonly translated as the "kingly" or "royal" way, but given that Jiang argues that the monarch should have a largely symbolic role, it may be misleading to use an English term that suggests the monarch exercises substantial political power. The first book of this translation series also translates "wang" as "humane authority" (Yan Xuetong [Daniel A. Bell and Sun Zhe, eds.; Edmund Ryden, trans.], *Ancient Chinese Thought, Modern Chinese Power* [Princeton, N.J.: Princeton University Press, 2011]).

14. In Chinese, the scholarly tradition of Confucianism is known as *Ruxue*. *Ru* is a tradition with Confucius as a central figure, but it predates Confucius (who viewed himself primarily as a transmitter of an earlier tradition) and was carried on as a tradition with different interpretations after Confucius. Since the "House of Confucians" connotes (to the Anglophone ear) the more narrow idea of a house composed of the followers of Confucius, we translate the *Tongruyuan* as the "House of *Ru*."

15. Functional constituencies are highly controversial in the Hong Kong context, and there may be similar problems if they are used in China as a whole: see my book *China's New Confucianism: Politics and Everyday Life in a Changing Society*, rev. ed. (Princeton, N.J.: Princeton University Press, 2010), 182–83.

16. Chapter 1, note 25.

17. Hahm Chaihark puts forward a similar proposal. In Choson dynasty Korea, the king was obliged to listen to policy lectures by Confucian scholars and was not allowed to hold audience with ministers unless he was accompanied by two court historians, one of whom recorded all the verbal transactions while the other recorded all physical movements. Hahm argues that "we should retrieve the notion that a ruler can and should be disciplined by being lectured to all the time, and put under constant surveillance." Hahm Chaihark, "Constitutionalism, Confucian Civic Virtue, and Ritual Propriety," in *Confucianism for the Modern World, ed.* Daniel A. Bell and Hahm Chaibong (Cambridge, UK: Cambridge University Press, 2003), 52.

18. Page 64 of this book and chapter 2, note 39.

19. Such claims make more sense of "civilizational" states like China, rather than recently created states like Singapore that are the self-conscious creation of identifiable "founding fathers."

20. The Thai monarchy is perhaps the closest model of what Jiang Qing has in mind for China. Just as the Thai monarch must be a Buddhist from a distinct lineage who stands above the fray and mediates political conflicts between real power holders as well as supports all traditions and religions in Thailand, so the Chinese monarch should be a Confucian from a distinct lineage who stands above the fray and mediates political conflicts between real power holders as well as supports all traditions and religions in China.

21. What Chan terms "civility" is similar in substance to what American liberal theorists such as Amy Gutmann and Stephen Macedo term "public reason."

22. John Rawls himself, however, would disagree with this implication. His last work—the *Law of Peoples*—is an argument that liberal societies should tolerate "decent" nondemocratic societies with an official state religion so long as they have consultative mechanisms and respect basic human rights. Jiang's "Confucian constitutionalism" is an excellent example of a "decent" society, except that Jiang would add that it is superior to liberal democracy, not a subpar society that should be "tolerated" by liberal societies.

23. In discussion, however, Bai Tongdong suggested that Confucianism might be more flexible than Jiang suggests. For example, Confucians might favor a complementarity of roles in marriage arrangements that need not map directly onto sex differences; hence, gay marriages that instantiate a complementarity of roles might be (legally) acceptable to Confucians.

24. Bai and Chan both appeal to Rawls to argue that any defense of Confucianism needs to be stripped of a priori foundations to be acceptable in a modern-day pluralistic context, but Bai is more optimistic about the fate of Confucianism in China in the sense that he believes a modernized version of pre-Qin nontranscendent Confucianism that captures the true spirit of Confucianism could command widespread assent in China (as opposed to a "piecemeal" defense of values derived from the Confucian tradition that aims for political consensus without moral consensus). Li, as we will see, goes even further than Bai, in the sense that he explicitly thinks it is possible to build a society built on a consensus of Confucian values (even though the political form would be democratic).

25. As Jiang himself points outs, both Bai and Li accuse Jiang of defending a view of a transcendent heaven that does not represent the true spirit of Confucianism, but whereas Bai accuses Jiang of employing a later Han Confucian reading of heaven that represented a distortion of classical Confucianism, Li accuses Jiang of invoking a reading of heaven that was even earlier than the pre-Qin classical period. Bai does note, however, that the Han reading is an apparent (politically motivated) move back to a pre-pre-Qin reading.

26. One might add that there are different levels of crises of popular legitimacy. It may be true that there is more popular support for the Chinese government than for most Western governments, but it is doubtful that there is more support for China's constitutional system as a long-term ideal compared to (for example) the support for the constitution in the United States. Put differently, Americans are likely to be satisfied with their form of government even if they are dissatisfied with their particular rulers, whereas the opposite may be true in China.

27. The same goes for his critics: their comments are excellent from an academic point of view, but they seem aimed at hacking away at the foundations of Jiang's theory with the hope that the whole edifice would collapse rather than learning from his theory.

28. I use the word "impression" because Jiang Qing has been open to modifying his views if he has felt that his critics have advanced arguments that have allowed him to improve his theory (e.g., he modified his view that the three houses should have equal power in response to the criticism that it would lead to political gridlock). See Jiang Qing, "Rujiao xianzheng de yili wenti yu yihui xingshi: huiying Bei Danning jiaoshou dui 'Yihui

Sanyuanzhi' de piping" ["Political Legitimacy and the Tricameral Parliament: Reply to the Criticism of Daniel A. Bell"] (unpublished manuscript). Plus, he openly says that the Way of the Humane Authority has incorporated some elements of modernity, such as democratic elections for the House of the People. Other aspects of his theory—like the fact that it is nonsexist in the sense he implicitly allows for the possibility that both women and men can be rulers—also seem to be informed by modern ideas of gender equality. So presumably Jiang should be open to further improvements to his theory in response to new developments and new arguments. One can infer that he did not modify his views in response to the four critics in this book because he thought they did not put forward any arguments that caused him to rethink and improve his theory. So that is why I ask if Jiang Qing could "compromise" without having to give up his normative commitments. From Jiang Qing's perspective, the result may not be as desirable as the Way of the Humane Authority, but from his critics' point of view, it would be an improvement.

29. Chapter 3, note 16.

30. Chapter 3, note 16.

31. Daniel Bardsley, "Plan for Church Higher Than Confucian Temple Causes Stir in China," *http://www.thenational.ae/news/worldwide/asia-pacific/plan-for-church-higher-than-confucian-temple-causes-stir-in-china?pageCount=0*, April 12, 2011 (accessed June 19, 2011).

32. In discussion, Jiang Qing said my own criticisms of Yu Dan were overly harsh, even though he largely agrees with the substance of the critique (see my book *China's New Confucianism*, appendix 1).

33. This is not to deny that some people benefitted from the Cultural Revolution. One successful businessman told me that he would still be toiling in the fields had it not been for the Cultural Revolution: his father was admitted to the elite Beijing University largely because of his peasant background, thus paving the way for upward mobility for himself and his family members. For a scholarly defense of the view that the rural poor and urban working class often benefitted from Mao's policies in the Cultural Revolution, see Mobo Gao, *The Battle for China's Past: Mao and the Cultural Revolution* (London: Pluto Press, 2008).

34. Chapter 8, note 41.

35. Elsewhere, Jiang has written, "[A]fter conservatism, socialism comes closest to Chinese thought in all of western thought. In fact, Chinese history shows that Confucianism is a natural form of socialism." He argues that such socialist values and concern for the poor and global justice are also traditional Confucian concerns. Moreover, Jiang argues that the "authentic critical spirit of original Marxism . . . is still required in China today" to address the huge gap between rich and poor in China. But Marxism cannot address the basic problem of legitimacy because it is foreign (and hence lacks historical legitimacy) and also because it is a form of secular atheism in which technology determines historical development (and hence lacks sacred legitimacy). See his article "Rujiao xianzheng de yili wenti yu yihui xingshi."

36. In the *Record of Rituals*, the most famous account of a Confucian political ideal begins with "tianxia wei gong" (the world for all) and is followed by the line "xuan xian yu neng" (the virtuous and the talented will be chosen [to rule]), suggesting that even an ideal that has been compared to "higher communism" would need a state governed by those with above-average moral judgment and intellectual ability.

37. Bryan Caplan has argued that American voters hold irrational beliefs that pose the greatest obstacle to sound economic policy, and he suggests that requiring poten-

tial voters to pass tests of economic literacy would lead to more sensible policies. Bryan Caplan, *The Myth of the Rational Voter: Why Democracies Choose Bad Policies* (Princeton, N.J.: Princeton University Press, 2007), 197. Such proposals are nonstarters in the American context, but in China they may hold some promise.

38. See, e.g., Joseph Chan, "Democracy and Meritocracy: Toward a Confucian Perspective," *Journal of Chinese Philosophy* 34, no. 2 (June 2007): 179–93; Bai Tongdong, "A Mencian Version of Limited Democracy," *Res Publica* 14, no. 1 (2008)): 19–34; and Chenyang Li, "Where Does Confucian Virtuous Leadership Stand?" *Philosophy East and West* 59, no. 4 (October 2009): 531–36. It is worth asking why Jiang's "liberal Confucian" critics reacted so strongly and negatively to Jiang's proposals even though they share his basic political aim of reconciling democracy and meritocracy. One reason might be that Jiang labels them as "liberals" rather than as different interpreters of the same Confucian tradition (as compromise terminology, they are referred to as "liberal Confucians" in this introduction). I once saw a similar reaction to a well-known orthodox rabbi who addressed a crowd of largely secular Jews at the University of Tel Aviv and questioned their Jewishness because they did not practice religious rites. Speaking for myself, I was charmed by the intelligence and humor of the speaker and thought he was making some good points and was somewhat surprised at the vehemently negative reaction of the audience (perhaps because I am only "half Jewish"—my father is Jewish, and my mother is Catholic—and I already consider myself to be both inside and outside the Jewish tradition, which may be similar to my relationship with Confucianism, and do not agonize too much about whether I have a "pure" Jewish or Confucian identity).

39. To borrow Rawlsian language, both sides can strive for an overlapping consensus on politics based on different versions of a comprehensive system of (religious or secular) value. Jiang may object to the (re)introduction of Rawls, but such strategies for seeking consensus in politics are older; for example, they were invoked as means for seeking consensus on the basic rights in the 1948 UN Universal Declaration of Human Rights (its drafters, including the Confucian philosopher P. C. Chang, allowed for disagreement about foundations). Besides, Jiang should not object to borrowing from aspects of Rawlsian liberalism if they help to promote his political aims just because it comes from Rawls (just as liberals should not endorse Rawlsian liberalism just because it comes from Rawls).

40. Given that the members of the House of *Ru* are supposed to focus on the needs of future generations and foreigners, it may also be desirable that the deputies be tested for basic knowledge of environmental science and international affairs.

41. Jiang argues that the American constitutional system prioritizes a Protestant value system, but it does not *explicitly* do so. In the same vein, the Chinese constitutional system could prioritize a Confucian value system without explicitly doing so.

42. But nineteenth-century "aristocratic" liberals such as John Stuart Mill and Alexis de Tocqueville explicitly allowed for elite rule in liberal societies (e.g., Mill suggested that educated people should have extra votes) and hence may have been more supportive of such proposals.

43. He does not, however, explicitly draw on contemporary legal (and social scientific) scholarship in support of his views on Confucian constitutionalism.

44. A more substantial modification would be to allow for the possibility that the Academy need not be composed exclusively of Confucian scholars, but Jiang is almost certain to reject such a modification (even if the Academy is still primarily composed of Confucians) because the members of the Academy are supposed to represent sacred Confucian values.

45. The U.S. presidential system may be defective in the sense that the U.S. president is both the head of state whom people project their emotions onto and the most politically powerful head of government. In practice, it may mean that Americans do not rationally scrutinize the president's policies as much as they should, especially regarding foreign policy.

46. Consider the serious doubts about the "playboy son" and likely successor to the current king of Thailand.

47. Even as an ideal, however, parts need to be further fleshed out. For example, the composition of the executive branch of government other than the symbolic monarch remains unclear (perhaps it can be composed of three people chosen from each of the three houses, like a Confucian-style politburo?).

48. This is not to deny that there has been substantial political reform the past three decades. Most important, there are now term and age limits for the top posts of the ruling Chinese Communist Party. There is also a competitive voting process for leaders within the highest echelons of the party (e.g., Hu Jintao is said to have lost the vote that was meant for him to choose his own successor; Hu's protégé Li Keqiang lost the vote to Xi Jinping). But such changes have not been openly debated, and they are not sufficiently substantial reforms from the point of view of most critics of the government (even from the point of view of Prime Minister Wen Jiabao, who has called for more political reforms).

49. For a recent essay that seeks inspiration from Kang Youwei's political ideals, see Ban Wang, "The Vision of International Morality in Kang Youwei's Book of the Great Community" (paper presented at the Tianxia Workshop, Stanford University, May 6–10, 2011).

CHAPTER 1

1. I have thought about the three sources of legitimacy of the Way of the Humane Authority for over a decade and discussed the issue with colleagues and friends, but had not yet written my ideas down. With the publication of *Political Confucianism*, which discusses politics in a rather different way, more people at home and abroad were interested in the Way of the Humane Authority, so I wrote a paper for the "International Conference on Contemporary Confucianism" in Hangzhou and set out the basic features of the Way of the Humane Authority to reply to scholars both at home and abroad.

2. Sébastien Billioud notes that Confucianism distinguished between external and internal kingship. The contemporary neo-Confucians have discussed the wisdom of Confucianism, the internal kingship, but have joined this to democracy as the external kingship. See Jiang Qing (Sébastien Billioud, trans.), "Le confucianisme de la Voie royale, direction pour le politique en Chine contemporaine," *Perspectives on the Political in China Today (Extrême-Orient Extrême-Occident)*, 31 (October 2009): 103–23, 103n3.

3. Sébastien Billioud notes that Jiang Qing follows Kang Youwei (1858–1927) in going back to the *Gongyang Commentary*, which treats the historical text of the Annals of the state of Lu as an esoteric teaching of Confucius, with moral lessons drawn applicable to present times. The *Commentary* was popular in the Han dynasty (206 BCE–220 CE). See ibid., 103n2, 104n5.

4. The founders of the three dynasties: Yu is supposed to have founded the Xia, Tang founded the Shang, and Kings Wen and Wu founded the Zhou.

5. James Legge, trans., *The Sacred Books of China*, vol. 4, book 28: *The State of Equilibrium and Harmony* (New York: Gordon Press, 1976), 324–25.

6. The translator notes that Billioud translates these terms according to the political

philosophy of Carl Schmitt (1888–1985) as *le politique* (*zheng Dao*) and *la politique* (*zhi Dao*). See Sébastien Billioud, in Jiang Qing, "Le confucianisme de la Voie royale," 108n8. See Carl Schmitt (George D. Schwab, trans.), *The Concept of the Political* (Chicago: University of Chicago Press, 2006).

7. "King Wan's Explanation of the Entire Hexagrams," in *The Book of Changes*, in Legge, *Sacred Books of China*, vol. 2, 213.

8. Louis Rougier, *La Mystique démocratique: ses origins, ses illusions* (Paris: Flammarion, 1929).

9. Francis Fukuyama, *The End of History and the Last Man* (London: Penguin, 1992).

10. The translator draws on Billioud's note that Jiang's language echoes that of Zhu Xi (1130–1200), who stressed the struggle between human desires and heavenly principles. See Sébastien Billioud, in Jiang Qing, "Le confucianisme de la Voie royale," 109n19.

11. In fact, this pressure comes from the steel, chemical, and auto industries and from the fact that most Americans are reluctant to reduce their standard of living.

12. Carl J. Friedrich, *The New Belief in the Common Man* (Boston: Little, Brown, 1942).

13. For instance, in the Western Middle Ages, sacred legitimacy was exalted as the only kind, leading to politics dominated by religious authority and oppression of reasonable human desires. The contemporary Western democracy, as discussed, has gone to another extreme. Or, in some Islamic countries, cultural legitimacy is exalted, and so those countries reject any change or reform of the cultural legacy. Such regimes do not accord with the will of the people and are obstinately conservative.

14. Although India and Japan did so reluctantly at first and only later by choice or partly so.

15. The translator draws on Billioud's note that the six offices represent heaven, earth, and the four seasons (*The Rites of Zhou*). See Sébastien Billioud, in Jiang Qing, "Le confucianisme de la Voie royale," 115n23.

16. The translator draws on Billioud's note about the *daishi* (Grand Teacher), *daifu* (Grand Counselor), and *daibao* (Grand Protector) of the Zhou kings. See ibid., 105n24.

17. The translator notes from Billioud's note that the Bright Hall is where the Zhou king conducted administrative affairs. See ibid., 116n25.

18. The translator draws on Billioud's note that this is a Song dynasty custom with origins in the Han. See ibid., 116n26.

19. The translator draws on Billioud's note that dynastic annals were kept by many early dynasties. The system was formalized in the Tang and called *True Records*. See ibid., 116n27.

20. The translator notes from Billioud's note that the four major sacrifices were at the altar of heaven to the south of the imperial city, the altar of earth in the north, the altar of the sun in the east, and the altar of the moon in the West. See ibid., 116n28.

21. The term *guoti* [national body] comes from the *Spring and Autumn Annals* and refers to the one body of the state that endures through the centuries. The state is the product of history and culture. It is an organic body. From the day the life of the state begins its organic life can never be cut off no matter what changes there are of dynasty, government, political authority, rulers, or the name of the state. The life of the state will always continue to exist forever. This is what the *Spring and Autumn Annals* means by saying, "[T]oday's state is that of the ancestors and of our descendants." China today continues the life of ancient China and hands this life on to China of the future. History and culture are the life of the state. China will always be China. Hence, the state is not only the product of history but also the body and inheritor of history and culture.

22. The eldest son of the descendants of Confucius has traditionally been honored

with the title "Duke Successor to the Sage."

23. According to the meaning of the *Spring and Autumn Annals*, Confucius was a king and so Confucius's descendants inherit his royal seat and should be kings. But the term "king" here is not to be understood in the common way. Rather, it stands for a historical and cultural kingship. Confucius inherited the cultural tradition of Fu Xi, Yao, Shun, Yu, Tang, Kings Wen and Wu, and the Duke of Zhou. These guarantee the legitimacy of the tradition. The descendants of Confucius chair the House of the Nation as a sign of the legitimacy of Chinese culture. Confucius was also descended from King Tang, founder of the Shang dynasty. Hence, he also inherited the rule of the ancient kings, which symbolizes the historical continuity of Chinese culture. His descendants as head of the House of the Nation, therefore, also represent the historical continuity of the nation. The continuity of this history is the cultural legitimacy of China.

24. The members of the House are chosen according to the following principles: "keeping alive the former kings" (*Spring and Autumn Annals*) for the descendants of rulers; "the three roots of the Rites" since the sages are the roots of culture and we should be grateful to them, for descendants of famous people and sages; the principle of compassion for those "whose renown has spread through generations" (*Book of History*) for descendants of patriots; the principle of "history as the mirror for running the state" for the history professors; the principle of "sustaining the old people of the state as advisors" for the retired officials; the principle of "choosing the worthy and elevating the capable" (*Spring and Autumn Annals*) for the worthy people in society; the traditional Chinese tolerance of religions for choosing religious leaders, with the Confucians representing the scholars of the palace and taking the lead and the other religions standing for the "hundred schools" under the direction of the former.

25. The tricameral system is different from Western democratic parliamentary systems. The U.S. Senate and House are chosen in different ways, but members all represent the popular will, which is the sole foundation of law. The restraint each chamber exercises on the other is simply a reflection of different opinions among the people and has no real significance. According to the Way of the Humane Authority, both are part of the House of the People.

In countries that still have a monarchy, such as the United Kingdom and Japan, the real power of the monarch is not the source of political legitimacy. Hence, the monarch cannot represent cultural legitimacy, nor exert any influence in the legislative process. The monarch is simply a ceremonial symbol of tradition and so cannot be compared to the House of the Nation. The House of Commons in the United Kingdom is very much like the House of the People in the Way of the Humane Authority. The House of Lords includes archbishops, bishops, aristocrats of the royal house, law lords, and other lords. To some extent it combines the sacred and cultural legitimacies, but since its existence is not clearly defined in law—it is simply something left behind by history—added to which the power of the Commons is always growing while that of the Lords is decreasing, the House of Lords has no effective role.

The Iranian parliamentary system has something like two houses. The parliament, the Islamic Consultative Assembly, is rather like a lower house that decides on legislation, while the Council of Guardians is rather like an upper house that assesses laws. Members of the Assembly are chosen by direct elections by all the people and represent popular legitimacy. The Council of Guardians is made up of religious leaders and legal experts. It represents both sacred and cultural legitimacy. However, since Iran is a theocracy, the only form of legitimacy is that of the sacred, and so the Council of Guardians has power over the Assembly and is not subject to its restraint. The two do not work in tandem. One leads the other. This is very different from the three-dimensional relationship between the House of *Ru* and the House of the People in the tricameral system. While in terms of content the Iranian and Western systems are very different, in their basic format they are not. Both exalt one kind of legitimacy: popular in the West, sacred in Iran. They both go against the principle of harmony and exhibit a biased form of legitimacy.

CHAPTER 2

1. This essay was written for a conference held at Qufu in Shandong, April 25–26, 2009, titled "Reform and Opening Up and China's Future: Confucian Ideas, Values, Motivations and Explorations." The conference was organized by Professor Fan Ruiping and Mr. Hong Xiuping and was sponsored by the Qufu Union of Confucian Culture.

2. Contemporary Chinese liberals, new Confucianists, and official circles in Hong Kong and Taiwan also share the same idea about issues of constitutional legitimacy.

3. We are very surprised that neither Kang Youwei nor Zhang Junmai added any Confucian element to the legitimization of their constitutions.

4. Ban Gu, *Han shu* [*Book of the Han History*] (Beijing: Shangwu Yinshuguan, 1941), book 30.

5. In today's world, among the types of constitution there are Christian constitutions and Islamic constitutions. Each type expresses the particular features of a given culture and civilization. Hence the term we must use is Confucian constitutionalism and not Confucianist constitutionalism or Confucian School constitutionalism because the latter two names refer only to the thoughts of a particular school of thought and do not represent Chinese culture and civilization in its entirety. Moreover, Confucian constitutionalism is the only thing that can respond to Christian or Islamic constitutionalism because in both these cases "Christian" and "Islamic" refer to civilizations formed in history and culture and not to mere schools of thought alone.

6. Ban Gu, *Han shu*, book 56.

7. *Shu King* in Legge, *Sacred Books of China*, vol. 1, part V, book 1, *The Great Declaration*, 128.

8. Translator's note: In this section, the author uses *rujia* and not *rujiao*. One wonders if that is an oversight.

9. *Shu King*, in Legge, *Sacred Books of China*, vol. 1, part II, book 2, *The Counsels of the Great Yu*, 47.

10. This is a comment on the *Qian* hexagram of the *Book of Changes*, which is the hexagram of heaven. Cheng Yi, *Zhouyi Shangjing shang* in *Zhouyi Chengshichuan* [*Cheng's Commentary on the Book of Changes*] (Taipei: Cheng Wen Chubanshe, 1976).

11. Mao Heng, *Maoshi zhushu* [*Mao's Commentary on Odes*], vol. 4 (Hong Kong: Zhonghua Shuju, 1964), 339.

12. For details on this point, see chapter 1.

13. The relationship of sovereignty to legitimacy is a complicated matter of political philosophy. It cannot be questioned that both exist in a tight relationship and in constitutional matters it is impossible to separate them. In general, "sovereignty" refers to the supreme real power of the ruler. To say that sovereignty comes from x is to refer to the origin of its legitimacy. If we say "from the people" then the people are the source of legitimacy, if "the ruler" then he is the source, and if "heaven" then heaven is the origin. Sovereignty is what carries the legitimacy. Without a sovereign the legitimacy does not exist. It would lack any power to rule and could not influence politics. It would be merely

a transcendent value. Legitimacy is what founds the value of sovereignty. Without it sovereignty would be naked brute force and politics would lack any correct norm to speak of. The state would be one that, in Mencius's words, had "lost the way" or that Augustine refers to as an "expanded band of robbers." From the point of view of political philosophy, the problem of the relationship between sovereignty and legitimacy is a fundamental issue for Confucian constitutionalism and something that we will encounter when discussing other issues.

14. In fact in Western democracies there are also subdelegations as in the American system where the people elect an electoral college, which then elects the president.

15. Dong Zhongshu, *Renyifa*, in *Chunqiu fanlu* [*Luxuriant Dew of the Spring and Autumn Annals*], book 8, sec. 9 (Shanghai: Shanghai Guji Chubanshe, 1989), 51.

16. See Richard John Neuhaus, *The Naked Public Square: Religion and Democracy in America* (Grand Rapids, Mich.: Eerdmans, 1984).

17. Modern Western constitutions, on the contrary, uphold limitation of power as a means to ensure the constitution meets its basic goal of power protecting rights.

18. Confucius encapsulated the spirit of this rule by scholars by saying "those who study and do well can be officials." The later imperial examination system provided a structure for this spirit. Rule by scholars is very different from the Western tradition of rule by wealth. From ancient Greece and Rome up until today in the West, the capitalist class has had a hold on politics and has obtained this by wealth. History shows us that the ways to obtain power are by violence, inheritance, usurpation, wealth, and the will of the people, whereas in Confucian rule by scholarship, power is obtained by learning. From the point of view of human history, that is pretty remarkable.

19. Huang Zongxi (Wm. Theodore de Bary, trans.), "Schools," in *Waiting for the Dawn: A Plan for the Prince* (New York: Columbia University Press, 1993), 104.

20. Ibid., 104.

21. Ibid., 107.

22. For instance, in its present development in Taiwan, the Control Yuan cannot impeach the president and so remains unable to supervise the work of the government.

23. In practice this means that, for all important discussions or decisions in the country, the Academy is to send two academicians to take part and keep a record: one to record the events and the other to record what is said. Within a legally fixed period of time, the records are then to be consigned to the archives of the Academy and sealed. The recording academicians are to be sworn to silence in the name of the sage kings. Access to the records is then denied to all, until such point as they are made available to later historians.

24. Ban Gu, *Yiwenzhi* [*Treatise on Literature*], in *Han shu*, 3115.

25. *The Collection of Treatises on the Rules of Propriety or Ceremonial Usages*, in Legge, *Sacred Books of China*, vol. 4, book 17, *The Record of Music*, 106.

26. The palace examinations were to select scholars for the Hanlin Academy. The emperor, or his representative, selected the best graduates of the triennial examinations for this Academy.

27. It is clear that the Academy functions very differently from Sun Yat-sen's Examination Yuan. Sun's Examination Yuan was rather like the old imperial system or that of the modern civil service exams.

28. The *Five Classics* are the *Book of Changes* (*Yijing*), the *Book of Odes* (*Shijing*), the *Classic of History* (*Shujing* or *Shangshu*), the *Book of Rites* (*Liji*), and the *Spring and Autumn Annals* (*Chunqiu*).

29. Huang Zongxi, *Waiting for the Dawn*.

30. Historically the system worked best in the Tang (618–907) and Song (960–1279)

dynasties, when the lecturers and emperors were in a teacher-friend relationship. In the Ming (1368–1644) and Qing (1644–1911), the emperor assumed a position of too much power, such that, during the lectures, the lecturers kowtowed to the emperor. The reason for this is that the scholar who was lecturing was considered a minister of the emperor and came from among the scholars of the executive under the emperor as in a cabinet or in the Hanlin Academy. He did not come from an independent supervisory body above the executive. Once the emperor assumed political power, the lectureship on the classics could not realize its full constitutional potential. In Confucian constitutionalism, however, the Academy is situated above, and is independent of, all other state institutions, hence the Chair of Classics can adequately fulfill its role by ensuring that at the level of the state's basic ritual order, it can independently, respectfully, and effectively regulate and educate the political leadership.

31. E.g., to Fu Xi, the Three Kings, Confucius, Mencius, Xunzi, Dong Zhongshu, Cheng Yi (1033–1107), Zhu Xi (1130–1200), Lu Xiangshan (1139–92), and Wang Yangming (1472–1528).

32. Translator's note: The Five Mountains are the Eastern Mountain (*Taishan*), the Western Mountain (*Huashan*), the Southern Mountain (*Hengshan*), the Northern Mountain (*Hengshan*), and the Central Mountain (*Songshan*). The Six Honored Ones (*Liu Zong*) are listed in various ways; a note on the *Classic of History* gives them as (1) the Four Seasons, (2) Cold and Hot, (3) the Sun, (4) the Moon, (5) the Planets, and (6) Water and Dryness.

33. For more on this, see chapter 3 of this book.

34. On this traditional ceremony, see my article "A Plan to Restablish China's Confucian Religion." Jiang Qing, "Chongjian rujiao jihua" ["A Plan to Reestablish China's Confucian Religion"], *Zhongguo rujiao yanjiu tongxun* [*News on Chinese Confucian Studies*] 1 (December 2005): 1–5.

35. It may be objected that, in the past, the emperor or government officials frequently presided at state ceremonies of a religious nature, so what is to prevent government institutions or officials doing the same today. A response to this objection has been suggested above. Here we draw it out in more detail. The reason why contemporary, as opposed to former, government institutions and their officials are unsuitable for presiding at such ceremonies is that politics have changed. In the past state and religion were united and the government aimed to implement the sacred values of the Confucian way, that is the principles of Yao, Shun, the Duke of Zhou, and Confucius. Moreover, the emperor saw himself as governing on behalf of heaven and deriving his sacred legitimacy from heaven. China of the past was not the secularized, rationalized state of today. It enjoyed a certain religious and sacred status. In carrying out sacrifices, emperors and government officials had a religious and sacred identity, and hence it was appropriate for them to carry out the ceremonies.

China today has already succumbed to the influence of Western political modernity with its increasing secularization, rationalization, impartiality, and accompanying exclusion of religion, the sacred, and values. State institutions no longer carry the religious values of Confucianism, and state officials bear only a rationalized political significance. It is, clearly, inappropriate that state leaders or government officials preside at state ceremonies in a nonreligious capacity. But this is not to exclude the possibility that one day Confucianism will revive throughout China and the way of Yao, Shun, Confucius, and Mencius will become the official learning of the state.

When Confucian constitutionalism is enshrined, then political and moral authority will be reunited and state institutions will once again be bearers of sacred, Confucian values and China will have returned to her own cultural specificity. China will once again be Confucian China. Furthermore, state leaders and government officials will nearly all have passed the Academy examinations and be scholars who believe in the transcendental values of Confucian religion. Then they will be qualified to preside at state ceremonies because they will enjoy a certain religious status. This union of political and moral authority is indeed what Confucianism seeks. Unfortunately, it has not materialized at present.

36. In democratic constitutions the people are above the parliament, whereas in Confucian constitutionalism scholarship is above the parliament. A parliament is not the ultimate source of authority; it is only the body that carries out sovereignty in practice.

37. The Chinese text gives the titles to the first and eleventh poems in the *Book of Odes*. The first is said to present ideal relations between husband and wife; the eleventh is its sequel, describing how the world was so perfect there were no faults to be observed.

38. Such as the legalization of homosexual marriage, the founding of one-parent families, the encouragement of sexual liberation or sexual freedom, the promotion of an open and legal sex industry, the cloning of human beings, research into genetic weapons, and blasphemy of the sages and worthy people.

39. It may be objected that this is a Taliban-style theocracy. Yet, unlike the Taliban, though the Academy upholds religion, it does so without exercising any power in carrying out daily affairs, or in performing legislative, executive, or judicial acts. The Taliban, by contrast, does hold such power, though it lacks the structural role of holding other powers in balance and hence does not act purely at the constitutional level. A Taliban-style regime may be described as a theocracy, but not one in which the Academy upholds religion.

If we take a step back and admit that, in fact, upholding religion does have a certain degree of judicial power, we must note that this judicial power is exercised according to the sacred way and principle of heaven. This kind of judicial power is not something that modern secular judiciaries enjoy, want, or have the capacity or qualifications to possess. Modern judiciaries have already become detached from religion and morality and are wholly secularized, rationalized, and neutral. Yet society cannot exist without a power that upholds religious and moral values, for without it society becomes oversecularized and rationalized and people fall into a moral abyss and the whole society collapses. For this reason, the Academy is the only body fit to uphold religious and moral values and ensure the state maintains its basic morality.

40. Below we make a few remarks about the formation of the Academy. The highest spiritual leader of the Academy, the Chief Libationer, could be publically proposed by the Confucians (*Rulin*). He would manage the affairs of the Academy and would serve for life. In the capital city, the Bright Hall would be erected as the seat of the Academy. Academicians would be chosen by the Chief Libationer from among the Confucians (*Rulin*) on account of their outstanding merit in both learning and practice and would run the daily business and teaching of the Academy. The state would finance the Academy, though the Chief Libationer would not receive a state salary as an indication of his transcendent and superior status.

Entering into more detail, we suggest that the Chief Libationer and academicians could be selected by a Confucian Scholars Committee (*Ruxuejia weiyuanhui*) formed of thirty persons selected jointly by the House of *Ru* and Confucians (*Rulin*) from the whole country, on the grounds of their outstanding merits in scholarship, practice, virtue, and competence. The Confucian Committee would then proceed to elect the Chief Libationer by secret ballot. He would serve for life unless he wished to resign on health or other grounds. The Confucian Committee would hold power of recall over the Chief Libationer. The academicians would have to be outstanding in both scholarship and practice. Persons could be recommended to this office by being nominated by the state, selected by the people, recommended by the Confucian Scholars (*ruxuejia*), by modern examinations, or by selection by the Chief Libationer. The election of the Chief Libationer would be like that of the Pope by the College of Cardinals in the Catholic Church, or like that of the Supreme Leader of Iran by the Assembly of Experts. At some later stage we could enter into more detail on the composition of the Academy and the creation of academicians. Here we present a simple sketch only.

41. For more information on the tricameral system, see chapter 1 of this book and my work *Zhengzhi ruxue: dangdai ruxue de zhuanxiang, tezhi yu fazhan* [*Political Confucianism: The Transformation, Special Characteristics, and Development of Contemporary Confucianism*] (Beijing: Sanlian Shudian, 2003).

CHAPTER 3

1. From May 3 to May 5, 2010, at the invitation of Professor Fan Ruiping, I took part in a Conference organized by the City University of Hong Kong under the title "Confucian Constitutionalism and China's Future." This chapter is my submission to the conference. Although I have taken part in many academic conferences, this one was different in that, despite the difficulty of the topic, my pen flowed freely, and I found that I wrote over sixty thousand characters. Were it not for Professor Fan's invitation, I might never have gotten around to putting down on paper my thoughts about such an important topic as republicanism under a symbolic monarch.

2. Other organizations may be formed or produced out of interests, reason, will, or belief, but not the state.

3. This is unlike the modern states produced by constitutions that are contractual in nature.

4. Heaven partakes in the formation and continuation of state history through the sage kings and sages who represent it, and so national history shares in the characteristics of heaven and is itself sacred, mysterious, whole, awe-inspiring, and enduring. State rituals also show these qualities since from ancient times rituals at the altars of state and at the altar of the national spirits are the best exemplars of the sacred, mysterious, whole, awe-inspiring, and enduring nature of state history. This phenomenon may be observed in many Confucian classics such as the *Book of Odes* and the *Book of History*, which record how the sacred decree of heaven was behind the formation and maintenance of many states.

5. The historical nature of the state and its continuance and eternal existence are connected. These features of the state affect the essence of the state, but the key term is that of historical identity, hence this chapter concentrates on historical identity as the essence of the state, though at times some of the other features will also be referred to.

6. For instance, ancient Greece has now become an Orthodox Christian state. Ancient Persia (Iran) has now become a Muslim state, and the ancient Buddhist states of the Silk Route have also become Islamic states.

7. For instance, it is impossible for today's Orthodox Greece to revert to the many gods of ancient Greece or for Islamic Iran to revert to polytheist ancient Persia. This is

because the historical nature of the state has already formed a firmly fixed nature, out of the mixture of historical rationality.

8. Gongyang Gao, *Gongyang chuan* in *Chunqiu* [*Gongyang Commentary* in the *Spring and Autumn Annals*] (Shanghai: Zhonghua Shuju, 1931).

9. The term "nation" is also distinct from that of "nationality" since its scope is much broader. In most countries the nation is composed of many nationalities. There are few countries, like Japan, composed of only one nationality. Nation is a historical concept and is formed by many nationalities coming together over the years; hence, it is the nation and not the nationalities who embody the historical nature of the state and hence the existence of the state. It may be that, among the many nationalities that compose the nation, a general awareness has built up over history, or an increase of population has led to oppression of minorities, or because of the great influence of a widespread and ancient culture, there is a dominant nationality, which forms the backbone of the nation and can naturally be taken as representative of the nation. For this reason the religion of the dominant nationality will naturally assume the characteristics of a national religion while the religions of the other nationalities are seen as the free beliefs of a given nationality and lacking in national status. The Chinese people of today is composed of fifty-six nationalities who together form the nation, but the Han people are the dominant nationality and hence represent the nation of China. The Confucian religion of the Han thus naturally becomes the state religion of China. This is not simply the result of abstract deduction; it is a fact of Chinese history.

10. For instance, under the Ming and Qing dynasties in China, the state erected in Beijing a temple for emperors and kings. Sacrifices offered to past emperors and kings by the emperor were an indication of the five thousand years of China's historical continuity. By honoring the rule of emperors throughout history, the sacrifice manifests the unbroken historical identity of the state, the reason being that the monarchical system is basically founded on the idea of national history as "one line through ten thousand generations."

11. There are different forms of democracy: procedural democracy, substantive democracy, explicit democracy, implicit democracy, effective democracy, sovereign democracy, democracy at the level of implementation or at the level of legitimization, democracy based on universal suffrage, democracy in which one party monopolizes the government, liberal democracy, and dictatorial democracy. Hence, in the matters of sovereignty, implementation, and legitimacy, a state under a chairman is also a form of democracy.

12. "Article 5: The President of the Republic shall ensure due respect for the Constitution. He shall ensure, by his arbitration, the proper functioning of the public authorities and the continuity of the State. He shall be the guarantor of national independence, territorial integrity and due respect for Treaties." Assemblée Nationale, "Constitution of October 4, 1958," http://www.assemblee-nationale.fr/english/8ab.asp, n.d. (accessed April 14, 2011).

13. That the constitution of the Fifth Republic accords the president the role of representing the continuity of the state is due to French constitutional history: an elected president has replaced the traditional hereditary monarchy. It is not purely a creation of de Gaulle himself.

14. While constitutional monarchies may not have written the continuity of the state into their constitutions, their hereditary monarchs are at least in a better position to represent historical continuity than an elected president ever could be.

In states run by a chairman, barring their ideology, there is no great difference from republican presidential systems. Both come from political modernity. The only difference lies in the method of election. In states run by a chairman, the chair is chosen by the People's Congress, whereas in republics the president is directly or indirectly chosen by all the people. However, in states run by a chairman, the difference between state and government is more marked because the role of the chairman as representative of the state would appear to be spelled out more clearly than the role of a president.

15. The first person to propose a republic under a symbolic monarch was Kang You-wei, at the height of the 1911 Revolution. At the time China's several-thousand-year-old monarchy had just fallen, and Kang was concerned how the spiritual and living body of the state and its historical continuity could be maintained in a constitution or in the way the state was set up. With profound historical wisdom, bold creativity, and a deep desire to save the nation, Kang proposed the very-Chinese idea of a republic under a symbolic monarch in the face of rush of pro-Western fever to imitate Western constitutions. His wisdom and courage still move those of us today who are seeking a Chinese-style constitution. Unfortunately, given the immense pressure at the time to save the nation, Kang had neither the time nor the right conditions to think about his plan in detail. He was able to draw up only a few simple structural principles. But those very principles are what can help us think today. They provide the wisdom needed for drawing up a constitution based on the specifics of Chinese history and culture. They serve as the point of departure for our efforts today to create a Chinese-style Confucian constitutionalism. As Kang gradually became accustomed to the Republic, he surprisingly did not mention the symbolic monarch but accepted the Western presidential model. This is evident from his draft constitution of 1903. But this fact does not diminish, in the slightest, the creativity and vitality of his original theory. We know that Kang Youwei was a thinker and political theorist imbued with passion and faith, rather than a bookish scholar or systematic academic. So Kang's intellectual contribution lies in his originality and depth and not in logical rigor or systematic thought. It is precisely those qualities that motivate our principles and thoughts today. Hence, in discussing the form of the state in Confucian constitutionalism, we are inheriting, deepening, developing, and completing Kang's reflections on the constitution.

16. The highest political hope of Confucianism is for the return of a sage king who will restore the direct rule of the sage kings. Confucian constitutionalism is the interim Way of the Humane Authority that prepares for this direct rule by the sage kings. The former entails personal rule by the sage kings, while the latter relies on the structural input of Confucian religion. Thus, republicanism under a symbolic monarch as presented by Confucian constitutionalism is not designed to last forever. It exists only in this interim period of republicanism.

17. In the United Kingdom and Japan and other countries that enjoy a constitutional monarchy, the monarch either constitutionally or by custom has only state power, which even if it is rarely used or used only on the advice or request of the government is said to be "symbolic." This does not mean that the head of state as "monarch" is completely powerless or unable to execute state power, and still less does it mean that the symbolic monarch has no influence on the life of the nation. It is a sort of unspoken tradition.

18. When he proposed the post of symbolic monarch, Kang Youwei envisaged giving it to the deposed emperor. In terms of recognizing the direct heir, there was no problem there, but it earned Kang the reputation of wishing to restore the monarchy even after the Republic was founded. Now, a hundred years later, the deposed emperor is already dead, and it would be impossible to find a symbolic monarch in the descendants of the Qing emperors. Not that it would be difficult to find a direct descendant given that we are dealing with a period of only a hundred years, but throughout that time there has been anti-

Manchu propaganda and the Qing dynasty has already been utterly demonized. Even today anti-Qing feeling runs high. The Qing rulers were Manchu and, though Kang Youwei proved that the Manchu, like the Han, were descendants of the Yellow Emperor, the narrow racist propaganda of the past century has become part of general belief, such that even today many people in China look on the Manchu Qing dynasty from a narrow racist perspective. Given this background, it is clearly unrealistic, and impossible, to find a suitable candidate for the symbolic monarch among the descendants of the Qing emperors.

19. The kings called themselves "Yin," but their dynasty was also known as "Shang," and it is commonly referred to in English by the latter name. However, for all practical purposes Yin and Shang are equivalent terms.

20. Under the feudal system, the rank Marquis is the second among the five. The first, third, fourth, and fifth ranks are Duke, Earl, Viscount, and Baron, respectively.

21. Qi was the elder brother, by a concubine, of the last king of the Shang/Yin dynasty. He was named Viscount of Wei. His name is recorded in the *Analects* 18.1.

22. Ban Gu, *Yang Hu Zhu Mei Yun chuan*, in *Han shu*, book 67.

23. According to the *Spring and Autumn Annals*, a duke is second in rank to a king. Confucius's heirs were dukes from this time in the Han and not as is said today ennobled only in the Song. Emperor Ren Zong of the Song ennobled the heir as the Duke: Heir of the Sage.

24. The descendants of all other historical figures, even if they claim to be of noble lineage, cannot claim descent from the ancient kings, and so their lineage has no political significance, nor can it permit them to take part in the public political arena or in the establishment of the basic structure of the state in the way that the heir can lay claim to. Hence, it is he who is qualified to meet the political test of the symbolic monarch.

25. In a broad sense, all Chinese people are descended from the Yellow Emperor, and so all Chinese people can trace their blood back to the Yellow Emperor, but since this blood has already flowed out to all Chinese people, it is significant only when talking about the origin of the nation as such. It is not relevant to the political culture or order of the state that has been formed over a long period of time in China. At least, it is not of determinate significance.

26. In fact, republicanism is not at variance with a peerage. The United Kingdom and other constitutional monarchies are proof of that. I will discuss this further in another paper.

27. See *The Collection of Treatises on the Rules of Propriety or Ceremonial Usages*, in Legge, *Sacred Books of China*, vol. 3, book 7, *Ceremonial Usages, Their Origin, Development, and Intention*.

28. Kang Youwei considered promoting him two degrees to the rank of emperor (*di*) and calling him the Emperor: Successor of the Sage.

29. Confucian texts speak of Confucius as a king, the King of Culture, the Uncrowned King, and the King of the Latter Days. Later the state elevated him to the status of King of Perfected Culture (*Wenxuanwang*). The title "emperor" (*di*) is reserved in ceremonial books to Yao and Shun. Confucius is a descendant of King Tang of the Shang and hence should be called "king" and not "emperor." Confucius's heir thus inherits his royal title both from Confucius and from King Tang.

30. This would be impossible for secular presidential systems or states with a chairman because for party political reasons neither president nor chairman can be superior to party politics. Both president and chairman also hold many powers that belong to parlia-

ment or the government. Furthermore, a president is elected by competition among all the people, while a chairman is proposed by the party. In both cases there is fierce competition. Moreover, once elected, president and chairman hold office for only a limited number of years. Being a country with a long history of centralized power, China is particularly susceptible to unrest and separation as a result of many political forces trying to seek the post of head of state and the supreme state power this brings. Therefore, only a system by which the King Successor of the Sage is the symbolic monarch is adapted to China's long, historical, and cultural tradition of centralized power.

31. Under Confucian constitutionalism parliamentary power and executive power are not purely secular powers. In the secular political power referred to here, what is meant are the modern Western or non-Western political powers guided or influenced by political modernity. In Confucian constitutionalism, the House of *Ru* and House of the Nation are not purely secular political institutions. Furthermore, in Confucian constitutionalism, government by scholar-officials is not purely secular power. Nonetheless, even in this Confucian constitutionalism there is a separation between state power and political power. State power has rather more of the sacred about it and political power comparatively less, though political power is not utterly void of the sacred. This is very different from totalitarianism, in which secular political power stifles all sacred space. This is a complex matter, and I have not said all that could be said on the matter. It will be left for a later discussion.

32. It is strange that when Sun Yat-sen, who overthrew the monarchy and founded a Republic, died in Beijing, members of the Republican Party set up a shrine in the temple of the past kings and emperors and held a funeral rite there. This shows that even the Republicans could not deny the historical nature of the Chinese state and, in their confusion, hoped that the Republic could continue the rule of the kings and emperors of the past. Of course this hope did not overcome the fact that the revolutionary consciousness that had thoroughly destroyed the monarchy had also destroyed its most important role, namely that of representing the historical nature of the state. Hence, the Republicans' hope of inheriting the five-thousand-year rule could not be realized and had to remain as only a hope.

33. In the constitutions of the United Kingdom and Japan today, the monarch can rely on custom or law to call the parliament, dismiss it, proclaim laws, nominate officials, approve foreign affairs documents, and carry out the role that the symbolic monarch has over parliament and government.

34. Let us speak no more of dying for the monarch, nor mention again the loyalty of Guan Yunchang and Zhuge Liang for Liu Bei and A-dou. Even what happened in the early years of the Republic when Liang Dingfen wept night and day alone at the emperor's tomb will never come to pass in our day. In that year the Qing troops entered Zhejiang, and Liu Jishan and his comrades died for their monarch as a sign of the death of the state. Another example is that when the Meiji Emperor died in Japan, there were Japanese generals who chose to die for the emperor. I wonder what the current "citizens" who are the "masters of the country" today would think of such loyalty!

35. Because the historical and cultural traditions of each country are different, the national ethos is also different. The United States is a rare example of a country with a short history and no tradition of monarchy. Its national ethos is such that its historical legitimacy may perhaps be based on representative republicanism on the basis of universal suffrage. But even if that is the case, one must still separate the state and the government and ensure a division in the constitution between representatives of each. The two should not be confused and focused only on the person of the president alone.

36. At present this kind of power is used by constitutional monarchs in the United Kingdom and in Thailand. In Confucian constitutionalism, both the symbolic monarch and the Academy can resolve ecological crises, but they do so in different ways and to different effect. The Academy has more effective teeth as it can effectively prevent parliament, government, and even the state from running counter to the way and principle of heaven and in effect the ecological values. Of course, the House of *Ru* also represents the legitimacy of the way of heaven and so can also solve ecological crises in a constitutional way. This problem is very complex and has many fine points to it. Since it is not the subject of this chapter, we will leave it at that.

37. After completing this essay, I noticed that there is a problem that affects the whole system of Confucian constitutionalism, which, although not the topic of this chapter, is nonetheless related to it and so should be briefly explained in order to get a better grasp of Confucian constitutionalism and republicanism under a symbolic monarch.

This problem is that of the five spheres of rule in Confucianism. In the system of Confucian thought there are five spheres of rule: the rule of the Way, of the state, of law, of politics, and of the government. In matters of legitimacy the superior legitimacy is enjoyed by the Way, then the state, down to the government.

These five spheres of rule are found in Confucian constitutionalism where different bodies represent different spheres of rule. The Academy represents the sphere of the Way, the symbolic monarch represents that of the state, a Confucian legal system represents that of the law, the parliament represents politics, and the scholar-officials represent the government. The hierarchy of legitimacy is reflected in the hierarchy of these bodies. In practice the Academy holds supervisory power, the symbolic monarch holds that of the state, the law courts hold judicial power, the parliament has political power, and the government has executive power. In terms of legitimacy, these powers are in descending order. But in the actual running of affairs, except for the supervisory power of the Academy, which always transcends the other bodies and is subject only to the way of heaven, the other powers are mutually exclusive.

Furthermore, of the five powers, four are active and one, that of the law, is passive, in that it is exercised only when a case is brought in court. Speaking of the law, there should be a constitution and a supreme law court that are grounded on Confucian principles. The first task of this is to define a Confucian constitution on the basis of which the supreme law court can exercise independent judicial judgment and investigate breaches of the constitution, and only in this way can it qualify as a Confucian judicial system with the characteristics of Chinese history and culture, and only then can the supreme court represent China's very own, independent rule of law. (It is not surprising that China must write her own Confucian constitution. In fact, the constitution of the United States is a Christian constitution. The difference is that a Confucian constitution should include some elements of modernity or of the West that do not clash with Confucian ideas.)

In this system the symbolic monarch is the only person who can represent the state. Unlike the British system in which the monarch rules "in parliament," in the Confucian system the king is above the parliament because the rule of the state is superior to the rule of politics, that is, historical legitimacy is higher than popular legitimacy. This is the special constitutional status of the symbolic monarch. Here I do not discuss the Confucian judicial system or the government by scholar-officials since these matters are also not the topic of this chapter.

CHAPTER 4

1. I am grateful to Elton Chan for translating parts of the original Chinese essay into English. I also thank Franz Mang and Elton Chan for assisting the research and writing of the Chinese article. The work is my responsibility alone. My work on this essay was supported by a grant from the Research Grants Council of the Hong Kong Special Administrative Region, China (HKU 741508H).

2. A recent articulation of this view is in the work of Yu Yingshi. See his *Xiandai ruxue lun* [*On Modern Confucianism*] (Hackensack, N.J.: Global Publishing, 1996), chap. 4.

3. See Li Minghui, *Dangdai ruxue de ziwo zhuanhua* [*Self-Transformation of Contemporary Confucianism*] (Beijing: Zhongguo shehui kexue chubanshe, 2001), 1–19.

4. See John Rawls, *Political Liberalism* (New York: Columbia University Press, 1993), 59.

5. For a detailed discussion of these two kinds of perfectionism, see my "Legitimacy, Unanimity, and Perfectionism," *Philosophy and Public Affairs* 29, no. 1 (2000): 5–42.

6. Edward Shils, *The Virtue of Civility* (Indianapolis: Liberty Fund, 1997), 26–28.

7. I have discussed the importance of civility in greater detail in my unpublished paper "In Defense of Moderate Perfectionism" (2009).

8. Chapter 2, note 5.

9. Jiang Qing, *Zhengzhi ruxue: dangdai ruxue de zhuanxiang, tezhi yu fazhan* [*Political Confucianism: The Transformation, Special Characteristics, and Development of Contemporary Confucianism*] (Beijing: Sanlian Shudian, 2003), 37.

10. For details on the Academy, see chapter 2 of this book. For details on the tricameral parliament, see chapter 1 of this book.

11. For details, see chapter 3 of this book.

12. See my "Moral Autonomy, Civil Liberties, and Confucianism," *Philosophy East and West* 52, no. 3 (July 2002): 302–4.

13. Jiang Qing, "Zhengzhi ruxue—xubian" ["Political Confucianism—A Sequel"] (unpublished manuscript), 47–48.

14. I am indebted to Elton Chan for providing the ideas in this section.

15. Wang Fuzhi, *Du Tongjian lun: Sung Wendi 13* [*On reading the Zizhi Tongjian: Emperor Wen of Liu Song*] (Beijing: Zhonghua shuju, 2002).

16. Anonymous (Fu Huisheng, trans.), *The Zhou Book of Change: The Survey I*, vol. 1 (Changsha: Hunan People's Publishing House, 2008).

17. Zheng Xuecheng, *Wenshi tongyi: yuandao* [*General Principle of Literature and History*] (Shenyang: Liaoning Jiaoyu Publishing, 1998), 33.

18. Ibid., 33.

19. Anonymous, *Zhou Book of Change*, vol. 1.

20. Legge, *Sacred Books of China*, vol. 4, book 28: *The State of Equilibrium and Harmony*, 305.

21. *Shu King*, in Legge, *Sacred Books of China*, vol. 1, part V, book 1, *The Great Declaration*, 128.

22. "For a man to give full realization to his heart is for him to understand his own nature, and a man who knows his own nature will know Heaven" (*Mencius* 7A:1).

23. Legge, *Sacred Books of China*, vol. 4, book 28, *The State of Equilibrium and Harmony*, 302.

24. Dong Zhongshu, *Tiendaosi*, in *Chunqiu fanlu*.

25. Wang Fuzhi, *Si Jie* (Beijing: Guji chubanshe, 1956).

26. Rawls, *Political Liberalism*, 38.

27. This paragraph is drawn from my unpublished paper "In Defense of Moderate Perfectionism," which gives a detailed defense of moderate perfectionism against liberal neutrality and comprehensive perfectionism.

28. Shils, *Virtue of Civility*, 49.

29. I have tried to do this in my earlier attempts. See "Is There a Confucian Perspective on Social Justice?" in *Western Political Thought in Dialogue with Asia*, ed. Takashi Shogimen and Cary J. Nederman (Lanham, Md.: Rowman & Littlefield, 2008), 261–77; "Democracy and Meritocracy"; "Giving Priority to the Worst Off: A Confucian Perspective on Social Welfare," in Bell and Hahm, *Confucianism for the Modern World*, 236–53; "Confucian Attitudes toward Ethical Pluralism," in *The Many and the One: Religious and Secular Perspectives on Ethical Pluralism in the Modern World*, ed. Richard Madsen and Tracy B. Strong (Princeton, N.J.: Princeton University Press, 2003), 129–53; "Moral Autonomy, Civil Liberties, and Confucianism"; "A Confucian Perspective on Human Rights for Contemporary China," in *The East Asian Challenge for Human Rights*, ed. Joanne R. Bauer and Daniel A. Bell (New York: Cambridge University Press, 1999), 212–37.

CHAPTER 5

1. Jiang Qing, "Zhengzhi ruxue—xubian" ["Political Confucianism—A Sequel"] (unpublished manuscript), 15; see also 328.

2. Ibid., 320.

3. Fukuyama, *End of History*.

4. Jiang Qing, "Zhengzhi ruxue," 35–38. See also chapter 1 of this book. In my own book *A New Mission of an Old State*, I also list a few more problems caused by a too strong emphasis on popular will in politics, such as problems related to budget deficits, foreign aid, and foreign policies (that need to be farsighted and stable). Bai Tongdong, *Jiubang xinming: gujin zhongxi canzhaoxia de gudian rujia zhengzhi zhexue* [*A New Mission of an Old State: The Contemporary and Comparative Relevance of Classical Confucian Political Philosophy*] (Beijing: Beijing Daxue Chubanshe, 2009), 65–68.

5. Thus in the following, when we use the word "Confucian" in Jiang's theory, it means *ru jiao*, and not *ru jia*.

6. Jiang Qing, "Zhengzhi ruxue," 57. See also chapter 1 of this book.

7. Jiang Qing, "Zhengzhi ruxue," 144. See also chapter 2 of this book.

8. Jiang Qing, "Zhengzhi ruxue," 50–52. See also chapter 1 of this book.

9. See chapter 1 of this book.

10. Jiang Qing, "Zhengzhi ruxue," 9 and 46.

11. For details, see ibid., 29 and chapter 1 of this book.

12. For details, see Jiang Qing, "Zhengzhi ruxue," 97 and 169–75 and chapter 3 of this book.

13. For details, see Jiang Qing, "Zhengzhi ruxue," 133 and 143 and chapter 2 of this book.

14. Jiang Qing, "Zhengzhi ruxue," 84, 134–38, 212–13, and 223.

15. Ibid., 228.

16. Ibid., 11.

17. John Rawls, *The Law of Peoples with "The Idea of Public Reason Revisited"* (Cambridge, Mass.: Harvard University Press, 1999).

18. Jiang Qing, "Zhengzhi ruxue," 254.

19. In the *Book of Odes*, there is a famous line, describing the state of Zhou, that reads, "Zhou is an old state, but its mandate/mission is ever renewing." James Legge (trans.), *The Book of Poetry*, in *The Chinese Classics*, vol. 4, ode 235 (Hong Kong: Hong Kong University Press, 1960), 427. This has become a motto for, among others, the contemporary Confucian philosophy of Feng Youlan that describes what he wishes to achieve. That is, he hopes to show the contemporary relevance of an old tradition, which is Confucianism. So, for him and for the author of this chapter, "old state" means the essence or spirit of Confucianism, and the new mission or new mandate means Confucianism contextualized in today's world and thus made relevant to it (which explains the title of my own book [Bai, *Jiubang xinming*] and what I intend to achieve in this chapter). But I think that Jiang is actually imposing an interpretation of Confucianism in an "old" context on today's world, which is why I call his project "an old mandate for a new state." There are puns based upon this famous line from the *Odes* throughout this chapter.

20. In the first part of one of my recent books in Chinese, *A New Mission of an Old State: The Contemporary and Comparative Relevance of Classical Confucian Political Philosophy*, I offer and defend a Confucian ideal state that is different from Western liberal democracies and human rights regimes.

21. Jiang Qing, "'Rujiao xianzheng' zhuti cankao wengao—yuanqi" ["The Reason of Writing on the Topic 'Political Confucianism'"] (unpublished manuscript), 103.

22. Jiang Qing, "Zhengzhi ruxue," 101; see also 232–33.

23. Ibid., 18 and 224.

24. Ibid., 330–31.

25. John Knoblock (trans.), *Xunzi: A Translation and Study of the Complete Works*, book 17, *Discourse on Nature* (Stanford, Calif.: Stanford University Press, 1988), 19–20.

26. Rawls, *Political Liberalism*.

27. Jiang Qing, "Zhengzhi ruxue," 262.

28. Mencius being one of the most important Confucians in the history of Confucianism.

29. Qian Mu, *Zhongguo lidai zhengzhi deshi* [*Merits and Problems of Chinese Dynasties*] (Beijing: Sanlian Shudian, 2005).

30. Jiang Qing, "Zhengzhi ruxue," 289.

31. Ibid., 27.

32. Ibid., 22–23, 27–28, 31, 67, 73, 91, and so on. See also chapter 3 of this book.

33. For the readers unfamiliar with Chinese philosophy, there is a notorious saying by some neo-Confucians that claims "to starve to death is a small matter, compared to saving one's chastity."

34. Jiang Qing, "Zhengzhi ruxue," 104.

35. In chapters 2 and 3 of my book, I offer reasons, both practical and from Confucian texts, why, in spite of the Confucian belief in the equality of human potential to become a sage, in spite of the Confucian emphasis on the government's obligation to educate everyone, and in spite of Western political theorists' attempt to reform democracy from within, the poor quality of average voters can never be improved to a level that meets the minimal requirements of a participatory democracy, and thus a hybrid regime is the only solution to the problem with popular democracy (Bai, *Jiubang xinming*, 21–77).

36. Jiang Qing, "Zhengzhi ruxue," 134–35.

37. Sheng Hong, "Jishan zhi jia, biyou yuqing—lun rujia xianzheng yuanze de lishi weidu" ["Families That Have Been Doing Charitable Things Will Be Particularly Blessed—On the Historical Dimension of Confucian Constitutionalism"] (unpublished manuscript).

38. For a detailed discussion, see Bai Tongdong, "Philosophical Reflections on National Identity," in *Teaching the Silk Road: Reflections and Pedagogical Essays for College Teachers*, ed. Jacqueline M. Moore and Rebecca Woodward Wendelken (Albany: State University of New York Press, 2010), 139–55.

39. Jiang Qing, "Zhengzhi ruxue," 74–78.

40. Ibid., 91–92.

41. Ibid., 78.

42. Ibid., 18 and 38.

CHAPTER 6

1. This essay evolved from a paper presented at the International Conference on Confucian Constitutional System and China's Future at the City University of Hong Kong, May 3–5, 2010. I would like to thank participants at the conference, especially Ruiping Fan, for their comments and critiques.

2. Here I use "conservative" as a value-neutral term.

3. I use "transcendent heaven" as a shorthand translation of Jiang's notion of transcendent, metaphysical, sacred, and personal heaven. In Jiang's system, the transcendent heaven in this sense is beyond the "heaven-earth-humanity" triad and hence not interrelated with earth or humanity.

4. Feng Youlan (Derk Bodde, trans.), *A History of Chinese Philosophy*, vol. 1 (Princeton, N.J.: Princeton University Press, 1952), 31 (Chinese transliteration has been modified to conform to modern usage).

5. Ibid., 57.

6. Meng Mo (ed.), *Mengwen Tongxiaoji* [*Scholarly Records of Meng Wentong*] (Beijing: Sanlian Shudian, 1993), 23–34.

7. Chen Lai, *Gudai zongjiao yu lunli—rujia sixiang de genyuan* [*Ancient Religions and Ethics—Roots of Confucian Thought*] (Beijing: Sanlian Shudian, 1996), 183, emphasis added.

8. Ouyang Zhenren, "Xianqin rujia wenxian zhong de 'tian'—jianlun Meng Wentong xiansheng dui xheyi wenti de sikao" ["The Concept of *Tian* in Pre-Qin Confucian Texts—Also on Meng Wentong's Opinions of the Matter"], http://www.mianfeilunwen.com/Zhexue/Zhongguo/30630.html, n.d. (accessed January 18, 2011) (my translation).

9. Cf. Zhang Dainian (Edmund Ryden, trans.), *Key Concepts in Chinese Philosophy* (New Haven, Conn.: Yale University Press, 2002), 4.

10. *Book of Changes: The Great Appendix* II.10, my translation. Cf. Z. D. Sung, *The Text of Yi King* (Taipei: Wenhua, 1988), 333.

11. Knoblock, *Xunzi*, 15.

12. Ibid., 14.

13. Dong Zhongshu, *Tiandi yinyang*, in *Chunqiu fanlu*, book 17, sec. 81, 99.

14. See the last section of this chapter.

15. Chenyang Li, *The Tao Encounters the West* (Albany: State University of New York Press, 1999).

16. Joseph Chan, "Democracy and Meritocracy."

17. For a more detailed account of this proposal, see Chenyang Li, "Minzhu de xingshi he rujia de neirong: zailun rujia yu minzhu de guanxi" ["Confucian Content and Democratic Form: Revisiting the Relationship of Confucianism and Democracy"], *Zhongguo zhexue yu wenhua* [*Chinese Philosophy and Culture*], 10 (2012).

CHAPTER 7

1. Yu Keping, *Democracy Is a Good Thing: Essays on Politics, Society, and Culture in Contemporary China* (Washington, D.C.: Brookings Institution, 2008).

2. Jiang Qing, *Zhengzhi ruxue: dangdai ruxue de zhuanxiang, tezhi yu fazhan* [*Political Confucianism: The Transformation, Special Characteristics, and Development of Contemporary Confucianism*] (Beijing: Sanlian Shudian, 2003).

3. Jiang Qing, *Gongyangxue yinlun* [*Introduction to the Gongyang Commentary on the Spring and Autumn Annals*] (Shenyang: Liaoning jiaoyu chubanshe, 1995).

4. Jiang Qing, "Wangdao zhengzhi shi dangjin zhongguo zhengzhi de fazhan fangxiang: 'rujiao xianzheng' de yili jichu yu 'yihui sanyuanzhi'" ["The Way of the Humane Authority Is the Way Ahead for China's Political Future: Political Legitimacy and the Tricameral Parliament"], *Yuan Dao* 10, no. 1 (2005): 79–94.

5. Jiang Qing, "'Rujiao xianzheng' zhuti cankao wengao—yuanqi" ["The Reason of Writing on the Topic 'Political Confucianism'"] (unpublished manuscript).

6. Jiang Qing, "Rujiao xianzheng de yili wenti yu yihui xingshi," 3.

7. Jiang Qing, *Zailun Zhengzhi Ruxue* [*Further discussion on Political Confucianism*] (Shanghai: Huadong Shifan Daxue Chubanshe, 2011), 5–6, 29.

8. It is a state where "a public and common spirit rule all under the sky; everyone is sincere and friendly; everyone has sense of shame and no one would violate laws so that no litigation and punishment are necessary; everyone acts as a gentleman treating all others equally."

9. Jiang Qing, "Wangdao tushui: 'rujiao xianzheng' de yili jichu yu 'yihui sanyuanzhi'" ["Explanation of the Way of the Humane Authority: Political Legitimacy and the Tricameral Parliament"] (unpublished manuscript), 12–13.

10. Jiang Qing, *Zhengzhi ruxue*, 202–5.

11. Feng Youlan (Derk Bodde, trans.), *A History of Chinese Philosophy*, vol. 1 (Princeton, N.J.: Princeton University Press, 1952), 31. The translation of these five expressions is that of Derk Bodde.

12. Jiang Qing, *Zailun Zhengzhi Ruxue* [*Further discussion on Political Confucianism*] (Shanghai: Huadong Shifan Daxue Chubanshe, 2011), 20.

13. Jiang Qing, *Zhengzhi ruxue*, 206–7.

14. Jiang Qing, *Zailun Zhengzhi Ruxue* [*Further discussion on Political Confucianism*] (Shanghai: Huadong Shifan Daxue Chubanshe, 2011), 11.

15. For details, see chapter 1 of this book.

16. Jiang Qing, "'Rujiao xianzheng' zhuti cankao wengao—yuanqi" ["The Reason of Writing on the Topic 'Political Confucianism'"] (unpublished manuscript), 1.

17. Rodney Barker, *Political Legitimacy and the State* (Oxford: Clarendon, 1990), 11.

18. Seymour Martin Lipset, *Political Man: The Social Bases of Politics*, 2nd ed. (London: Heinemann, 1983), 64.

19. Joseph Schumpeter, *Capitalism, Socialism and Democracy* (New York: Harper, 1942). From Aristotle's time all the way up to the beginning of the nineteenth century, most political thinkers, whether they were supporters or opponents of democracy, always associated democracy with sortition rather than election. In this book, Schumpeter challenged what he called the "classical doctrine" of democracy and asserted that the idea of "rule by the people" was neither possible nor desirable. Instead, he advocated a minimalist model of democracy whereby the participatory role of the people was reduced to taking part in periodic elections, which was a mechanism for competition between elite.

20. Chen Jie, Yang Zhong, and Jan Hillard, "Assessing Political Support in China: Citizens' Evaluations of Governmental Effectiveness and Legitimacy," *Journal of Contemporary China* 6, no. 16 (November 1997): 551–66; Shi Tianjian, "Cultural Values and Political Trust: A Comparison of the People's Republic of China and Taiwan," *Comparative Politics* 33, no. 4 (July 2001): 401–19; Tang Wenfang, "Political and Social Trends in the Post-Deng Urban China: Crisis or Stability?" *China Quarterly* 168 (2001): 890–909; Chen Jie, *Popular Political Support in Urban China* (Washington, D.C.: Woodrow Wilson Center Press, 2004); Li Lianjiang, "Political Trust in Rural China," *Modern China* 30, no. 2 (April 2004): 228–58; Wang Zhengxu, "Political Trust in China: Forms and Causes," in *Legitimacy: Ambiguities of Political Success or Failure in East and Southeast Asia*, ed. Lynn White (Singapore: World Scientific, 2005); Tang Wenfang, *Public Opinion and Political Change in China* (Stanford, Calif.: Stanford University Press, 2005); Joseph Fewsmith, "Assessing Social Stability on the Eve of the 17th Party Congress," *China Leadership Monitor* 20 (2007): 1–24; Shi Tianjian, "China: Democratic Values Supporting an Authoritarian System," in *How East Asians View Democracy*, ed. Chu Yun-han, Larry Diamond, Andrew J. Nathan, and Doh Chull Shin (New York: Columbia University Press, 2008), 209–37; Bruce Gilley, "Legitimacy and Institutional Change: The Case of China," *Comparative Political Studies* 41, no. 3 (2008): 259–84; Bruce Gilley, *The Right to Rule: How States Win and Lose Legitimacy* (New York: Columbia University Press, 2009).

21. For instance, Shi Tianjian's "Establishing Evaluative Criteria: Measuring Political Stability and Political Support in the PRC" has not been published.

22. Heike Holbig and Bruce Gilley, "In Search of Legitimacy in Post-revolutionary China: Bringing Ideology and Governance Back In," *GIGA Working Papers* 127 (March 2010): 6.

23. Bruce Gilley, "The Meaning and Measure of State Legitimacy: Results for 72 Countries," *European Journal of Political Research* 45 (2006): 499–525.

24. Chu Yun-han et al., *How East Asians View Democracy*.

25. See Comparative Study of Electoral Systems, "Satisfaction with Democracy," http://www.umich.edu/~cses/resources/results/CSESresults_SatisfactionWithDemocracy.htm, October 24, 2005 (accessed May 7, 2011).

26. Damarys Canache, Jeffery J. Mondak, and Mitchell A. Seligson, "Meaning and Measurement in Cross-National Research on Satisfaction with Democracy," *Public Opinion Quarterly* 65, no. 4 (Winter 2001): 506–28.

27. For the original data, see ASEP/JDS Data Bank, "Confidence in the Government," http://www.jdsurvey.net/jds/jdsurveyActualidad.jsp?Idioma=I&SeccionTexto=0404, 2010 (accessed May 7, 2011).

28. Fareed Zakaria, *The Future of Freedom: Illiberal Democracy at Home and Abroad* (New York: Norton, 2003), 241.

29. Pew Research Center for the People & the Press, "The People and Their Government: Distrust, Discontent, Anger and Partisan Rancor," http://people-press.org/reports/pdf/606.pdf, April 18, 2010 (accessed May 7, 2011).

30. To have access to the data, please visit Norwegian Social Science Data Services, "European Social Survey Education Net," http://essedunet.nsd.uib.no/, 2011 (accessed May 7, 2011).

31. Aristotle argues, "The appointment of magistrates by lot is thought to be democratic, and the election of them oligarchic." See his *The Politics* (Cambridge, UK: Cambridge University Press, 1988), VI, 9, 1294b.

32. John P. McCormick, "Contain the Wealthy and Patrol the Magistrates: Restoring Elite Accountability to Popular Government," *American Political Science Review* 100, no. 2 (May 2006): 149–50.

33. Wang Shaoguang, "Jingti dui minzhu de xiushi" ["Guarded Against modifications to Democracy"], *Dushu [Reading]*, no. 4 (2003).

34. Hsu Cho-yun, *Wangu jianghe: Zhongguo lishi wenhua de zhuanzhe yu kaizhan [The Eternal Rivers: The Turning Point and Evolution of Chinese Historical Culture]* (Shanghai: Shanghai wenyi chubanshe, 2006), 49.

35. See Daniel A. Bell, *Beyond Liberal Democracy: Political Thinking for an East Asian Context* (Princeton, N.J.: Princeton University Press, 2006), 152–79, etc.

36. Hu Qiaomu, "Mao zhuxi zai zhuiqiu yizhong shehuizhuyi" ["Chairman Mao in the Search of an Ideal Socialism"], in *Hu Qiaomu tan zhonggong dangshi [Hu Qiaomu Talks about the History of the Chinese Communist Party]* (Beijing: Renmin chubanshe, 1999), 70–72.

37. Mao Zedong, "Dui 'heshi zhengzhi zhanxian shang he sixiang zhanxian shang de shehuizhuyi geming' yiwen de piyu he xiugai" ["Comments and Revisions on the Draft 'This Is a Socialist Revolution on the Front of Political and Ideological Battlefields'"], http://www.hprc.org.cn/hybldrzz/dhgj/mzdzz/wg6/200908/t20090810_24920.html, September 15, 1957 (accessed May 7, 2011).

38. Zhonghua renmin gonghe guo shixuehui (ed.), *Mao Zedong dou shehuizhuyi zhengzhixue pizhu he tanhua [Mao Zedong's Remarks on and Discussions about Socialist Political Economy]* (Beijing: Zhonghua renmin gongheguo shixuehui, 1998), 40–41.

39. Mao Zedong, "Dui zonghouqinbu guanyu jinyibu gaohao budui nongfuye shengchan baogao de piyu" ["Comments on the Report of the General Logistics Department on Further Improvement of PLA's Agricultural and Sideline Production"], in *Jianguo yilai Mao Zedong wengao [Mao Zedong's Manuscripts since the Foundation of the PRC]*, vol. 12 (Beijing: Zhongyang wenxian chubanshe, 1998), 54.

40. Mao Zedong, "Guanyu lilun wenti de tanhua yaodian" ["Main Points of a Discussion on Theoretic Issues"], in *Jianguo yilai Mao Zedong wengao [Mao Zedong's Manuscripts since the Foundation of the PRC]*, vol. 13 (Beijing: Zhongyang wenxian chubanshe, 1998), 413.

41. Central Committee of the Chinese Communist Party, "Zhonggong zhongyang tongzhi: Maozhuxi zhongyao zhishi" ["The Notice of the Central Committee of the Chinese Communist Party: Chairman Mao's Important Instructions"], *Zhonggong zhongyang 1976 nian sihao wenjian [Documents of the Central Committee of the Chinese Communist Party, no. 4, 1976]* (March 3, 1976). Based on Mao Zedong's several talks during the months from October 1975 through January 1976, this document was personally endorsed by Mao himself.

42. Kang Xiaoguang, "Weilai 3–5 nian zhongguo dalu zhengzhi wendingxin fenxi" ["An Analysis on China's Political Stability in the Coming 3–5 Years"], *Zhanglue yu guanli [Strategy and Management]*, no. 3 (2002): 1–15.

43. Sun Chengbin, Tian Yu, and Zou Shengwen, "Gengduo xinmiankong 'liangxiang' Zhongguo zhengzhi wutai: shiyijie quanguo rendadaibiao gouchen teshe fenxi" ["More New Faces Showing Up on China's Political Stage: An Analysis of the Composition of the National People's Congress Deputies"], http://news.xinhuanet.com/politics/2008-02/28/content_7687622.htm, February 28, 2008 (accessed May 7, 2011).

44. National Political Consultative Conference, "Zhongguo zhengxie de goucheng" ["The Composition of the National Political Consultative Conference"] http://www.cppcc.gov.cn/page.do?pa=402880631d247e3e011d24ad4ee60072&guid=4625e9e517

e64bddacod3ea06e09fb8f&og=40288063Id2d9ofdoIId2de66e59027e, December 19, 2008 (accessed May 17, 2011).

45. Gaetano Mosca, *The Ruling Class* (New York: McGraw-Hill, 1960).

46. Vilfredo Pareto, *The Rise and Fall of Elites: An Application of Theoretical Sociology* (New Brunswick, N.J.: Transaction, 1991).

47. Wang Shaoguang, *Qumei yu chaoyue: fansi minzhu, ziyou, pingdeng, gongminshehui* [*Disenchantment and Transcendence: Reflections on Democracy, Freedom, Equality, Civil Society*] (Beijing: Zhongxin chubanshe, 2009), 227–33.

48. Sean Loughlin and Robert Yoon, "Millionaires Populate U.S. Senate: Kerry, Rockefeller, Kohl among the Wealthiest," http://www.cnn.com/2003/ALLPOLI-TICS/06/13/senators.finances/, June 13, 2003 (accessed May 17, 2011); Paul Singer, Jennifer Yachnin, and Casey Hynes, "The 50 Richest Members of Congress," http://www.rollcall.com/features/Guide-to-Congress_2008/guide/28506-1.html?type=printer_friendly, September 22, 2008 (accessed May 17, 2011).

49. Agence France Presse, "Millionaires Fill US Congress Halls," http://www.commondreams.org/headlineso4/0630-05.htm, June 30, 2004 (accessed May 17, 2011).

50. Wang Shaoguang, *Qumei yu chaoyue*, 241–42.

51. Larry M. Bartels, *Unequal Democracy: The Political Economy of the New Gilded Age* (Princeton, N.J.: Princeton University Press, 2008).

52. Mark Murray, "Obama Blasts GOP for Ignoring Economy," http://firstread.msnbc.msn.com/archive/2008/09/03/1334964.aspx, September 3, 2008 (accessed May 17, 2011).

53. Bartels, *Unequal Democracy*, 260–70.

54. Jiang Qing, *Zhengzhi ruxue*, 341–58.

55. Ibid., 18–23.

56. Ibid., 109.

57. *The Anecdotal History of the Scholars* (*Rulin Waishi*) is a novel by Wu Jingzi (1701–54).

58. The Ye Shaoweng of the Song dynasty accused Zhu Xi in his *Sichao jianwenlu* as follows: He maltreated his elderly mother and was lacking in piety toward his parents. He played with a Buddhist nun and seduced her into becoming his concubine. He opened his door to students, whose families offered him gifts worth tens of thousands of taels of silver. The reference to his maltreatment of his mother refers to his not giving good rice to her to eat. See Ye Shaoweng, *Sichao jianwenlu* [*Records of Observation in Four Dynasties*] (Taipei: Guang Wen Shu Ju, 1986). Zhu Xi himself did not deny some of those allegations. He said that he had reflected on his conduct and expressed his willingness to repent. Hong Mai in his *Yijianzhi* also records Zhu Xi's hypocrisy and small-mindedness. See Hong Mai, *Yijianzhi* (Shanghai: Commercial Press, 1937).

59. Longchan, "'Xuezhe shetou' Zheng Jiadong" ["Scholar Smuggler Zheng Jiadong"], *Sanlian shenghuo zhoukan* [*SDX Life Weekly*], no. 25 (2005).

60. Alfred Kroeber and Clyde Kluckhohn, *Culture: A Critical Review of Concepts and Definitions* (Cambridge, Mass.: Harvard University, Peabody Museum of American Archeology and Ethnology, 1952).

61. The distinction between great and little traditions is one made by Robert Redfield. See his *Peasant Society and Culture: An Anthropological Approach to Civilization* (Chicago: University of Chicago Press, 1956).

62. Bell, *China's New Confucianism*, 22.

63. Baidu has an English introduction about its products at "The Baidu Story," http://ir.baidu.com/phoenix.zhtml?c=188488&p=irol-homeprofile, 2011 (accessed May 17,

2011).

64. Jiang Qing, "Wangguanxue, Zhengzhi baoshou yu hefaxing chongjian: Nandou zhoukan Jiang Qing zhuanfang" ["Reconstructing the Palace School, Political Conservatism and Legitimacy: Southern Weekly's Interview with Jiang Qing"], http://www.rjfx.net/dispbbs.asp?boardID=25&ID=7051&page=1, August 30, 2007 (accessed May 17, 2011).

65. Bai Tongdong, "Yige rujiao banben de youxian minzhu: Yige gengxianshi de wutoubang" ["A Confucian Version of the Limited Democracy: A More Realistic Utopia"] in his *Jiubang xinming*, chap. 3.

66. Two legendary sage kings in ancient China.

67. Wang Shaoguang, "Jianshou fangxiang, tansuo daolu: Zhongguo shehuizhuyi liushinian" ["Adhere to the Direction, Exploring New Road: The Practice of Socialism in China in the Last 60 Years"], *Zhongguo shehui kexue* [*China Social Sciences*], no. 5 (2009).

68. Erik Olin Wright, "The Real Utopias Project," http://www.ssc.wisc.edu/~wright/RealUtopias.htm, n.d. (accessed May 17, 2011).

69. See Wang Shaoguang, *Qumei yu chaoyue*; and *Minzhu sijiang* [*Four Lectures on Democracy*] (Beijing: Sanlian Shudian, 2008).

CHAPTER 8

1. Robert N. Bellah, "Civil Religion in America," *Journal of the American Academy of Arts and Sciences* 96, no. 1 (Winter 1967): 1–21.

2. See Neuhaus, *Naked Public Square*.

3. See Alasdair MacIntyre, *After Virtue: A Study in Moral Theory* (Notre Dame, Ind.: University of Notre Dame Press, 1984) and *Whose Justice? Which Rationality?* (Notre Dame, Ind.: University of Notre Dame Press, 1988); Leo Strauss, *On Tyranny* (New York: Free Press, 1991) and *What Is Political Philosophy? And Other Studies* (Chicago: University of Chicago Press, 1988).

4. James Legge (trans.), *The Book of Historical Documents*, in *The Chinese Classics*, vol. 3, *The Announcement of T'ang* (Hong Kong: Hong Kong University Press, 1960), 186.

5. James Legge (trans.), *The Book of Poetry*, in *The Chinese Classics*, vol. 4, ode 191 (Hong Kong: Hong Kong University Press, 1960), 312.

6. Ibid., ode 255, 505.

7. Direct rule by sage kings is the highest historical ideal, but rule by sages or scholar-officials is a practical goal that can be realized in history.

8. For instance, besides the basic demand of respect for parents, the *Classic of Filial Piety* explains carrying out filial piety as exerting social responsibility, accepting the political duty of running the state, and fulfilling the transcendent, sacred meaning of life by realizing religious and moral values. This is what is meant by the *Classic of Filial Piety* when it says filial piety "commences with the service of parents; it proceeds to the service of the ruler; it is completed by establishment of the character." In Legge, *Sacred Books of China*, vol. 1, 466–67. These are the familial, sociopolitical, and religious dimensions of piety.

Again the *Classic of Filial Piety* goes on to say, "When we have established our character by the practice of the (filial) course, so as to make our name famous in future ages, and thereby glorify our parents." Ibid., 466. This means that the way to carry out piety is by realizing religious and moral values and thus accomplishing one's transcendent sacred life and thereby ensuring that the life of one's parents endures forever. The *Classic of Filial Piety* goes on to speak of the Duke of Zhou who "at the border altar sacrificed to Hau-ki as the correlate of Heaven, and in the Brilliant Hall he honoured king Wan, and sacrificed to him as the correlate of God." Ibid., 477. The *Analects* speaks of Yu as "showing great piety to ghosts and spirits" (*Analects* 8.21). These passages refer to the religious dimension of piety.

In four chapters, "Xiaozhi" (Filial Piety in Government), "Shengzhi" (The Government of the Sages), "Ganying" (The Influence of Filial Piety and the Response to It), and "Sangqin" (Filial Piety in Mourning for Parents), the *Classic of Filial Piety* variously discusses the piety of social public responsibility and political duty and the piety of the realization of transcendent sacred values and eternal life.

Again, the *Record of Rites of the Elder Dai* has a theory of the three roots of rites, one of which is stated as "the prince as teacher is the root of ruling." Dai De, *Da Dai Liji* [*Record of Rites of the Elder Dai*] (Taipei: Shangwu Yìnshuguan, 1984), 41. By the prince as teacher is meant the union of virtue and status as with the sage kings. "Ruling" here refers to the educational and moral transformation of society and politics, which is the same as the culture of the sages mentioned above. On the basis of these three roots of rites, Confucianism has formed the idea of the three returns for rites. This means that by sacrificial rites to the three roots, to heaven-earth, ancestors, and the prince as teacher, one can show piety in response to the grace by which heaven and earth have formed humanity and all that is, piety in response to the grace of life given to us by our ancestors, and piety in response to the grace by which the prince as teacher undertakes the educational and moral transformation of society by means of the culture of the sages and thus ensures the stability and harmony of society. Here, the response to the sages embodies the cultural aspect of piety, which is involved in offering sacrifices to the sages, and the responses to heaven and earth and to ancestors express the religious aspect of piety. Hence, we can say that response is piety and that the three forms of response are piety toward heaven and earth, toward ancestors, and toward the sages. These three forms of piety were later inscribed on a tablet as Heaven Earth Parents Prince Teacher and form part of the common faith of Chinese people.

Furthermore, the *Record of Rites of the Elder Dai* says, "Grass and trees are felled in season; birds and beasts are killed in season. The master said; 'to fell one tree or kill one beast not in season is to fail in piety.'" Ibid.,186. What is spoken of here is the way of treating things with filial piety, a piety directed toward nature. Moreover, in the faith of piety that involves responding to heaven and earth, heaven and earth are both the transcendent sacred religious origin and the natural world of sun, moon, stars, mountains, and rivers. So the piety of responding to heaven includes the ecological sense of treating things with piety.

9. The *Classic of Filial Piety* tells the story of a conversation between Zengzi and Confucius. Zengzi asked "[i]f (simple) obedience to the orders of one's father can be pronounced filial piety." Confucius replied, "[T]he father who had a son that would remonstrate with him would not sink into the gulf of unrighteous deeds. Therefore when a case of unrighteous conduct is concerned, a son must by no means keep from remonstrating with his father. . . . Hence, since remonstrance is required in the case of unrighteous conduct, how can (simple) obedience to the orders of a father be termed filial piety?" Legge, *Sacred Books of China*, vol. 1, 484. From this we can see that even in the family circle obedience to parents is not unconditional. The conduct of the parents must be in accord with right living if the children are to obey. It is not a case of simple obedience alone.

10. Bai Tongdong and Li Chenyang share a sympathetic understanding of Confucianism and appreciate many Confucian values. However, the framework and direction of their basic political thinking is still that of liberalism. Among academics in China to-

day there is a Chinese liberalism and a Confucian liberalism. Bai and Li can perhaps be accommodated under both of these labels. In my reply to Joseph Chan, I have already discussed some of the basic principles of liberalism, and so here I do not repeat what was said there insofar as it also applies to Bai and Li. Instead, I concentrate on the important points raised by the two, which have not yet been discussed.

11. Ban Gu, *Dong Zhongshu chuan*, in *Han shu*, book 56.

12. A peaceful transition of political power, by abdication and succession or by hereditary succession, is one way in which heaven exercises its sovereignty. There are many other ways too, such as in giving life to all that is, in revealing auspicious omens, and in sending down disasters.

13. *The Great Declaration* in *The Book of History*.

14. See my discussion in chapter 2.

15. "Explain" here has two meanings: it means to interpret and to deconstruct, or to deconstruct while interpreting. For more details see my paper "Yi Zhongguo jieshi Zhongguo: huigui Zhongguo ruxue xijuan de jieshi xiyong" ["Explaining China from a Chinese Perspective: Returning to the Internal Logic of Chinese Confucianism"], http://www.chinamengzi.net/Library/ddmjsj/jqwj/200707/1797.html, July 23, 2007 (accessed April 15, 2011).

16. Mencius is talking about the undoing of political power by heaven and not by men. The human undoing of power, evidenced in the historical examples of the revolutions led by Tang and Wu, was but a form of implementation of the will of heaven.

17. Mencius says that heaven is what acts without action.

18. "King Wan's Explanation of the Entire Hexagrams," in *The Book of Changes*, in Legge, *Sacred Books of China*, vol. 2, 213.

19. Because today's academic world has rejected metaphysics, it has deconstructed the united purpose of the universe and the universal significance of the world, with the result that the world and human history have fallen into a chaos and absurdity without purpose, meaning, or value. This type of thought is very prolific and should be discussed elsewhere.

20. Li Chenyang, "Tian-di-ren zhi tian, haishi chaoyue tian-di-ren zhi tian?—jianlun 'minzhu de xingshi he rujia de neirong'" ["Heaven of the 'Heaven-Earth-Humanity' Triad or Transcendent Heaven? Also on the Discussion of 'Confucian Content with Democratic Form'"] (unpublished manuscript), 4.

21. Chapter 6.

22. Li Chenyang, "Tian-di-ren zhi tian," 13.

23. Friedrich, *New Belief*.

24. Chen Shui-bian was president of the Republic of China (Taiwan) from 2000 to 2008.

25. Li Chenyang, "Tian-di-ren zhi tian."

26. The House of Representatives, "Honoring the 2,560th Anniversary of the Birth of Confucius and Recognizing His Invaluable Contributions to Philosophy and Social and Political Thought," http://www.gpo.gov/fdsys/pkg/bills-111hres784ih/pdf/bills-111hres784ih.pdf, n.d. (accessed June 14, 2011).

27. "Supplementary to the Thwan and Yao on the First and Second Hexagrams, and Showing How They May Be Interpreted of Man's Nature and Doings," in *The Book of Changes*, in Legge, *Sacred Books of China*, vol. 2, 409.

28. See Mou Zongsan, *Zhengdao yu zhidao* [*The Way of Politics and the Way of Governance*] (Taipei: Taiwan xuesheng shuju, 1996).

29. See Fok Tou-hui, "Keyi you youzhi minzhu ma?" ["Can There Be Elite Democracy?"], *Fadeng* 338 (August 1, 2010). Translator's note: Fok Tou-hui is the head of the

Dharmasthiti College of Cultural Studies.

30. Translator's note: Fan Yafeng is the head of Christian Human Rights Lawyers of China, the Shengshan (Holy Mountain) Culture Research Institute, and the Shengshan (Holy Mountain) Church.

31. Translator's note: Tu Weiming is a lifetime professor of philosophy and dean of the Institute for Advanced Humanistic Studies at Peking University and research professor and senior fellow of Asia Center at Harvard University. He thinks that there can be Confucian democracy, Confucian liberalism, even a Confucian Christian, in which "Confucian" is an adjective and the Western terms "democracy" and "liberalism" are the nouns.

32. See Gan Yang, *Women zai chuangzao chuantong* [*We Are Creating Tradition*] (Taipei: Lianjing Chubanshe, 1989). Translator's note: Gan Yang is at Sun Yat-sen University in Guangzhou.

33. Translator's note: This is a remaking of the famous phrase of Zhang Zhidong (1835–1909) in his book *Exhortation to Study* of 1898: "Chinese learning as substance; Western learning as means." See Zhang Zhidong, *Quanxiaopian* [*Exhortation to Study*] (Shanghai: Shanghai Shudian Chubanshe, 2002).

34. Translator's note: Chen Yinke (1890–1969), educated in Western learning, retained a preference for traditional cultural norms.

35. Li Chenyang, "Tian-di-ren zhi tian," 12.

36. The view that Confucianism has already lost all creativity in political matters is not only the view of Professor Li and the other scholars mentioned above. Two classic examples of this attitude can be seen in Yu Ying-shih's theory of the social role of Confucianism and Lee Ming-huei's theory of Confucianism as a form of pure criticism alone. Yu Ying-shih thinks that under suppression from authoritarian monarchs, Confucianism was forced out of the political sphere into that of society and that only in society can it still exercise a function. Lee Ming-huei thinks that the basic political framework today is already that of democracy, so Confucianism can only resign itself to fully accepting this situation and not pretend to exert any creativity. This does not mean that Confucianism is totally useless since it can still act as a critic of democracy. From these views, we can see that Confucian-inclined Chinese intellectuals today have accepted a mitigated version of Fukuyama's thesis in the realm of politics and lost any creative awareness or creativity based on the political ideas of Confucianism itself. Translator's note: Yu Ying-shih (1930–) taught at several universities, retiring from Princeton in 2001. Lee Ming-huei (1953–) is in Taiwan and is an expert on Confucianism and Kant.

37. Over the past sixty years, China's national ideological attitude has been one of atheism and materialism. It is this attitude that determines that China cannot resolve the problem of the lack of sacred legitimacy.

38. Chapter 7.

39. Mao's May 7th Directive refers to Mao's letter to Lin Biao, then the vice chairman of the Chinese Communist Party Committee, regarding educational policy, dated May 7, 1966, during the Cultural Revolution. For a Chinese version of the letter, see Anonymous, "Wuqi zhishi" ["May 7th Directive"], http://baike.baidu.com/view/423078.htm, n.d. (accessed June 21, 2011).

40. This point is evident from the *Analects*, Mencius, the chapter on the Confucians in the *Record of Rites*, the Four Sentence Doctrine of Zhang Zai (also known as Heng Qu), the Memorials of Wang Yangming, and the history books throughout the ages.

41. Let us imagine that we ask Professor Wang to work on the assembly line in a factory in Dongguan and let an assembly worker from a factory in Dongguan go to lecture

in the Chinese University of Hong Kong. This was the ideal of great equality of the Cultural Revolution in which intellectuals and manual laborers exchanged positions. This is impossible.

42. Professor Wang is correct in noting that "Chinese" refers to the way of earth and historical and cultural legitimacy. There is no need to say any more about this here.

43. A political ideology founded on money and wealth is not only that of the West today. It has also been the ideology of the West in the past. Ancient Greece and Rome had this wealth-based attitude to politics. Likewise, the political attitude that relies on rule by the worthy and capable is not only part of my Confucian constitutionalism. It is the tradition of rule by learning that has been a constant thread throughout the five thousand years of Chinese history. For details on this matter, one may refer to my discussion in chapter 2.

44. *The Collection of Treatises on the Rules of Propriety or Ceremonial Usages*, in Legge, *Sacred Books of China*, vol. 4, book 17, *The Record of Music*, 112.

ENGLISH AND FRENCH WORKS

Agence France Presse, "Millionaires Fill US Congress Halls," *http://www.commondreams* *.org/headlineso4/0630-05.htm*, June 30, 2004 (accessed May 17, 2011).

Alitto, Guy S., *The Last Confucian* (2nd ed.; Berkeley: University of California Press, 1986).

Angle, Stephen, "Rethinking Confucian Authority and Rejecting Confucian Authoritarianism," in Liu Xiaogan (ed.), *Zhongguo zhexue yu wenhua (di ba ji): Tang Junyi yu Zhongguo zhexue yanjiu [Chinese Philosophy and Culture (v.8): Tang Junyi and the Studies of Chinese philosophy]* (Guilin: Guangxi shifan daxue chubanshe, 2010), 27–55.

Anonymous (Fu Huisheng, trans.), *The Zhou Book of Change: The Survey I*, vol. 1 (Changsha: Hunan People's Publishing House, 2008).

Aristotle, *The Politics* (Cambridge, UK: Cambridge University Press, 1988).

ASEP/JDS Data Bank, "Confidence in the Government," *http://www.jdsurvey.net/jds* */jdsurveyActualidad.jsp?Idioma=I&SeccionTexto=0404*, 2010 (accessed May 7, 2011).

Assemblée Nationale, "Constitution of October 4, 1958," *http://www.assemblee-nationale* *.fr/english/8ab.asp*, n.d. (accessed April 14, 2011).

Bai Tongdong, "Philosophical Reflections on National Identity," in Jacqueline M. Moore and Rebecca Woodward Wendelken (eds.), *Teaching the Silk Road: Reflections and Pedagogical Essays for College Teachers* (Albany: State University of New York Press, 2010), 139–55.

——, "A Mencian Version of Limited Democracy," *Res Publica* 14, no. 1 (2008): 19–34.

Baidu, "The Baidu Story," *http://ir.baidu.com/phoenix.zhtml?c=188488&p=irol-homeprofile*, 2011 (accessed May 17, 2011).

Bardsley, Daniel, "Plan for Church Higher Than Confucian Temple Causes Stir in China," *http://www.thenational.ae/news/worldwide/asia-pacific/plan-for-church-higher-than-confucian-temple-causes-stir-in-china?pageCount=0*, April 12, 2011 (accessed June 19, 2011).

Barker, Rodney, *Political Legitimacy and the State* (Oxford: Clarendon, 1990).

Bartels, Larry M., *Unequal Democracy: The Political Economy of the New Gilded Age* (Princeton, N.J.: Princeton University Press, 2008).

Bell, Daniel A., *Beyond Liberal Democracy: Political Thinking for an East Asian Context* (Princeton, N.J.: Princeton University Press, 2006).

——, *China's New Confucianism: Politics and Everyday Life in a Changing Society* (rev. ed.; Princeton, N.J.: Princeton University Press, 2010).

——, "A Visit to a Confucian Academy," *http://www.dissentmagazine.org/online* *.php?id=146*, September 22, 2008 (accessed June 19, 2011).

Bellah, Robert N., "Civil Religion in America," *Journal of the American Academy of Arts and Sciences* 96, no. 1 (Winter 1967): 1–21.

Canache, Damarys, Jeffery J. Mondak, and Mitchell A. Seligson, "Meaning and Measurement in Cross-National Research on Satisfaction with Democracy," *Public Opinion Quarterly* 65, no. 4 (Winter 2001): 506–28.

Caplan, Bryan, *The Myth of the Rational Voter: Why Democracies Choose Bad Policies* (Princeton, N.J.: Princeton University Press, 2007).

Chan, Joseph, "Confucian Attitudes toward Ethical Pluralism," in Richard Madsen and Tracy B. Strong (eds.), *The Many and the One: Religious and Secular Perspectives on Ethical Pluralism in the Modern World* (Princeton, N.J.: Princeton University Press, 2003), 129–53.

———, "A Confucian Perspective on Human Rights for Contemporary China," in Joanne R. Bauer and Daniel A. Bell (eds.), *The East Asian Challenge for Human Rights* (Cambridge, UK: Cambridge University Press, 1999), 212–37.

———, "Democracy and Meritocracy: Toward a Confucian Perspective," *Journal of Chinese Philosophy* 34, no. 2 (2007): 179–93.

———, "Giving Priority to the Worst Off: A Confucian Perspective on Social Welfare," in Daniel A. Bell and Hahm Chaibong (eds.), *Confucianism for the Modern World* (Cambridge, UK: Cambridge University Press, 2003), 236–53.

———, "In Defense of Moderate Perfectionism" (unpublished manuscript, 2009).

———, "Is There a Confucian Perspective on Social Justice?" in Takashi Shogimen and Cary J. Nederman (eds.), *Western Political Thought in Dialogue with Asia* (Lanham, Md.: Rowman & Littlefield, 2008), 261–77.

———, "Legitimacy, Unanimity, and Perfectionism," *Philosophy and Public Affairs* 29, no. 1 (2000): 5–42.

———, "Moral Autonomy, Civil Liberties, and Confucianism," *Philosophy East and West* 52, no. 3 (July 2002): 281–310.

Chen Jie, *Popular Political Support in Urban China* (Washington, D.C.: Woodrow Wilson Center Press, 2004).

Chen Jie, Yang Zhong, and Jan Hillard, "Assessing Political Support in China: Citizens' Evaluations of Governmental Effectiveness and Legitimacy," *Journal of Contemporary China* 6, no. 16 (November 1997): 551–66.

Chu Yun-han, Larry Diamond, Andrew J. Nathan, and Doh Chull Shin (eds.), *How East Asians View Democracy* (New York: Columbia University Press, 2008).

Comparative Study of Electoral Systems, "Satisfaction with Democracy," http://www.umich.edu/~cses/resources/results/CSESresults_SatisfactionWithDemocracy.htm, October 24, 2005 (accessed May 7, 2011).

Confucius (D. C. Lau, trans.), *The Analects* (Hong Kong: Chinese University Press, 1992).

Feng Youlan (Derk Bodde, trans.), *A History of Chinese Philosophy*, vol. 1 (Princeton, N.J.: Princeton University Press, 1952).

Fewsmith, Joseph, "Assessing Social Stability on the Eve of the 17th Party Congress," *China Leadership Monitor* 20 (2007): 1–24.

Friedrich, Carl J., *The New Belief in the Common Man* (Boston: Little, Brown, 1942).

Fukuyama, Francis, *The End of History and the Last Man* (London: Penguin, 1992).

Gao Mobo, *The Battle for China's Past: Mao and the Cultural Revolution* (London: Pluto Press, 2008).

Gilley, Bruce, "Legitimacy and Institutional Change: The Case of China," *Comparative Political Studies* 41, no. 3 (2008): 259–84.

———, "The Meaning and Measure of State Legitimacy: Results for 72 Countries," *European Journal of Political Research* 45 (2006): 499–525.

———, *The Right to Rule: How States Win and Lose Legitimacy* (New York: Columbia University Press, 2009).

Hahm Chaihark, "Constitutionalism, Confucian Civic Virtue, and Ritual Propriety," in Daniel A. Bell and Hahm Chaibong (eds.), *Confucianism for the Modern World* (Cambridge, UK: Cambridge University Press, 2003), 31–53.

Holbig, Heike, and Bruce Gilley, "In Search of Legitimacy in Post-revolutionary China: Bringing Ideology and Governance Back In," *GIGA Working Papers* 127 (March 2010): 5–34.

House of Representatives, "Honoring the 2,560th Anniversary of the Birth of Confucius and Recognizing His Invaluable Contributions to Philosophy and Social and Political Thought," *http://www.opencongress.org/bill/111-hr784/text*, n.d. (accessed June 14, 2011).

Huang Zongxi (Wm. Theodore de Bary, trans.), *Waiting for the Dawn: A Plan for the Prince* (New York: Columbia University Press, 1993).

Jiang Qing (Sébastien Billioud, trans.), "Le confucianisme de la Voie royale, direction pour le politique en Chine contemporaine," *Perspectives on the Political in China Today (Extrême-Orient Extrême-Occident)* 31 (October 2009): 103–23.

Knoblock, John (trans.), *Xunzi: A Translation and Study of the Complete Works* (Stanford, Calif.: Stanford University Press, 1988).

Kroeber, Alfred and Clyde Kluckhohn, *Culture: A Critical Review of Concepts and Definitions* (Cambridge, Mass.: Harvard University, Peabody Museum of American Archeology and Ethnology, 1952).

Legge, James (trans.), *The Chinese Classics* (Hong Kong: Hong Kong University Press, 1960).

——— (trans.), *The Sacred Books of China* (New York: Gordon Press, 1976).

Li Chenyang, *The Tao Encounters the West* (Albany: State University of New York Press, 1999).

———, "Where Does Confucian Virtuous Leadership Stand?" *Philosophy East and West* 59, no. 4 (October 2009): 531–36.

Li Lianjiang, "Political Trust in Rural China," *Modern China* 30, no. 2 (April 2004): 228–58.

Lipset, Seymour Martin, *Political Man: The Social Bases of Politics*, 2nd ed. (London: Heinemann, 1983).

Loughlin, Sean, and Robert Yoon, "Millionaires Populate U.S. Senate: Kerry, Rockefeller, Kohl among the Wealthiest," *http://www.cnn.com/2003/ALLPOLITICS/06/13/senators.finances/*, June 13, 2003 (accessed May 17, 2011).

MacIntyre, Alasdair, *After Virtue: A Study in Moral Theory* (Notre Dame, Ind.: University of Notre Dame Press, 1984).

———, *Whose Justice? Which Rationality?* (Notre Dame, Ind.: University of Notre Dame Press, 1988).

McCormick, John P., "Contain the Wealthy and Patrol the Magistrates: Restoring Elite Accountability to Popular Government," *American Political Science Review* 100, no. 2 (May 2006): 147–63.

Mencius (D. C. Lau, trans.), *Mencius* (Hong Kong: Chinese University Press, 2003).

Mosca, Gaetano, *The Ruling Class* (New York: McGraw-Hill, 1960).

Murray, Mark, "Obama Blasts GOP for Ignoring Economy," *http://firstread.msnbc.msn.com/archive/2008/09/03/1334964.aspx*, September 3, 2008 (accessed May 17, 2011).

Neuhaus, Richard John, *The Naked Public Square: Religion and Democracy in America* (Grand Rapids, Mich.: Eerdmans, 1984).

Norwegian Social Science Data Services, "European Social Survey Education Net," *http://essedunet.nsd.uib.no/*, 2011 (accessed May 7, 2011).

Pareto, Vilfredo, *The Rise and Fall of Elites: An Application of Theoretical Sociology* (New Brunswick, N.J.: Transaction, 1991).

Pew Research Center for the People & the Press, "The People and Their Government: Distrust, Discontent, Anger and Partisan Rancor," *http://people-press.org/reports/pdf/606.pdf*, April 18, 2010 (accessed May 7, 2011).

Rawls, John, *The Law of Peoples with "The Idea of Public Reason Revisited"* (Cambridge, Mass.: Harvard University Press, 1999).

———, *Political Liberalism* (New York: Columbia University Press, 1993).

Redfield, Robert, *Peasant Society and Culture: An Anthropological Approach to Civilization* (Chicago: University of Chicago Press, 1956).

Rougier, Louis, *La Mystique démocratique: ses origins, ses illusions* (Paris: Flammarion, 1929).

Schmitt, Carl (George D. Schwab, trans.), *The Concept of the Political* (Chicago: University of Chicago Press, 2006).

Schumpeter, Joseph, *Capitalism, Socialism and Democracy* (New York: Harper, 1942).

Shi Tianjian, "Cultural Values and Political Trust: A Comparison of the People's Republic of China and Taiwan," *Comparative Politics* 33, no. 4 (July 2001): 401–19.

———, "Establishing Evaluative Criteria: Measuring Political Stability and Political Support in the PRC" (unpublished manuscript).

Shils, Edward, *The Virtue of Civility* (Indianapolis: Liberty Fund, 1997).

Singer, Paul, Jennifer Yachnin, and Casey Hynes, "The 50 Richest Members of Congress," *http://www.rollcall.com/features/Guide-to-Congress_2008/guide/28506-1.html?type=printer_friendly*, September 22, 2008 (accessed May 17, 2011).

Strauss, Leo, *On Tyranny* (New York: Free Press, 1991).

———, *What Is Political Philosophy? And Other Studies* (Chicago: University of Chicago Press, 1988).

Sung, Z. D., *The Text of Yi King* (Taipei: Wenhua, 1988).

Tang Wenfang, "Political and Social Trends in the Post-Deng Urban China: Crisis or Stability?" *China Quarterly* 168 (2001): 890–909.

———, *Public Opinion and Political Change in China* (Stanford, Calif.: Stanford University Press, 2005).

Wang Ban, "The Vision of International Morality in Kang Youwei's Book of the Great Community" (paper presented at the Tianxia Workshop, Stanford University, May 6–10, 2011).

Wang Ruichang, "The Rise of Political Confucianism in Contemporary China," in Fan Ruiping (ed.), *The Renaissance of Confucianism in Contemporary China* (Dordrecht: Springer, 2011), 33–45.

Wang Zhengxu, "Political Trust in China: Forms and Causes," in Lynn White (ed.), *Legitimacy: Ambiguities of Political Success or Failure in East and Southeast Asia* (Singapore: World Scientific, 2005).

Wright, Erik Olin, "The Real Utopias Project," *http://www.ssc.wisc.edu/~wright/RealUtopias.htm*, n.d. (accessed May 17, 2011).

Yan Xuetong (Daniel A. Bell and Sun Zhe, eds.; Edmund Ryden, trans.), *Ancient Chinese Thought, Modern Chinese Power* (Princeton, N.J.: Princeton University Press, 2011).

Yu, Erika, and Meng Fan, "A Confucian Coming of Age," in Fan Ruiping (ed.), *The Renaissance of Confucianism in Contemporary China* (Dordrecht: Springer, 2011), 241–57.

Yu Keping, *Democracy Is a Good Thing: Essays on Politics, Society, and Culture in Contemporary China* (Washington, D.C.: Brookings Institution, 2008).

Zakaria, Fareed, *The Future of Freedom: Illiberal Democracy at Home and Abroad* (New York: Norton, 2003).

Zhang Dainian (Edmund Ryden, trans.), *Key Concepts in Chinese Philosophy* (New Haven, Conn.: Yale University Press, 2002).

CHINESE WORKS

Anonymous, "Wuqi zhishi" ["May 7th Directive"], *http://baike.baidu.com/view/423078 .htm*, n.d. (accessed June 21, 2011).

Bai Tongdong, *Jiubang xinming: gujin zhongxi canzhaoxia de gudian rujia zhengzhi zhexue* [*A New Mission of an Old State: The Contemporary and Comparative Relevance of Classical Confucian Political Philosophy*] (Beijing: Beijing Daxue Chubanshe, 2009).

Ban Gu, *Han shu* [*Book of Han History*] (Beijing: Shangwu Yìnshuguan, 1941).

Central Committee of the Chinese Communist Party, "Zhonggong zhongyang tongzhi: Maozhuxi zhongyao zhishi" ["The Notice of the Central Committee of the Chinese Communist Party: Chairman Mao's Important Instructions"], in *Zhonggong zhongyang 1976 nian sihao wenjian* [*Documents of the Central Committee of the Chinese Communist Party, no. 4, 1976*] (March 3, 1976).

Chen Lai, *Gudai zongjiao yu lunli—rujia sixiang de genyuan* [*Ancient Religions and Ethics—Roots of Confucian Thought*] (Beijing: Sanlian Shudian, 1996).

Chen Lai and Gan Yang (eds.), *Kongzi yu dangdai Zhongguo* [*Confucius and Contemporary China*] (Beijing: Xinzhi sanlian shudian, 2008).

Cheng Yi, *Zhouyi Shangjing shang* in *Zhouyi Chengshichuan* [*Cheng's Commentary on the Book of Changes*] (Taipei: Cheng Wen Chubanshe, 1976).

Dai De, *Da Dai Liji* [*Record of Rites of the Elder Dai*] (Taipei: Shangwu Yìnshuguan, 1984).

Dong Zhongshu, *Chunqiu fanlu* [*Luxuriant Dew of the Spring and Autumn Annals*] (Shanghai: Shanghai Guji Chubanshe, 1989).

———, *Chunqiu fanlu* [*Luxuriant Dew of the Spring and Autumn Annals*] (Taipei: Sanmin shuju, 2007).

Fan Ruiping (ed.), *Rujia shehui yu daotong fuxing* [*Confucian Society and the Revival of Dao*] (Shanghai: Huadong shifan daxue chubanshe, 2008).

Fok Tou-hui, "Keyi you youzhi minxhu ma?" ["Can There Be Elite Democracy?"], *Fadeng* 338 (August 1, 2010).

Gan Chunsong, "Qingmo minchu kongjiao hui shijian yu Rujia xiandai zhuandai de kunjing" ["The Establishment of Confucian Religious Associations in the Late Qing and Early Republican Period and the Difficulty of Transforming Confucianism Today"], *Qilu Xuekan* 3.186 (2005): 24–25.

Gan Yang, *Women zai chuangzao chuantong* [*We Are Creating Tradition*] (Taipei: Lianjing Chubanshe, 1989).

Gongyang Gao, *Gongyang chuan* in *Chunqiu* [*Gongyang Commentary* in the *Spring and Autumn Annals*] (Shanghai: Zhonghua Shuju, 1931).

Hong Mai, *Yijianzhi* [*Record of the Listener*] (Shanghai: Shangwu Yìnshuguan, 1937).

Hsu Cho-yun, *Wangu jianghe: Zhongguo lishi wenhua de zhuanzhe yu kaizhan* [*The Eternal Rivers: The Turning Point and Evolution of Chinese Historical Culture*] (Shanghai: Shanghai wenyi chubanshe, 2006).

Hu Qiaomu, "Mao zhuxi zai zhuiqiu yizhong shehuizhuyi" ["Chairman Mao in the Search of an Ideal Socialism"], in *Hu Qiaomu tan zhonggong dangshi* [*Hu Qiaomu Talks about the History of the Chinese Communist Party*] (Beijing: Renmin chubanshe, 1999), 70–72.

Jiang Qing, "Chongjian rujiao jihua" ["A Plan to Reestablish China's Confucian Religion"], *Zhongguo rujiao yanjiu tongxun* [*News on Chinese Confucian Studies*] 1 (December

2005): 1–5.Jiang Qing, *Gongyangxue yinlun* [*Introduction to the Gongyang Commentary on the Spring and Autumn Annals*] (Shenyang: Liaoning jiaoyu chubanshe, 1995).

———, "Rujiao xianzheng de yili wenti yu yihui xingshi: huiying Bei Danning jiaoshou dui 'yihui sanyuanzhi' de piping" ["Political Legitimacy and the Tricameral Parliament: Reply to the Criticism of Daniel A. Bell"] (unpublished manuscript).

———, "'Rujiao xianzheng' zhuti cankao wengao—yuanqi" ["The Reason of Writing on the Topic 'Political Confucianism'"] (unpublished manuscript).

———, *Shengming xinyang yu wangdao zhengzhi: rujia wenhua de xiandai jiazhi* [*Faith in Spiritual Life and Politics Way of the Humane Authority: The Modern Value of Confucian Culture*] (Taiwan: Yang Zheng Tang Chuban, 2004).

———, "Wangdao tushui: 'rujiao xianzheng' de yili jichu yu 'yihui sanyuanzhi'" ["Explanation of the Way of the Humane Authority: Political Legitimacy and the Tricameral Parliament"] (unpublished manuscript).

———, "Wangdao zhengzhi shi dangjin zhongguo zhengzhi de fazhan fangxiang: 'rujiao xianzheng' de yili jichu yu 'yihui sanyuanzhi'" ["The Way of the Humane Authority Is the Way Ahead for China's Political Future: Political Legitimacy and the Tricameral Parliament"], *Yuan Dao* 10, no. 1 (2005): 79–94.

———, "Wangguanxue, zhengzhi baoshou yu hefaxing chongjian: Nandou zhouka Jiang Qing zhuanfang" ["Reconstructing the Palace School, Political Conservatism and Legitimacy: Southern Weekly's Interview with Jiang Qing"], *http://www.rjfx.net/dispbbs.asp?boardID=25&ID=7051&page=1*, August 30, 2007 (accessed May 17, 2011).

———, "Yi Zhongguo jieshi Zhongguo: huigui Zhongguo ruxue xijuan de jieshi xiyong" ["Explaining China from a Chinese Perspective: Returning to the Internal Logic of Chinese Confucianism"], *http://www.chinamengzi.net/Library/ddmjsj/jqwj/200707/1797.html*, July 23, 2007 (accessed April 15, 2011).

———, *Zhengzhi ruxue: dangdai ruxue de zhuanxiang, tezhi yu fazhan* [*Political Confucianism: The Transformation, Special Characteristics, and Development of Contemporary Confucianism*] (Beijing: Sanlian Shudian, 2003).

———, "Zhengzhi ruxue—xupian" ["Political Confucianism—A Sequel"] (unpublished manuscript).

Kang Xiaoguang, "Weilai 3–5 nian zhongguo dalu zhengzhi wendingxin fenxi" ["An Analysis on China's Political Stability in the Coming 3–5 Years"], *Zhanglue yu guanli* [*Strategy and Management*], no. 3 (2002): 1–15.

Li Chenyang, "Minzhu de xingshi he rujia de neirong: zailun rujia yu minzhu de guanxi" ["Confucian Content and Democratic Form: Revisiting the Relationship of Confucianism and Democracy"], *Zhongguo zhexue yu Wenhua* [*Chinese Philosophy and Culture*] 10 (2012).

Li Minghui, *Dangdai ruxue de ziwo zhuanhua* [*Self-Transformation of Contemporary Confucianism*] (Beijing: Zhongguo shehui kexue chubanshe, 2001).

Longchan, "'Xuezhe shetou' Zheng Jiadong" ["Scholar Smuggler Zheng Jiadong"], *Sanlian shenghuo zhoukan* [*SDX Life Weekly*], no. 25 (2005): 50–53.

Mao Heng, *Maoshi zhushu* [*Mao's Commentary on Odes*], vol. 4 (Hong Kong: Zhonghua Shuju, 1964).

Mao Zedong, "Dui 'heshi zhengzhi zhansian shang he sixiang zhanxian shang de shehuizhuyi geming' yiwen de piyu he xiugai" ["Comments and Revisions on the Draft 'This Is a Socialist Revolution on the Front of Political and Ideological Battlefields'"], *http://www.hprc.org.cn/hybldrzz/dhgj/mzdzz/wg6/200908/t20090810_24920.html*, September 15, 1957 (accessed May 7, 2011).

———, "Dui zonghouqinbu guanyu jinyibu gaohao budui nongfuye shengchan baogao de piyu" ["Comments on the Report of the General Logistics Department on Further Improvement of PLA's Agricultural and Sideline Production"], in *Jianguo yilai Mao Zedong wengao* [*Mao Zedong's Manuscripts since the Foundation of the PRC*], vol. 12 (Beijing: Zhongyang wenxian chubanshe, 1998), 53–56.

———, "Guanyu lilun wenti de tanhua yaodian" ["Main Points of a Discussion on Theoretical Issues"], in *Jianguo yilai Mao Zedong wengao* [*Mao Zedong's Manuscripts since the Foundation of the PRC*], vol. 13 (Beijing: Zhongyang wenxian chubanshe, 1998), 413–15.

Meng Mo (ed.), *Mengwen Tongxiaoji* [*Scholarly Records of Meng Wentong*] (Beijing: Sanlian Shudian, 1993).

Mou Zongsan, *Zhengdao yu zhidao* [*The Way of Politics and the Way of Governance*] (Taipei: Taiwan xuesheng shuju, 1996).

National Political Consultative Conference, "Zhongguo zhengxie de goucheng" ["The Composition of the National Political Consultative Conference"], *http://www.cppcc. gov.cn/2011/11/23/art11322013701379833.shtml*, December 19, 2008 (accessed May 17, 2011).

Ouyang Zhenren, "Xianqin rujia wenxian zhong de 'tian'—jianlun Meng Wentong xiansheng dui xheyi wenti de sikao" ["The Concept of *Tian* in Pre-Qin Confucian Texts—Also on Meng Wentong's Opinions of the Matter"], *http://www.mianfeilunwen.com/ Zhexue/Zhongguo/30630.html*, n.d. (accessed January 18, 2011).

Qian Mu, *Zhongguo lidai zhengzhi deshi* [*Merits and Problems of Chinese Dynasties*] (Beijing: Sanlian Shudian, 2005).

Sheng Hong, "Jishan zhi jia, biyou yuqing—lun rujia xianzheng yuanze de lishi weidu" ["Families That Have Been Doing Charitable Things Will Be Particularly Blessed—On the Historical Dimension of Confucian Constitutionalism"] (unpublished manuscript).

Sun Chengbin, Tian Yu, and Zou Shengwen, "Gengduo xinmiankong 'liangxiang' Zhongguo zhengzhi wutai: shiyijie quanguo rendadaibiao gouchen teshe fenxi" ["More New Faces Showing Up on China's Political Stage: An Analysis of the Composition of the National People's Congress Deputies"], *http://news.xinhuanet.com/politics 2008-02/28/content_7687622.htm*, February 28, 2008 (accessed May 7, 2011).

Wang Fuzhi, *Du Tongjian lun: Sung Wendi 13* [*On Reading the Zizhi Tongjian: Emperor Wen of Liu Song*] (Beijing: Zhonghua shuju, 2002).

———, *Si jie* (Beijing: Guji chubanshe, 1956).

Wang Shaoguang, "Jianshou fangxiang, tansuo daolu: Zhongguo shehuizhuyi liushinian" ["Adhere to the Direction, Exploring New Road: The Practice of Socialism in China in the Last 60 Years"], *Zhongguo shehui kexue* [*China Social Sciences*], no. 5 (2009): 4–19.

———, "Jingti dui minzhu de xiushi" ["Guarded against Modifications to Democracy"], *Dushu* [*Reading*], no. 4 (2003): 9–18.

———, *Minzhu sijiang* [*Four Lectures on Democracy*] (Beijing: Sanlian Shudian, 2008).

———, *Qumei yu chaoyue: fansi minzhu, ziyou, pingdeng, gongminshehui* [*Disenchantment and Transcendence: Reflections on Democracy, Freedom, Equality, Civil Society*] (Beijing: Zhongxin chubanshe, 2009).

Ye Shaoweng, *Sichao jianwenlu* [*Records of Observation in Four Dynasties*] (Taipei: Guang Wen Shu Ju, 1986).

Yu Yingshi, *Xiandai ruxue lun* [*On Modern Confucianism*]) (Hackensack, N.J.: Global Publishing, 1996).

Zhang Zhidong, *Quanxiaopian* [*Exhortation to Study*] (Shanghai: Shanghai Shudian Chubanshe, 2002).

Zheng Xuecheng, *Wenshi tongyi: yuandao* [*General Principle of Literature and History*] (Shenyang: Liaoning Jiaoyu Chubanshe, 1998).

Zhonghua renmin gonghe guo shixuehui (ed.), *Mao Zedong dou shehuizhuyi zhengzhixue pizhu he tanhua* [*Mao Zedong's Remarks on and Discussions about Socialist Political Economy*] (Beijing: Zhonghua renmin gongheguo shixuehui, 1998).

Jiang Qing is the founder and master of the Confucian academy *Yangming Jingshe* in Guizhou province. Before establishing the academy, he taught at the Southwest University of Political Science and Law and the Shenzhen College of Administration. His publications include *Gongyangxue yinlun* [*Introduction to the Gongyang Commentary on the Spring and Autumn Annals*], *Zhengzhi ruxue: dangdai ruxue de zhuanxiang, tezhi yu fazhan* [*Political Confucianism: The Transformation, Special Characteristics, and Development of Contemporary Confucianism*], and *Shengming xinyang yu wangdao zhengzhi: rujia wenhua de xiandai jiazhi* [*Faith in Spiritual Life and Politics of the Kingly Way: The Modern Value of Confucian Culture*]. Email: jq5301@163.com.

Bai Tongdong is a professor of philosophy at Fudan University in China. The English and revised version of his book (published in Chinese by Peking University Press), *A New Mission of an Old State: Classical Confucian Political Philosophy in a Contemporary and Comparative Context*, is being reviewed for publication, and his short introduction to Chinese political philosophy, *China: The Middle Way of the Middle Kingdom*, will be published by Zed Books. Email: baitongdong@gmail.com.

Daniel A. Bell is Zhiyuan Chair Professor of the Arts and Humanities at Jiaotong University (Shanghai) and professor of philosophy and director of the Center for International and Comparative Political Philosophy at Tsinghua University (Beijing). His recent books include *Beyond Liberal Democracy*, *China's New Confucianism*, the coauthored *The Spirit of Cities*, and the coedited *Ancient Chinese Thought, Modern Chinese Power* (all published with Princeton University Press). Email: daniel.a.bell@gmail.com.

Joseph Chan is professor and head of the Department of Politics and Public Administration at the University of Hong Kong. He has published extensively in the area of Confucian political philosophy and is working on a monograph that critically reconstructs and develops Confucian political ideas for modern times. Email: jcwchan@hku.hk.

Ruiping Fan is professor of philosophy in the Department of Public and Social Administration of the City University of Hong Kong. He edited *Confucian Bioethics* and *The Renaissance of Confucianism in Contemporary China*. His most recent book is *Reconstructionist Confucianism: Rethinking Morality after the West*. Email: safan@cityu.edu.hk.

Chenyang Li is associate professor and founding director of the philosophy program at Nanyang Technological University, Singapore. Prior to his work at NTU, he was professor and chair of the Philosophy Department at Central Washington University (1999–2010), where he received Distinguished Research Professor Award, Outstanding Department Chair Award, and Keys to Success Award (Student Service). Among his publications are *The Tao Encounters the West* and *The Sage and the Second Sex* (ed.) as well as over fifty journal articles and book chapters. He was an ACE fellow (2008–9) and the first president of the Association of Chinese Philosophers in North America (1995–97). Email: cyli@ntu.edu.sg.

Edmund Ryden lectures in the Department of Law at Fu Jen Catholic University. His previous translations include *Key Concepts in Chinese Philosophy* by Zhang Dainian (Yale and Beijing), *Laozi: Daodejing* (Oxford), and *Ancient Chinese Thought, Modern Chinese Power* by Yan Xuetong (Princeton). Email: edmundrdn@gmail.com

Wang Shaoguang is a chair professor and chairperson in the Department of Government and Public Administration and the director of the Universities Service Centre for China Studies at the Chinese University of Hong Kong, a nonofficial member of HKSAR's Commission on Strategic Development, and the chief editor of *The China Review*, an interdisciplinary journal on greater China. He has authored and coauthored more than twenty books, including *Failure of Charisma: The Chinese Cultural Revolution in Wuhan* (Oxford University Press, 1995), *The Political Economy of Uneven Development: The Case of China* (M. E. Sharpe, 1999), and *Minzhu sijiang* [*Four Lectures on Democracy*] (in Chinese, 2008). Email: b887706@mailserv.cuhk.edu.hk.

Erika Yu is senior research assistant in the Department of Public and Social Administration at the City University of Hong Kong. She recently coauthored the paper "A Confucian Coming of Age." Email: erikayu@gmail.com.